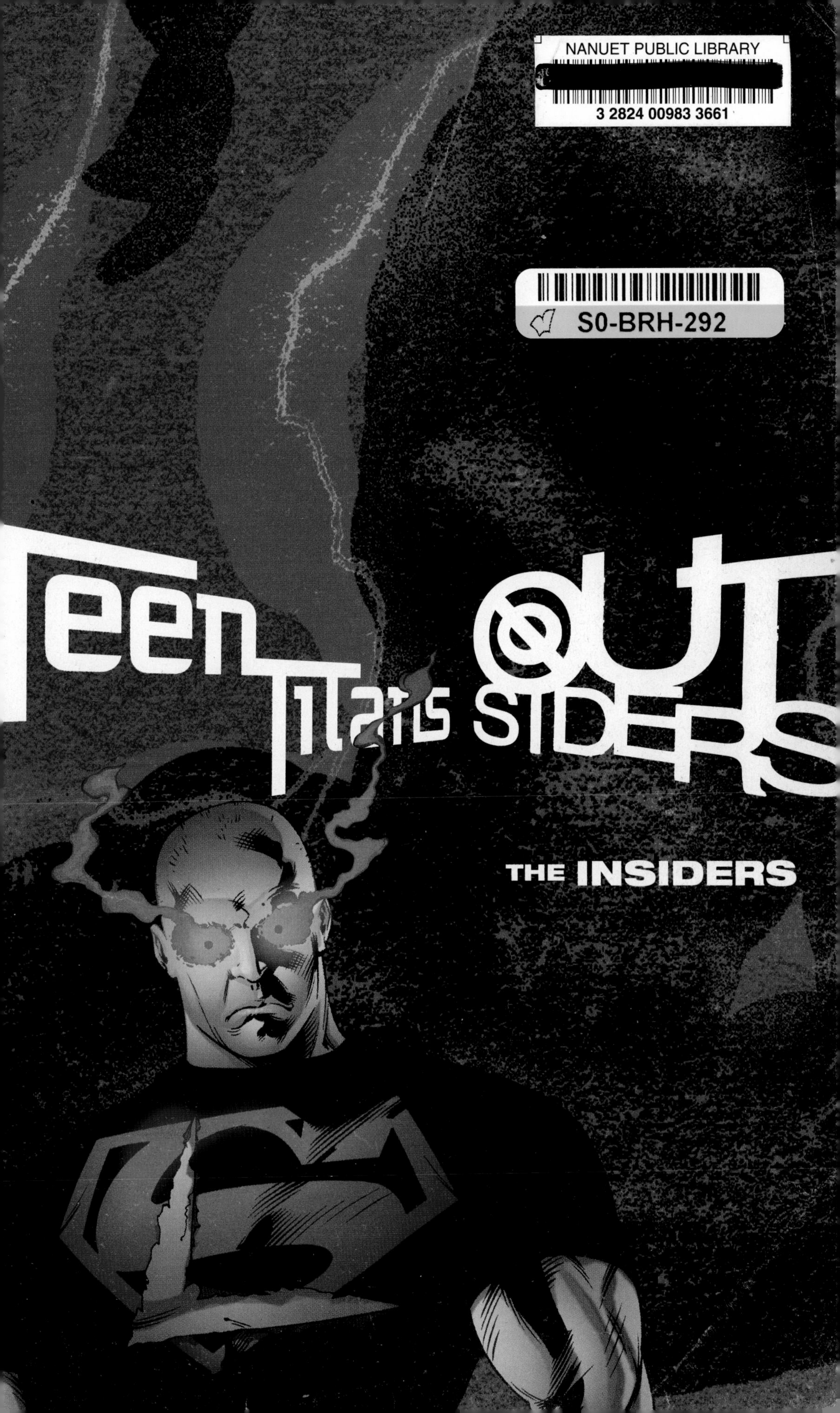
Teen Titans Outsiders
THE INSIDERS

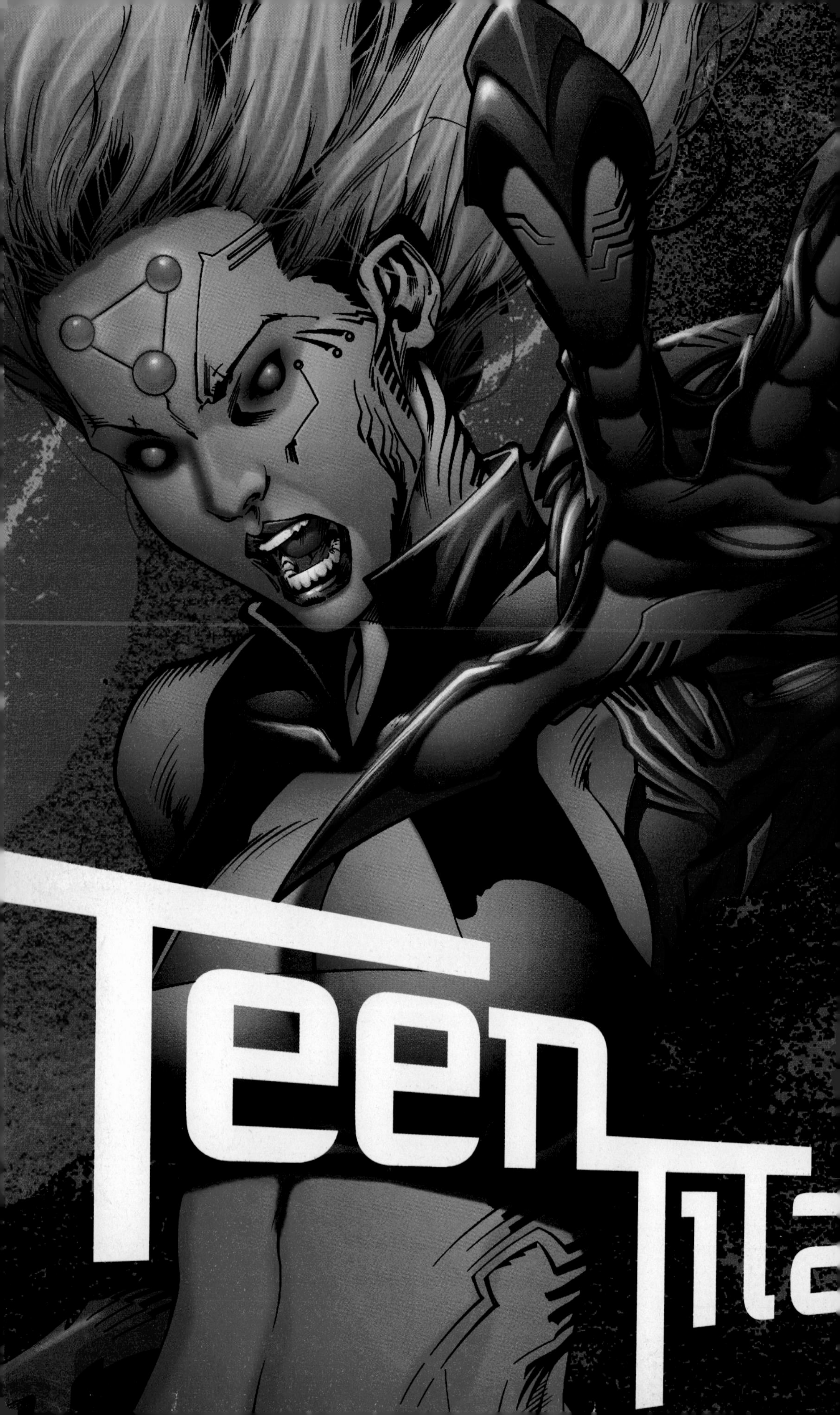
Teen
Tita

PARTS ONE & THREE
GEOFF JOHNS **Writer**
MATTHEW CLARK **Penciller**
ART THIBERT **Inker**
JEROMY COX **Colorist**
COMICRAFT **Letterer**

PARTS TWO & FOUR
JUDD WINICK **Writer**
CARLOS D'ANDA **Artist**
GUY MAJOR **Colorist**
PHIL BALSMAN **Letterer**
MIKE MCKONE & MARLO ALQUIZA **Original covers**

SOUL SEARCHING
GEOFF JOHNS **Writer**
TONY DANIEL **Penciller**
MARLO ALQUIZA **Inker**
JEROMY COX **Colorist**
COMICRAFT **Letterer**
TONY DANIEL & MARLO ALQUIZA **Original Cover**

LETTING IT GO
JUDD WINICK **Writer**
MATTHEW CLARK **Penciller**
ART THIBERT **Inker**
JEROMY COX **Colorist**
PAT BROSSEAU **Letterer**
DANIEL ACUÑA **Original Cover**

OUTSIDERS 5

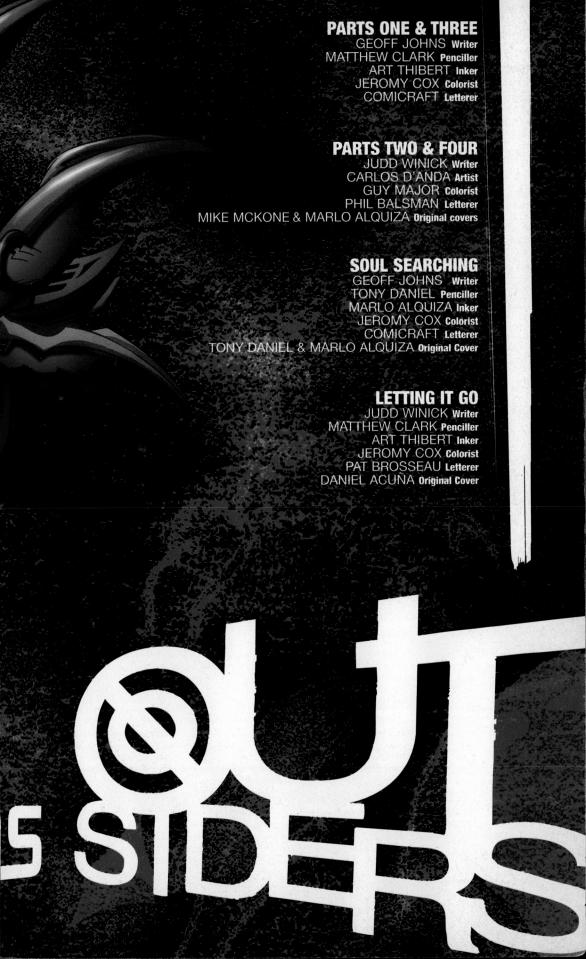

DAN DIDIO
Senior VP-Executive Editor

EDDIE BERGANZA
JOAN HILTY
Editors-original series

TOM PALMER, JR.
Associate Editor-original series

JEANINE SCHAEFER
RACHEL GLUCKSTERN
Assistant Editors-original series

ROBERT GREENBERGER
Senior Editor-collected edition

ROBBIN BROSTERMAN
Senior Art Director

LOUIS PRANDI
Art Director

PAUL LEVITZ
President & Publisher

GEORG BREWER
VP-Design & DC Direct Creative

RICHARD BRUNING
Senior VP-Creative Director

PATRICK CALDON
Executive VP-Finance & Operations

CHRIS CARAMALIS
VP-Finance

JOHN CUNNINGHAM
VP-Marketing

TERRI CUNNINGHAM
VP-Managing Editor

STEPHANIE FIERMAN
Senior VP-Sales & Marketing

ALISON GILL
VP-Manufacturing

RICH JOHNSON
VP-Book Trade Sales

HANK KANALZ
VP-General Manager, WildStorm

LILLIAN LASERSON
Senior VP & General Counsel

JIM LEE
Editorial Director-WildStorm

PAULA LOWITT
Senior VP-Business & Legal Affairs

DAVID MCKILLIPS
VP-Advertising & Custom Publishing

JOHN NEE
VP-Business Development

GREGORY NOVECK
Senior VP-Creative Affairs

CHERYL RUBIN
Senior VP-Brand Management

JEFF TROJAN
VP-Business Development, DC Direct

BOB WAYNE
VP-Sales

TEEN TITANS/OUTSIDERS:
THE INSIDERS
Published by DC Comics. Cover, introduction,
and compilation copyright © 2006
DC Comics. All Rights Reserved.

Originally published in single magazine form
in TEEN TITANS 24-26, OUTSIDERS 24-25, 28.
Copyright © 2005 DC Comics. All Rights
Reserved. All characters, their distinctive
likenesses and related elements featured in
this publication are trademarks of
DC Comics. The stories, characters and
incidents featured in this publication are
entirely fictional. DC Comics does not read or
accept unsolicited submissions of ideas,
stories or artwork.

DC Comics, 1700 Broadway,
New York, NY 10019
A Warner Bros. Entertainment Company
Printed in Canada. First Printing.
ISBN: 1-4012-0926-1
ISBN - 13 978-1-4012-0926-1

Cover illustration by Daniel Acuña

Teen Titans Logo designed by Terry Marks

Outsiders Logo designed by Glenn Parsons

TEEN TITANS

Each new generation of heroes must fight evil in fresh ways. As much as their predecessors may teach them, there is much more they can teach one another. Thus were born the Teen Titans. Over the years the lineup has changed, but the need for guidance remains, as does the spirit of comradery and friendship.

BEAST BOY

Garfield Logan was poisoned with sakutia by a rare African primate. His geneticist parents used an experimental treatment to save his life, and in so doing imbued him with green skin and the ability to transform himself into any animal life form. When his parents died in an accident, he was adopted by Rita Farr and Steve Dayton of the Doom Patrol. Gar desperately wants to be an actor but finds himself most comfortable in the role of hero, serving with the various incarnations of the Titans. At age 19, Beast Boy finds himself acting as the mediator between the older and younger Titans, a task he readily accepts.

CYBORG

Victor Stone's parents were research scientists for S.T.A.R. Labs. During an experiment his mother accidentally unleashed a destructive force that killed her instantly and destroyed most of Vic's body. His father saved the youth's life by grafting cybernetic components to his body, leaving Vic feeling utterly alienated from his fellow man. He only came to accept his fate when he joined the Titans. Through many changes, Vic has remained committed to the team. Currently, Cyborg has taken it upon himself to re-form the Titans and usher in today's incarnation of the teenaged super-heroes at the new Titans Tower in San Francisco.

KID FLASH

Bart Allen has quite a legacy to live up to. His grandfather was Barry Allen, the second Flash. Born in the 30th century, Bart was brought to the 21st century by his grandmother to be properly schooled in the use of his natural super-speed. For a time, he operated as Impulse, under the tutelage of Max Mercury, Zen master of speed. A dramatic turn of events led Bart to decide it was time to grow up, and toward that goal he has speed-read and memorized the contents of the San Francisco Public Library. He has the knowledge but now needs the experience that will make him worthy of the Flash mantle. Taking the next step in the process, he changed his name to Kid Flash.

RAVEN

The daughter of a human mother and the demon Trigon, Raven has spent much of her life trying to escape her father's influence. She was warned to always keep her anger and frustrations in check, lest she give in to her father's demonic influence. When Trigon set his sights on Earth, she got there ahead of him, helping form one version of the Titans in order to stop him. Since then, she has opposed Trigon frequently, losing her mortal body in the process. Without a body to inhabit, Raven's soul-self wandered the world aimlessly until recently. Now she's trying to adapt to her new surroundings.

ROBIN

Perhaps the best prepared of the younger heroes, Tim Drake has been trained by the best – Batman and the first Robin, Dick Grayson. Tim wants to fight crime, and uses his quick mind and strong body in addition to a veritable arsenal he keeps at his fingertips. Robin remains a mystery to those around him, but since receiving word of his father's death, he has finally begun to open up to his teammates. Yet even when the Titans began to believe they could predict his next move, they generally found out they were mistaken.

SPEEDY

Mia Dearden was a street child, doing drugs and turning tricks before she encountered Oliver Queen. He saw in her a soul in need of help, and brought her into his home. Thus she entered the world of heroes. Learning from Queen, his son Connor Hawke, and adopted son Roy Harper, Mia chose a new path for herself as Speedy, the latest in a line of extraordinary archers. The Titans give her a peer group she's never had before.

SUPERBOY

In the wake of Superman's death, a clone was formed using DNA drawn not only from Superman, but from his archfoe Lex Luthor, as well. Being a hybrid human/Kryptonian, Superboy possesses a different set of abilities including flight, strength, speed, limited near and something he calls tactile telekinesis. The clone strives to do the right thing but frequently acts without thinking. Superman recently asked his adoptive parents, the Kents, to help raise the teen. He also entrusted the youth, now called Conner, with Krypto's care.

WONDER GIRL

Cassie Sandsmark was thrilled to befriend Diana, the Themysciran princess known as Wonder Woman — so much so that during a crisis, she borrowed the Sandals of Hermes and the Gauntlet of Atlas in order to aid Diana. Emboldened by her success, she asked Zeus for additional powers. Amused and impressed, he granted her strength and flight, and she became the heroine known as Wonder Girl. Cassie's secret identity was exposed, and arrangements were made for her to attend private school. Cassie continues to grow into her extraordinary role, discovering the extent of her powers and finding new allies and enemies lurking among ancient myths. These foes include the war god Ares, who for reasons unknown, gave her a golden lasso. She has also faced an astonishing revelation — that

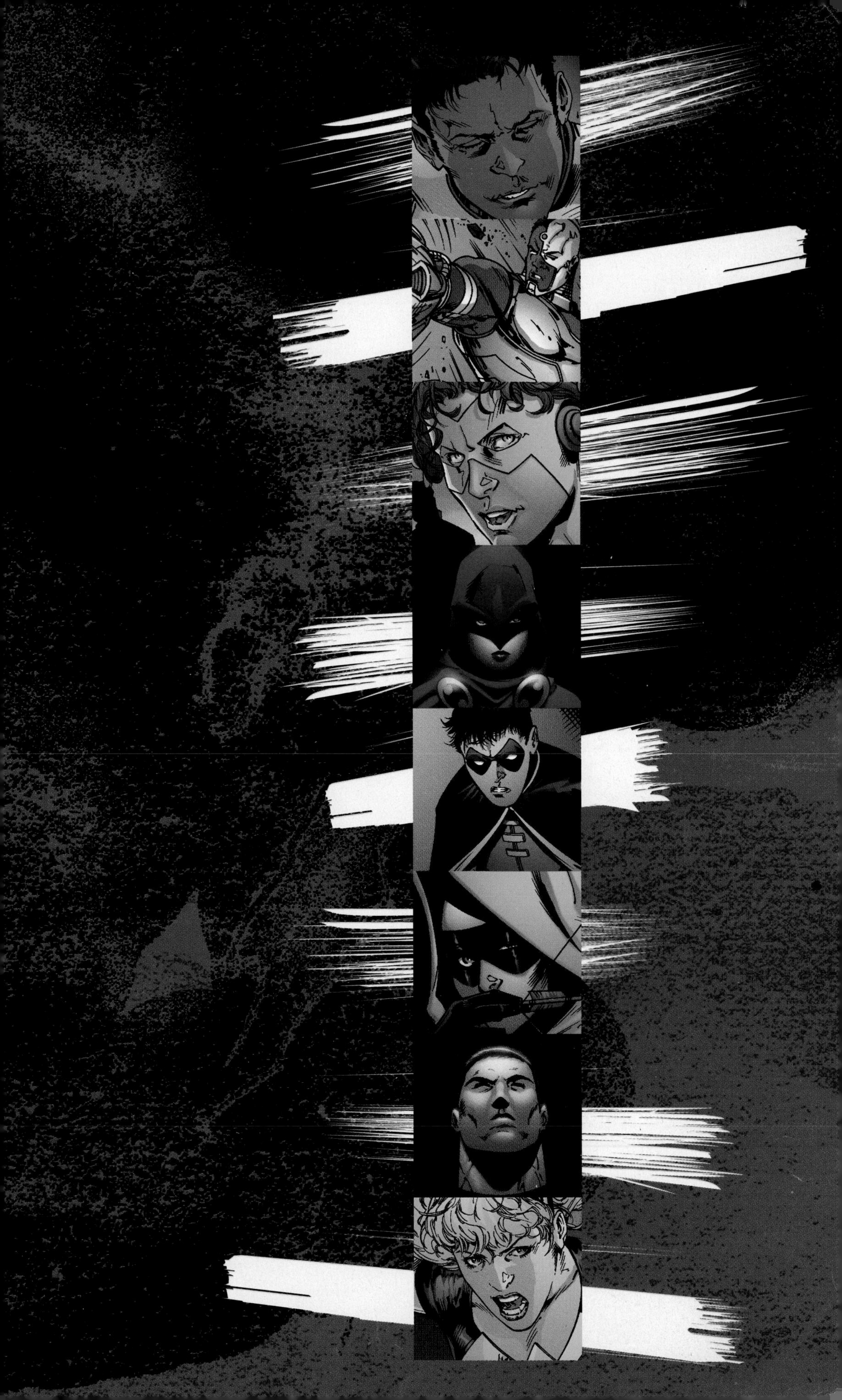

THE OUTSIDERS

The lives of several heroes, and the super-teams to which they belonged, were shattered during the events of TEEN TITANS/OUTSIDERS: THE LIFE AND DEATH OF DONNA TROY — leaving those heroes who were still standing to pick up the pieces. While Arsenal was willing to continue with the Titans, Nightwing couldn't bear to let another catastrophe hit their close-knit family, and disbanded the group known as Young Justice. Months later, Arsenal took it upon himself to recruit a new band of heroes whose mission would be to stop criminals before they could strike. This new team would be composed of crimefighters who would act strictly as co-workers rather than an extended family. Eventually, Arsenal convinced Nightwing to lead these newly assembled Outsiders…

NIGHTWING

Former partner to Batman as Robin, Dick Grayson has left Gotham City for the nearby city of Blüdhaven where he fights crime as Nightwing. He is a master of several martial arts disciplines, and is armed with escrima sticks, batarangs, jumplines and gas capsules. As the head of the new Outsiders (which he named as a nod to Batman's former team), Dick sees this group as hunters — they will seek out the world's villains and bring them in.

ARSENAL

Idolizing Green Arrow, orphan Roy Harper had mastered archery when he was a teenager on a Navajo reservation. Harper became billionaire Oliver Queen's ward, and his guardian named him Speedy because of the quickness he exhibited with his bow. Renaming himself Arsenal, Harper went on to work for the U.S. government, lead the Titans, and fall in love with the assassin Cheshire. Together they have a child, Lian.

JADE

Jenny-Lynn Hayden's normal adolescence came to an abrupt end when the green birthmark on her left palm began to pulse, giving her power over a strange green energy similar to the type used by Green Lanterns. Jenny-Lynn, along with her long-lost brother Todd (a.k.a. Obsidian), learned that their biological father was the World War II-era Green Lantern, Alan Scott. After being a member of the group Infinity Inc., and the girlfriend of Green Lantern Kyle Rayner, Jenny-Lynn felt she needed to define herself on her own and joined the Outsiders.

SHIFT

Metamorpho was a member of the original Outsiders, who could transform his body into any element on the periodic table. When the Outsiders disbanded, he joined the Justice League for a mission which left him a comatose, inert mass. Fragments of Metamorpho were scattered all over the United States, and the hero collected each one he could find. But one fragment developed into a full-bodied replica of Metamorpho, with no memories of his own. This replica joined the new Outsiders, and has since learned the truth of his origin. Now called Shift, he too has the ability to transform his body into any element he wishes.

THUNDER

The only child of veteran hero Jefferson Pierce — a.k.a. Black Lightning — Anissa Pierce discovered when she was only eleven years old that she had the power to increase her density. Longing to become a hero like her father, Anissa was forbidden to even consider crimefighting until she finished college. On the night of her graduation, she donned a costume for the first time and took to the streets. She discovered that a quick increase of her body's density, combined with the slamming down of her foot, produced a shock wave that toppled her adversaries. Pierce chose a code name that both honors her father and is a nod to her "signature move."

GRACE

Almost nothing is known about Grace's background and upbringing, and she's not very forthcoming. What is known is that the seven-foot-tall super-strong powerhouse used to work security for Chaney's — the night club hotspot for metahumans in Metropolis. She's also had a "history" with Arsenal. When Harper approached her with an offer to join the Outsiders, Grace only accepted after learning that the job paid three times as much as being a bouncer.

INDIGO

The blue-skinned android known as Indigo arrived mysteriously from the distant future. Almost immediately, Indigo found herself in defensive mode and facing off against The Titans and Young Justice. In the process she indirectly caused the deaths of Omen and Donna Troy at the hands of a renegade Superman robot she restarted. She ultimately defeated the robot, then shut down. Arsenal oversaw her repairs at S.T.A.R. Labs, and now — with no memory of the damage she caused, or even of her own history — Indigo serves as a member of the Outsiders, utilizing powers of flight, force fields and energy blasts.

STARFIRE

Princess Koriand'r of Tamaran was sacrificed by her father to save their world. Subjected to horrendous experiments, she gained the ability to generate energy bolts, this in addition to her natural gift of flight. Escaping her tormentors, she made her way to Earth and found a new life as Starfire. Her world is now gone, a victim of the alien warlord Imperiex. Starfire tends to be impatient, which has recently led to her leaving the Titans and working with the Outsiders.

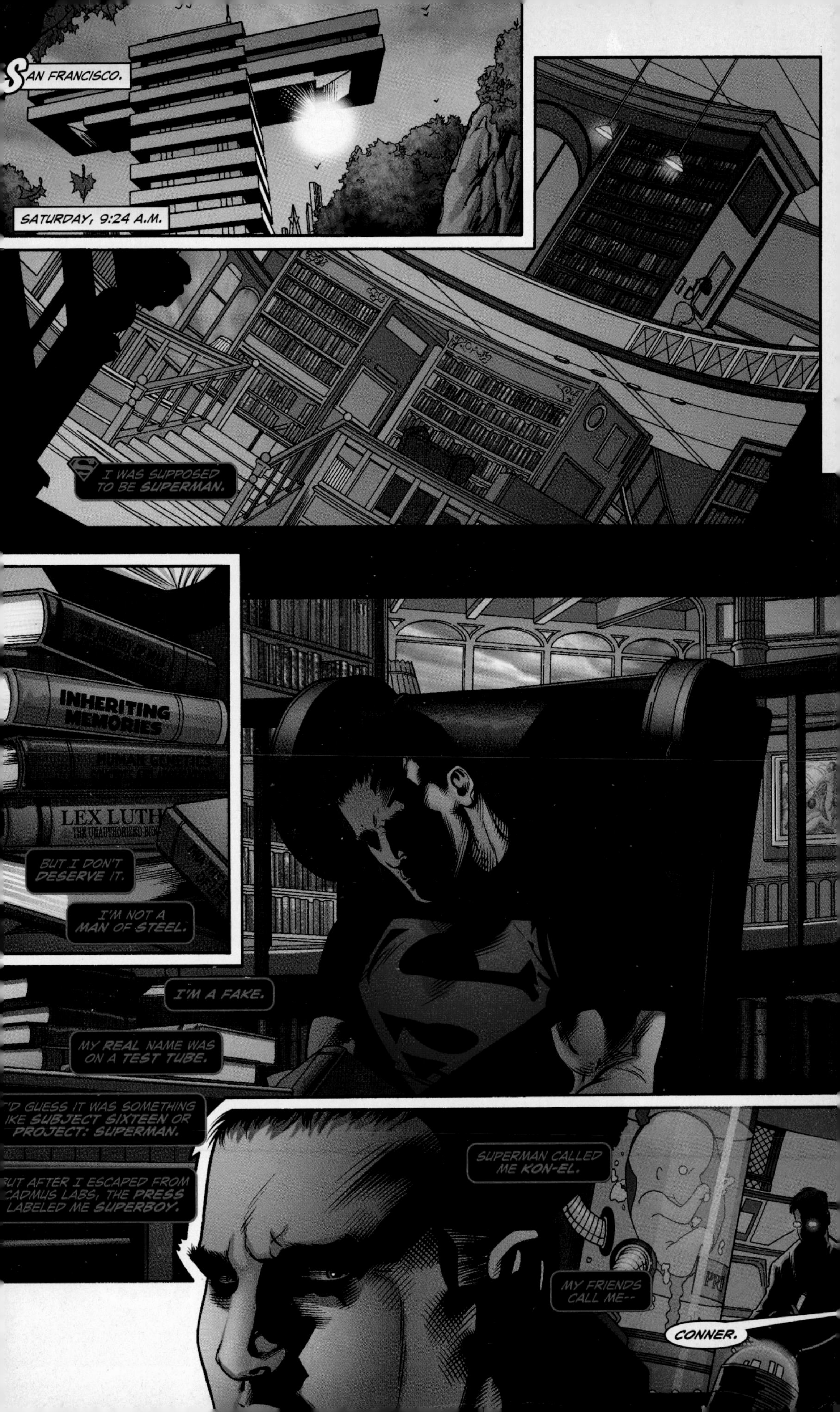
SAN FRANCISCO.
SATURDAY, 9:24 A.M.
I WAS SUPPOSED TO BE SUPERMAN.
INHERITING MEMORIES
HUMAN GENETICS
LEX LUTH
THE UNAUTHORIZED BIO
BUT I DON'T DESERVE IT.
I'M NOT A MAN OF STEEL.
I'M A FAKE.
MY REAL NAME WAS ON A TEST TUBE.
I'D GUESS IT WAS SOMETHING LIKE SUBJECT SIXTEEN OR PROJECT: SUPERMAN.
BUT AFTER I ESCAPED FROM CADMUS LABS, THE PRESS LABELED ME SUPERBOY.
SUPERMAN CALLED ME KON-EL.
MY FRIENDS CALL ME--
CONNER.

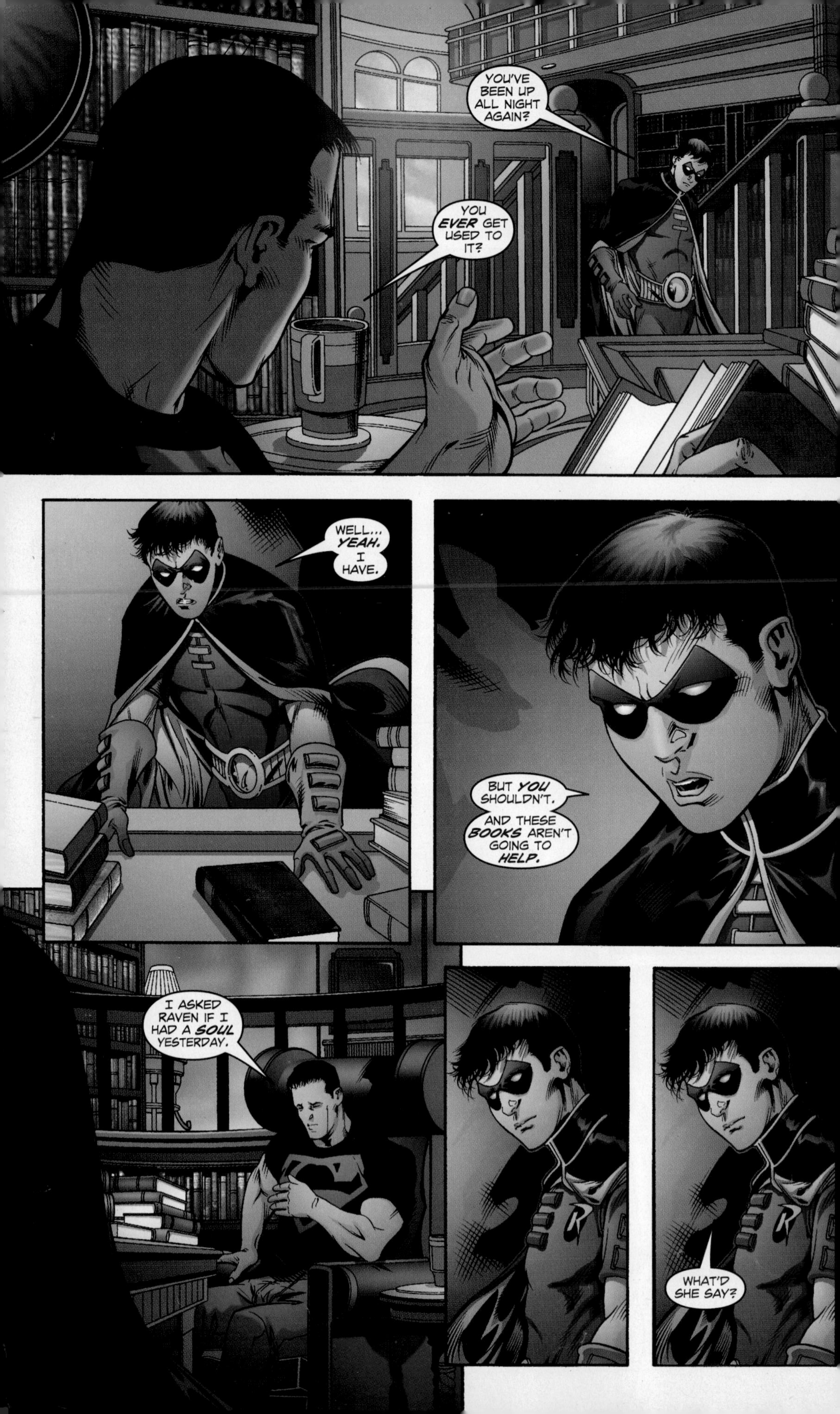
YOU'VE BEEN UP ALL NIGHT AGAIN?
YOU EVER GET USED TO IT?
WELL... YEAH. I HAVE.
BUT YOU SHOULDN'T.
AND THESE BOOKS AREN'T GOING TO HELP.
I ASKED RAVEN IF I HAD A SOUL YESTERDAY.
WHAT'D SHE SAY?

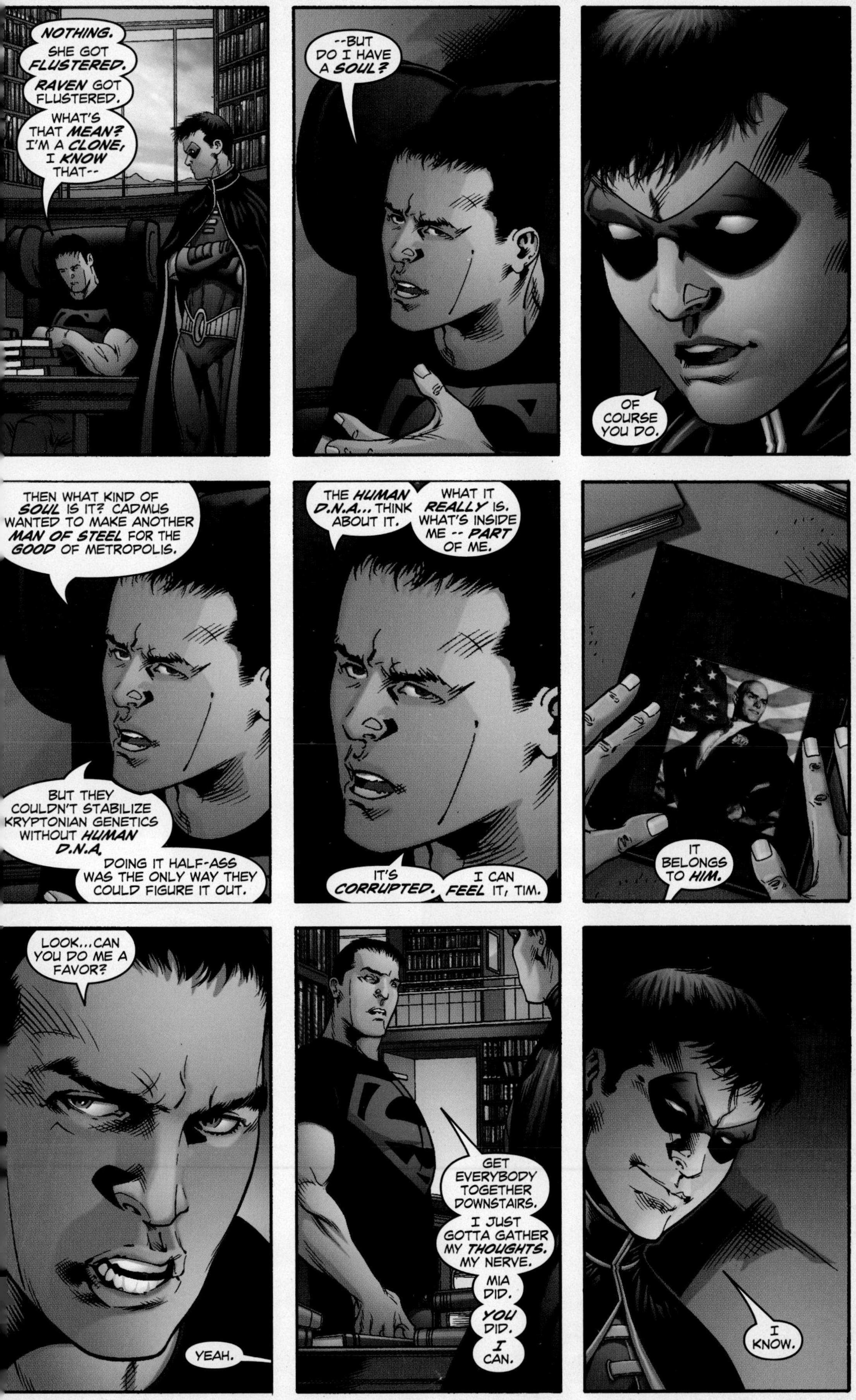
NOTHING.
SHE GOT FLUSTERED.
RAVEN GOT FLUSTERED.
WHAT'S THAT MEAN? I'M A CLONE, I KNOW THAT--
--BUT DO I HAVE A SOUL?
OF COURSE YOU DO.
THEN WHAT KIND OF SOUL IS IT? CADMUS WANTED TO MAKE ANOTHER MAN OF STEEL FOR THE GOOD OF METROPOLIS.
BUT THEY COULDN'T STABILIZE KRYPTONIAN GENETICS WITHOUT HUMAN D.N.A.
DOING IT HALF-ASS WAS THE ONLY WAY THEY COULD FIGURE IT OUT.
THE HUMAN D.N.A... THINK ABOUT IT.
WHAT IT REALLY IS. WHAT'S INSIDE ME -- PART OF ME.
IT'S CORRUPTED.
I CAN FEEL IT, TIM.
IT BELONGS TO HIM.
LOOK...CAN YOU DO ME A FAVOR?
YEAH.
GET EVERYBODY TOGETHER DOWNSTAIRS.
I JUST GOTTA GATHER MY THOUGHTS. MY NERVE.
MIA DID.
YOU DID.
I CAN.
I KNOW.

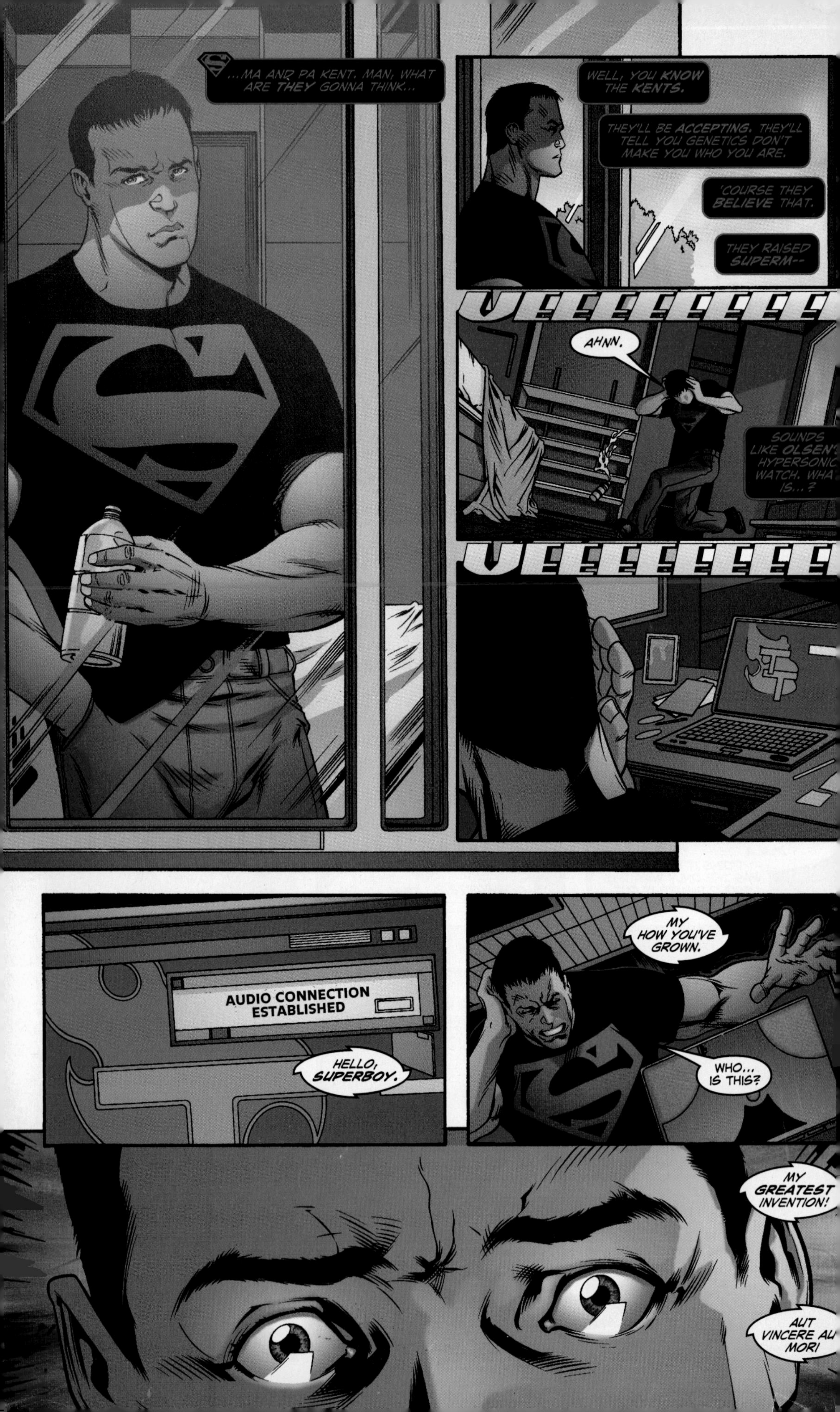
...MA AND PA KENT. MAN, WHAT ARE THEY GONNA THINK...
WELL, YOU KNOW THE KENTS.
THEY'LL BE ACCEPTING. THEY'LL TELL YOU GENETICS DON'T MAKE YOU WHO YOU ARE.
'COURSE THEY BELIEVE THAT.
THEY RAISED SUPERM--
VEEEEEEEEEE
AHNN.
SOUNDS LIKE OLSEN'S HYPERSONIC WATCH. WHA IS...?
VEEEEEEEEEE
AUDIO CONNECTION ESTABLISHED
HELLO, SUPERBOY.
MY HOW YOU'VE GROWN.
WHO... IS THIS?
MY GREATEST INVENTION!
AUT VINCERE AU MORI

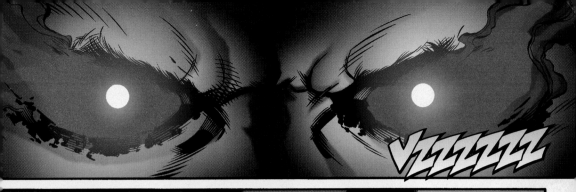

VZZZZZZ

AUDIO CONNECTION
TERMINATED

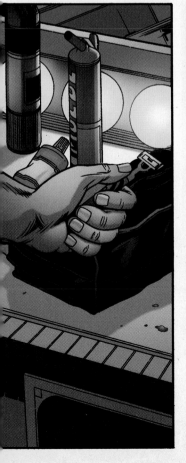

SKKKT

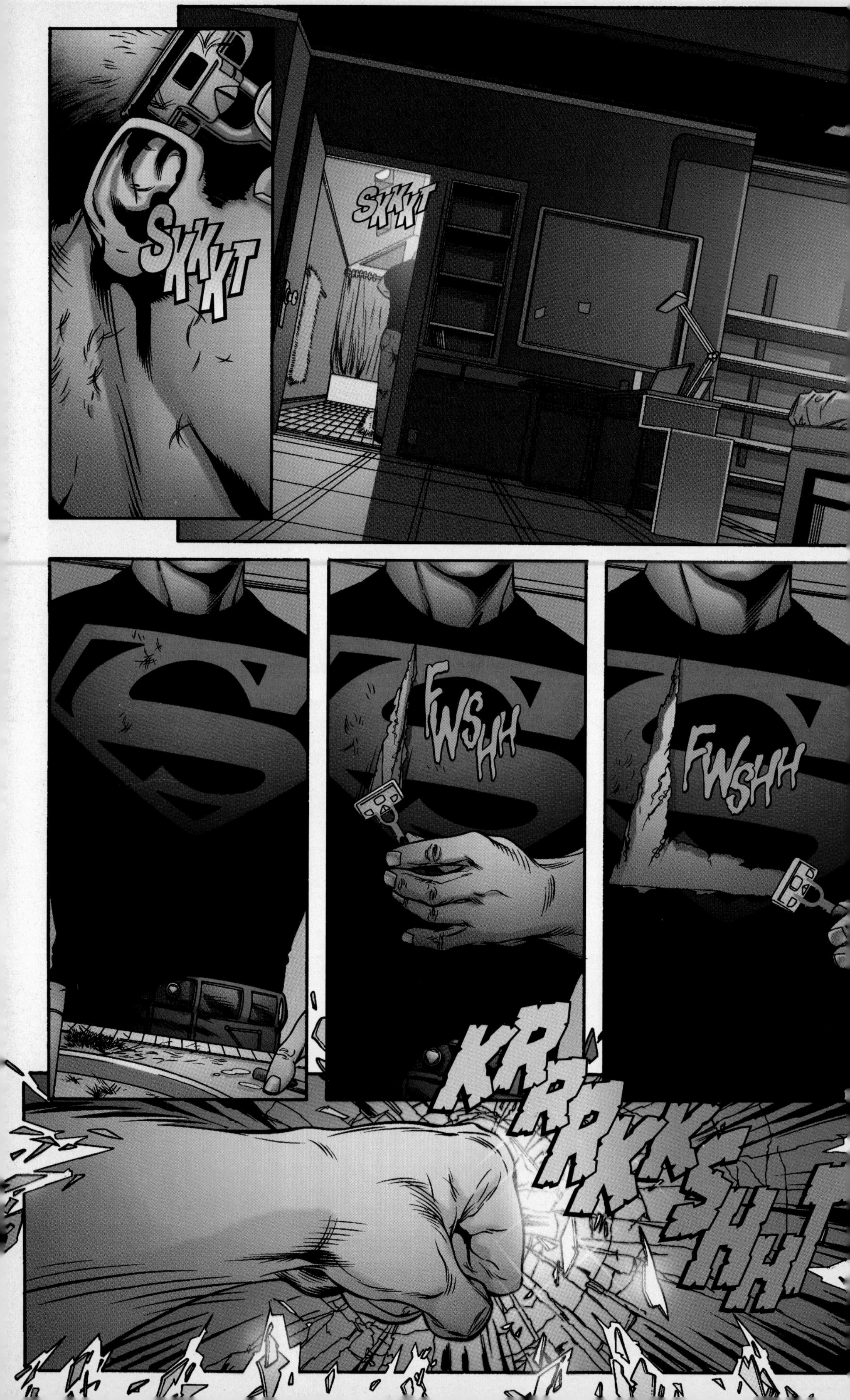
SKKKT
SKKKT
FWSHH
FWSHH
KRRKKSHHT

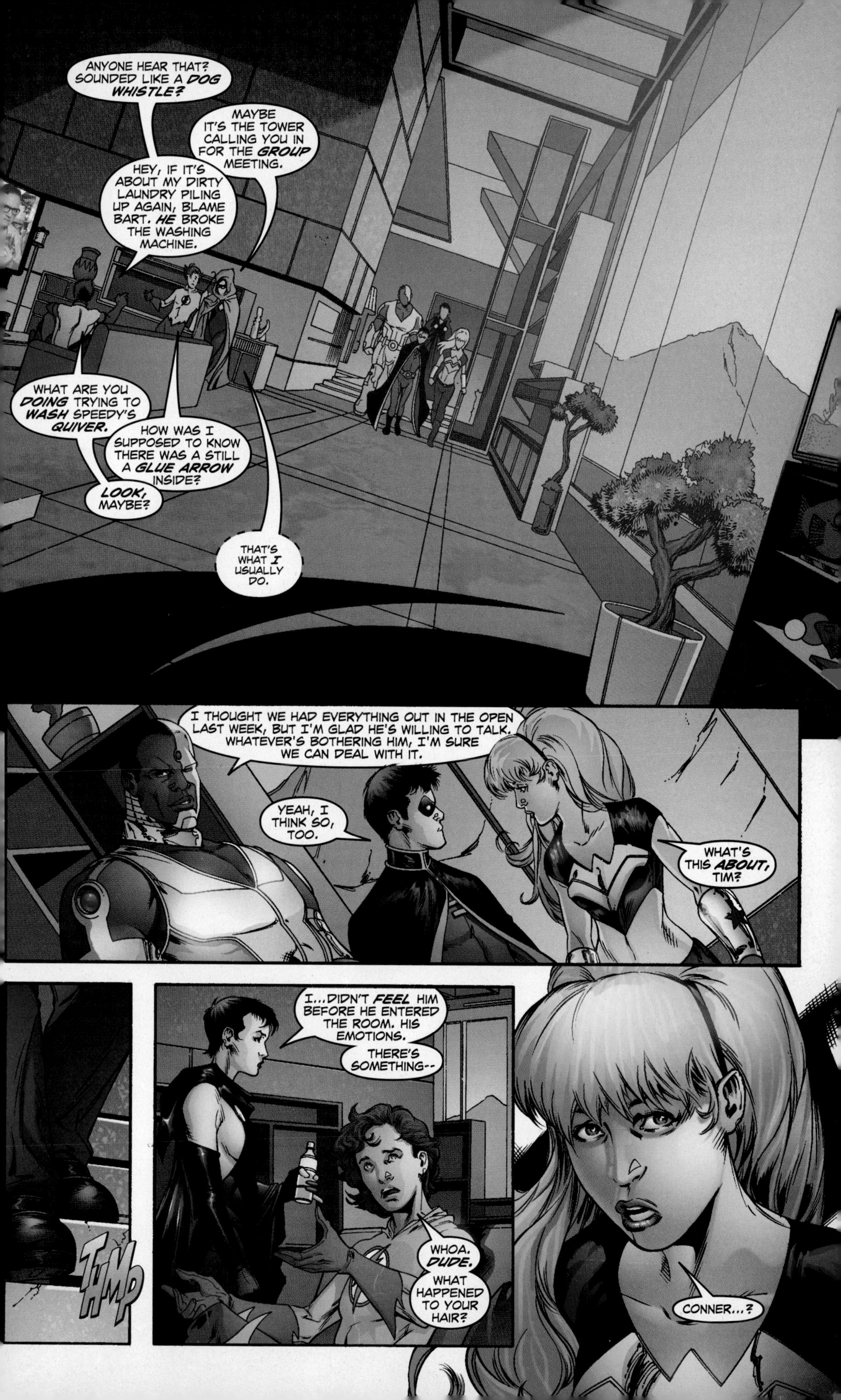

ANYONE HEAR THAT? SOUNDED LIKE A DOG WHISTLE?
MAYBE IT'S THE TOWER CALLING YOU IN FOR THE GROUP MEETING.
HEY, IF IT'S ABOUT MY DIRTY LAUNDRY PILING UP AGAIN, BLAME BART. HE BROKE THE WASHING MACHINE.
WHAT ARE YOU DOING TRYING TO WASH SPEEDY'S QUIVER.
HOW WAS I SUPPOSED TO KNOW THERE WAS A STILL A GLUE ARROW INSIDE?
LOOK, MAYBE?
THAT'S WHAT I USUALLY DO.
I THOUGHT WE HAD EVERYTHING OUT IN THE OPEN LAST WEEK, BUT I'M GLAD HE'S WILLING TO TALK. WHATEVER'S BOTHERING HIM, I'M SURE WE CAN DEAL WITH IT.
YEAH, I THINK SO, TOO.
WHAT'S THIS ABOUT, TIM?
THMP
I...DIDN'T FEEL HIM BEFORE HE ENTERED THE ROOM. HIS EMOTIONS.
THERE'S SOMETHING--
WHOA. DUDE.
WHAT HAPPENED TO YOUR HAIR?
CONNER...?

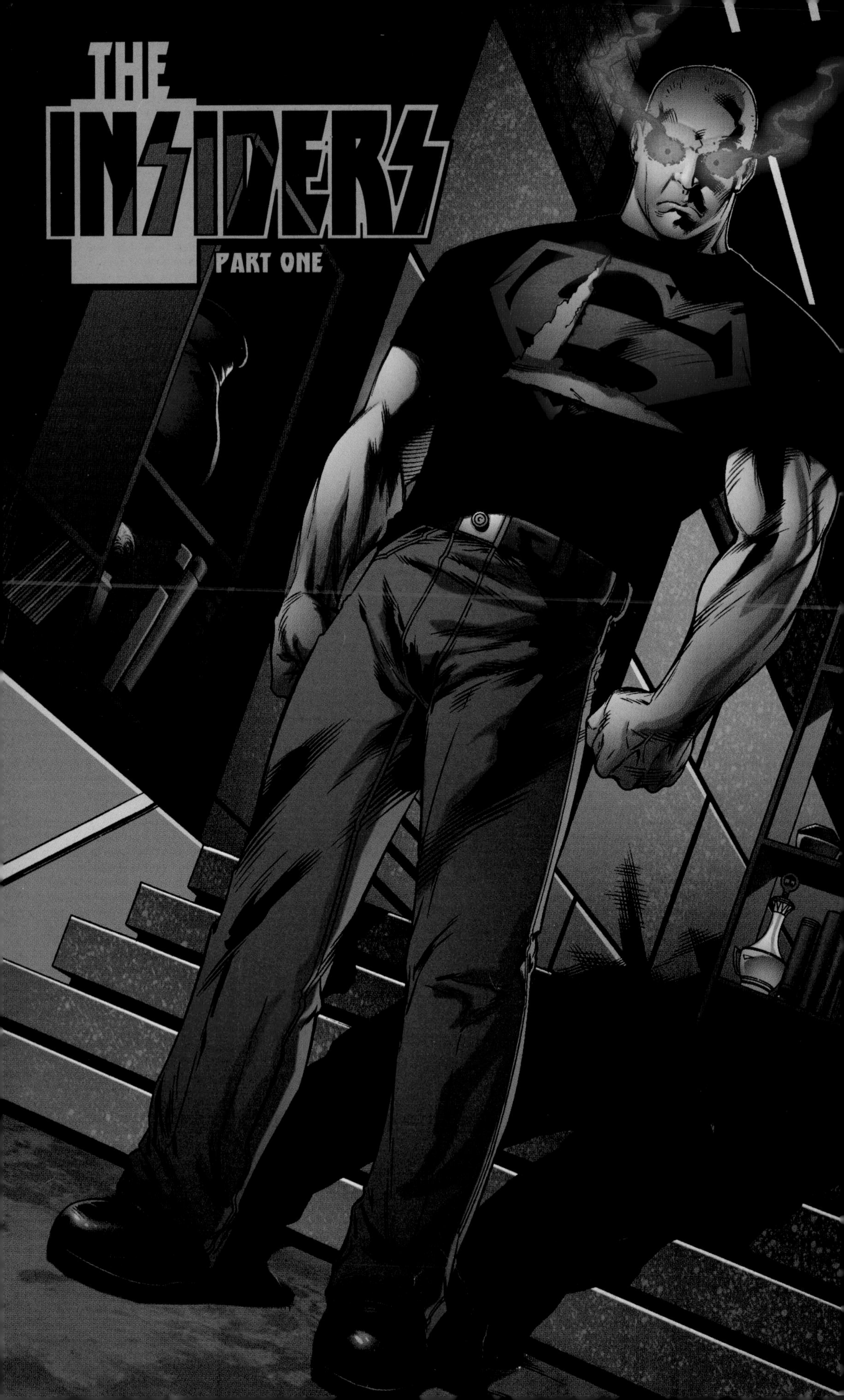
THE INSIDERS
PART ONE

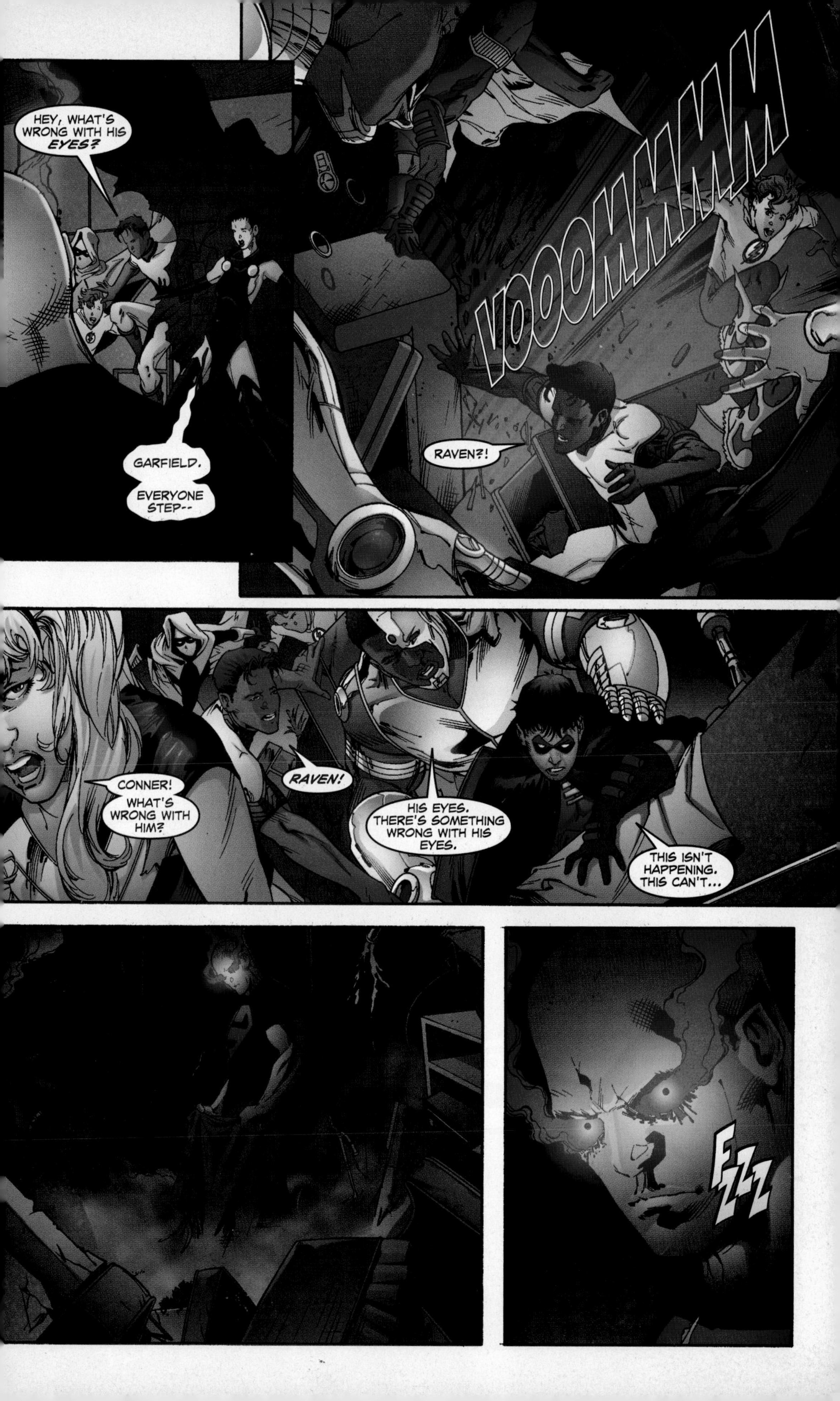

HEY, WHAT'S WRONG WITH HIS *EYES?*
GARFIELD.
EVERYONE STEP--
VOOOMMMM
RAVEN?!
CONNER! WHAT'S WRONG WITH HIM?
RAVEN!
HIS EYES. THERE'S SOMETHING WRONG WITH HIS EYES.
THIS ISN'T HAPPENING. THIS CAN'T...
FZZZ

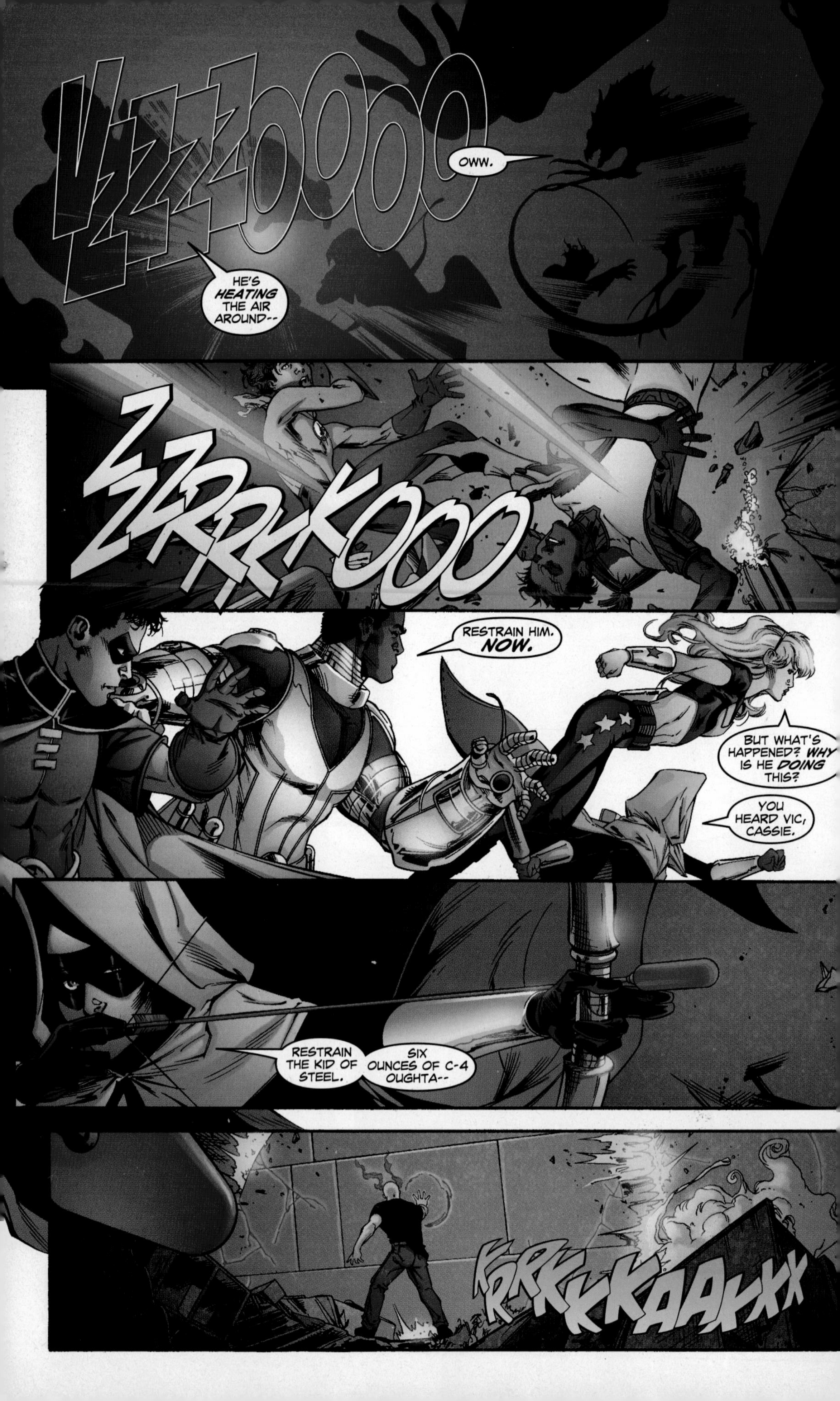
VZZZZOOOOO
OWW.
HE'S HEATING THE AIR AROUND--
ZZRRKOOO
RESTRAIN HIM. NOW.
BUT WHAT'S HAPPENED? WHY IS HE DOING THIS?
YOU HEARD VIC, CASSIE.
RESTRAIN THE KID OF STEEL.
SIX OUNCES OF C-4 OUGHTA--
KRRKKAAKKK

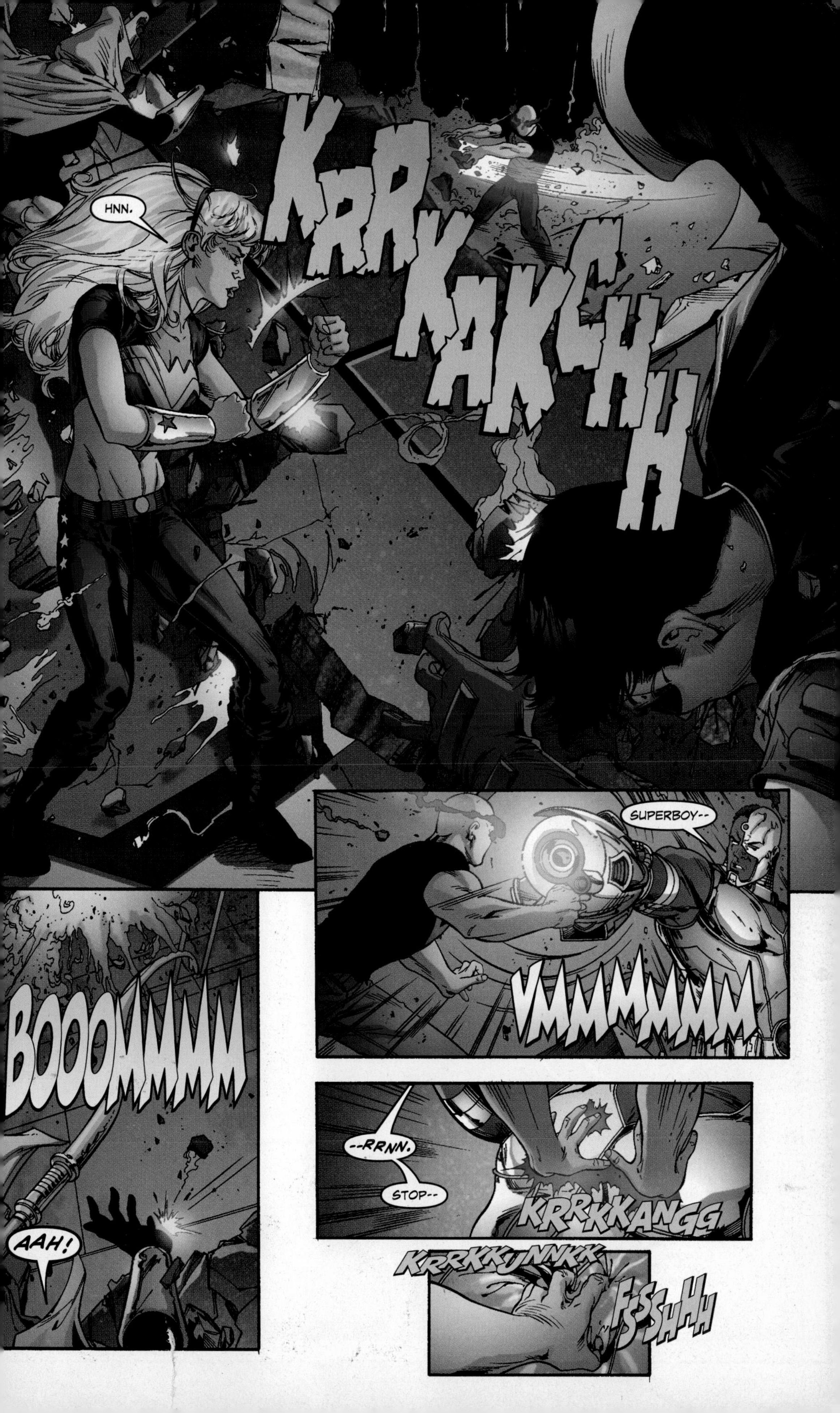
HNN.
KRRKAKCHHH
SUPERBOY--
VMMMMMMM
BOOOMMMM
AAH!
--RRNN.
STOP--
KRRKKANGG
KRRKKUNNKK
FSSSHHH

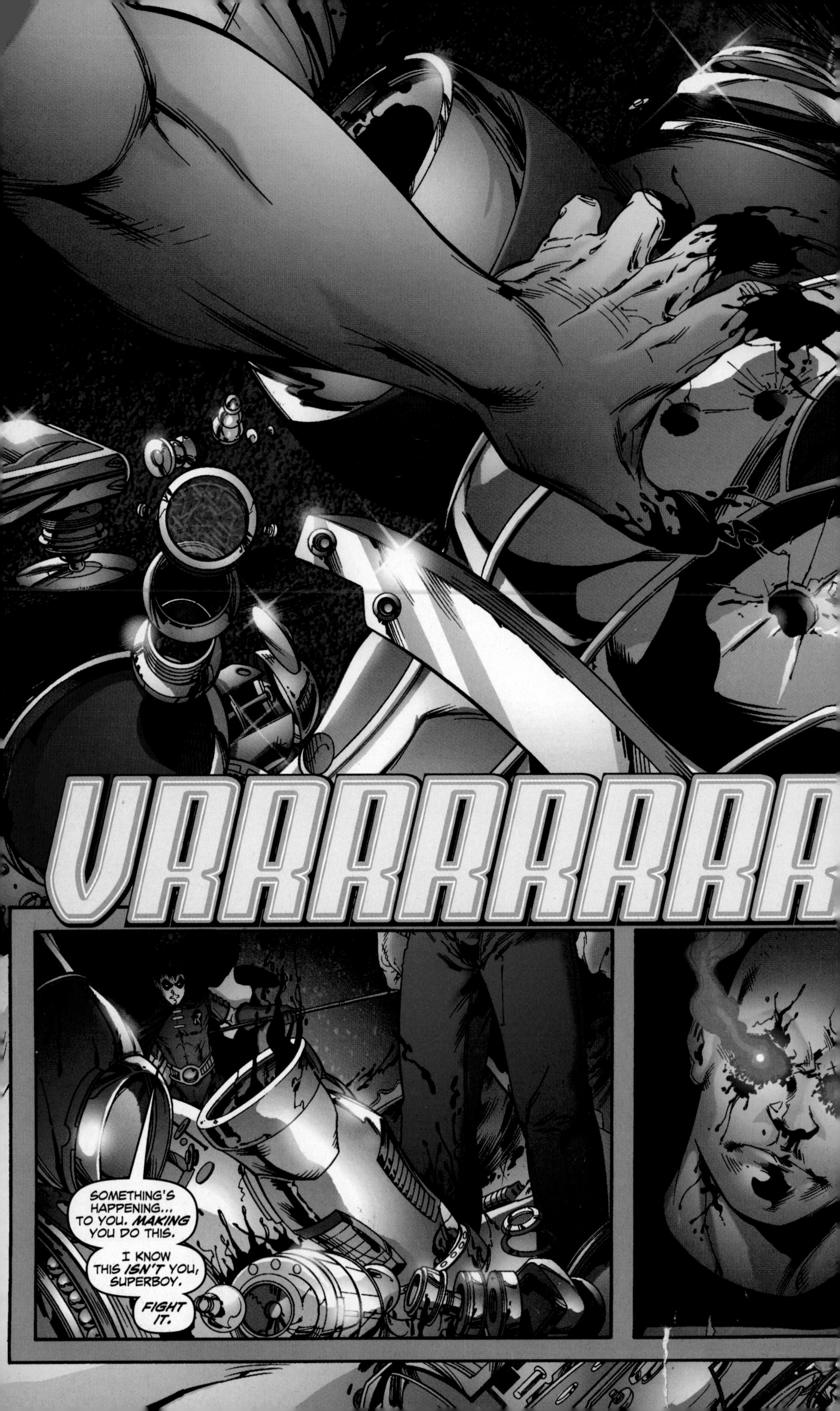
VRRRRRRRRR
SOMETHING'S HAPPENING... TO YOU. *MAKING* YOU DO THIS.
I KNOW THIS *ISN'T* YOU, SUPERBOY.
FIGHT IT.

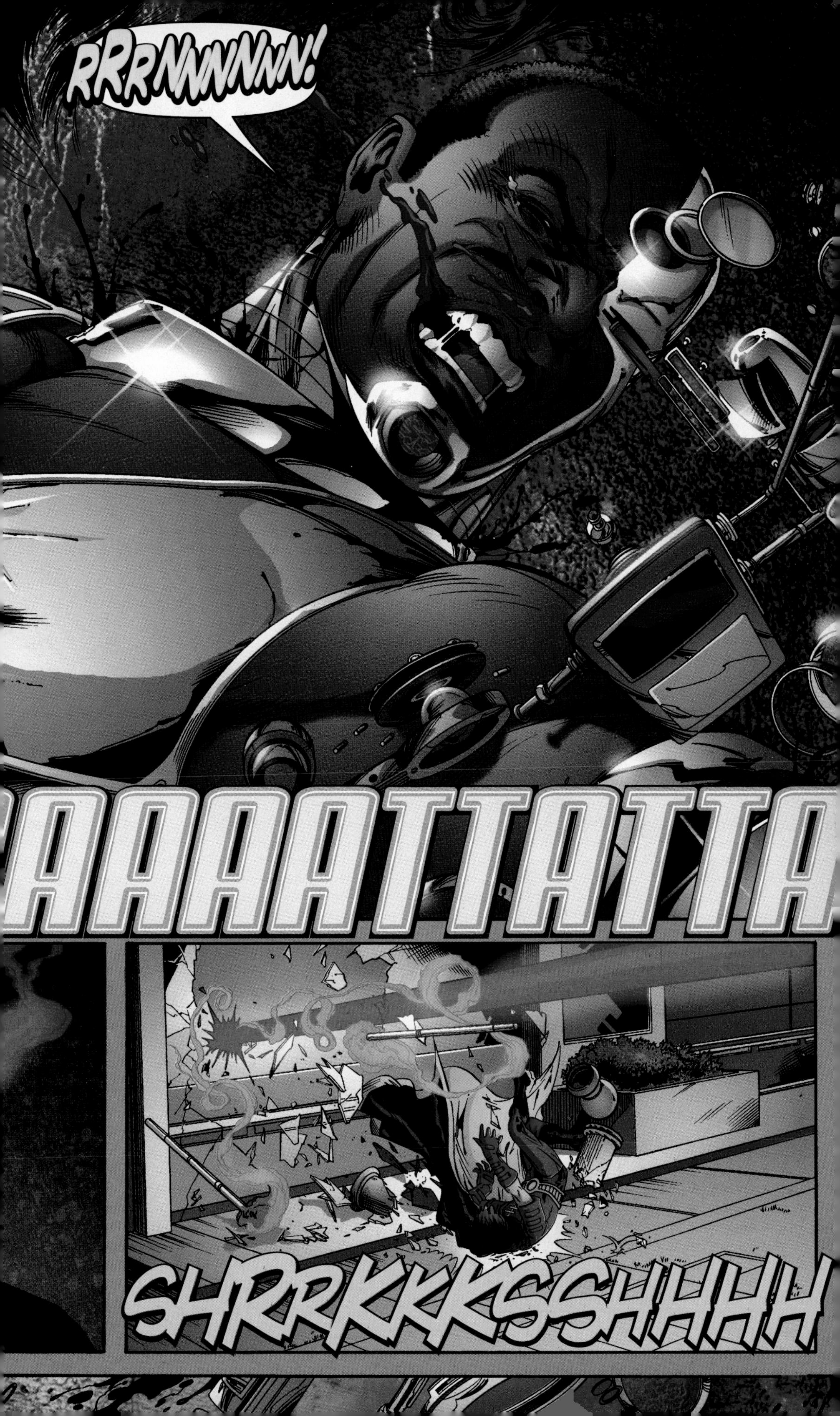
RRRNNNNNNN!
AAAAATTATTA
SHRRKKKSSHHHH

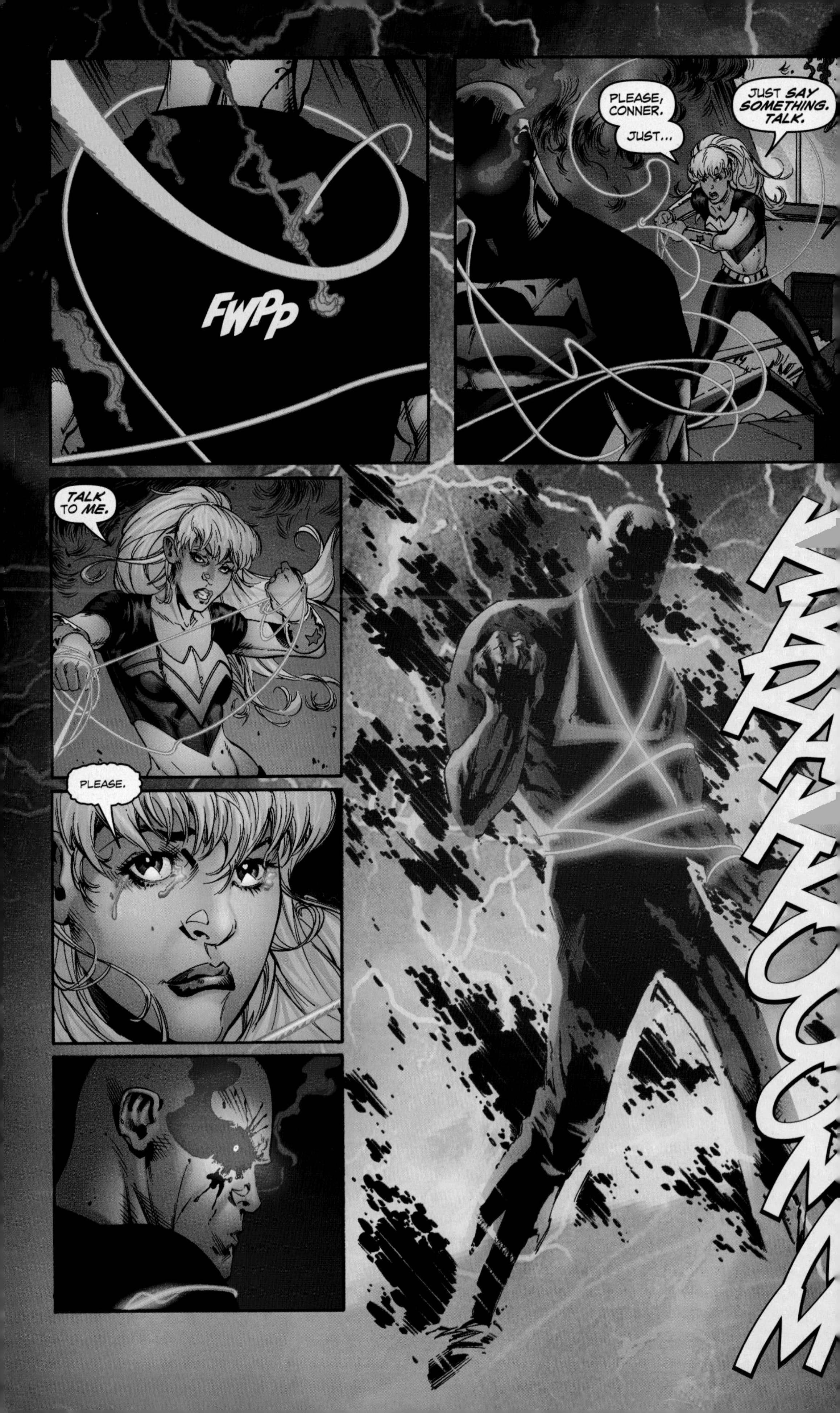
FWPP
PLEASE, CONNER.
JUST...
JUST SAY SOMETHING. TALK.
TALK TO ME.
PLEASE.

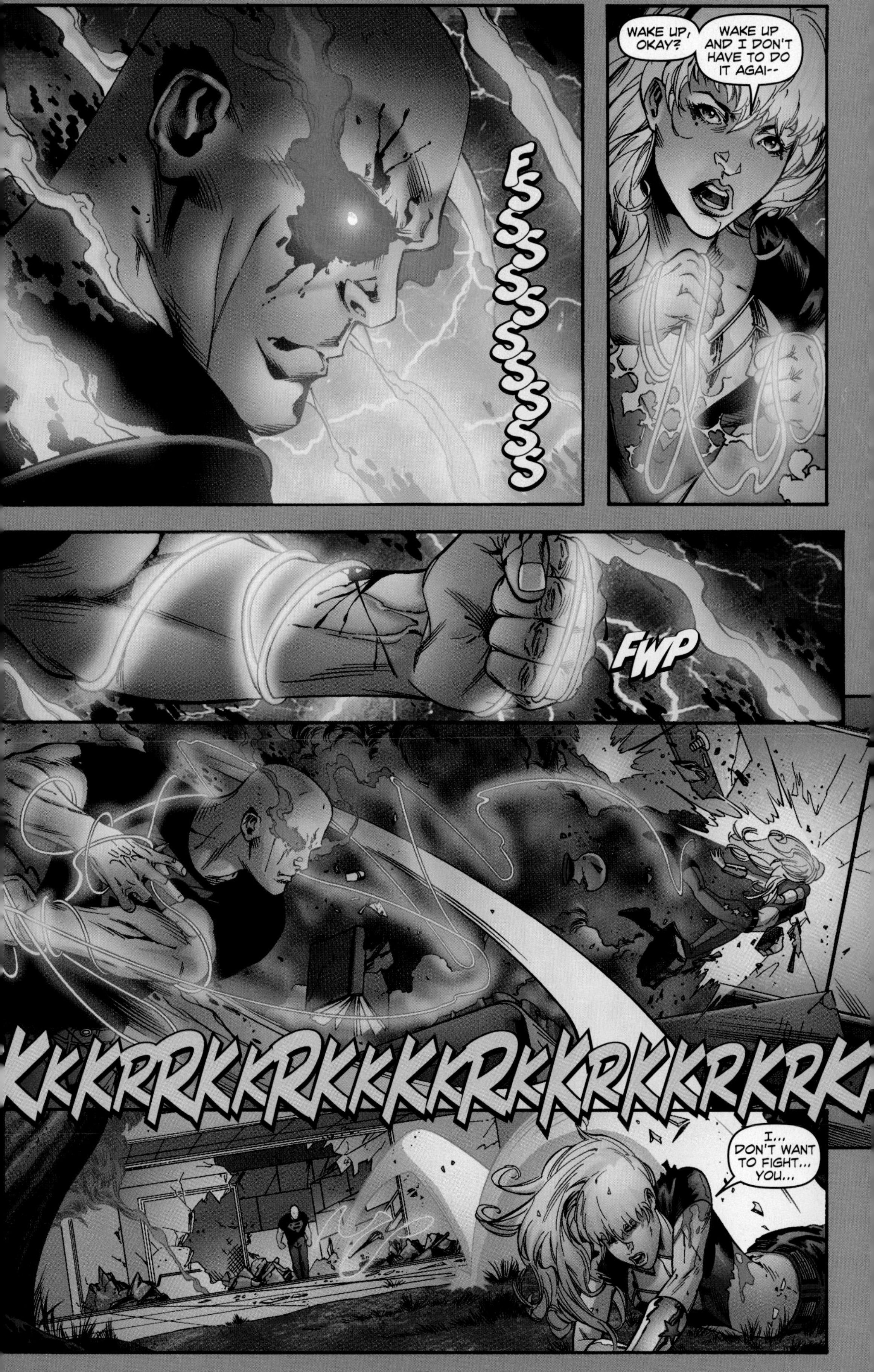
FSSSSSSSSSS
WAKE UP, OKAY?
WAKE UP AND I DON'T HAVE TO DO IT AGAI--
FWP
KKKRRKKKRKKKKKRKKRKKKRKRK
I... DON'T WANT TO FIGHT... YOU...

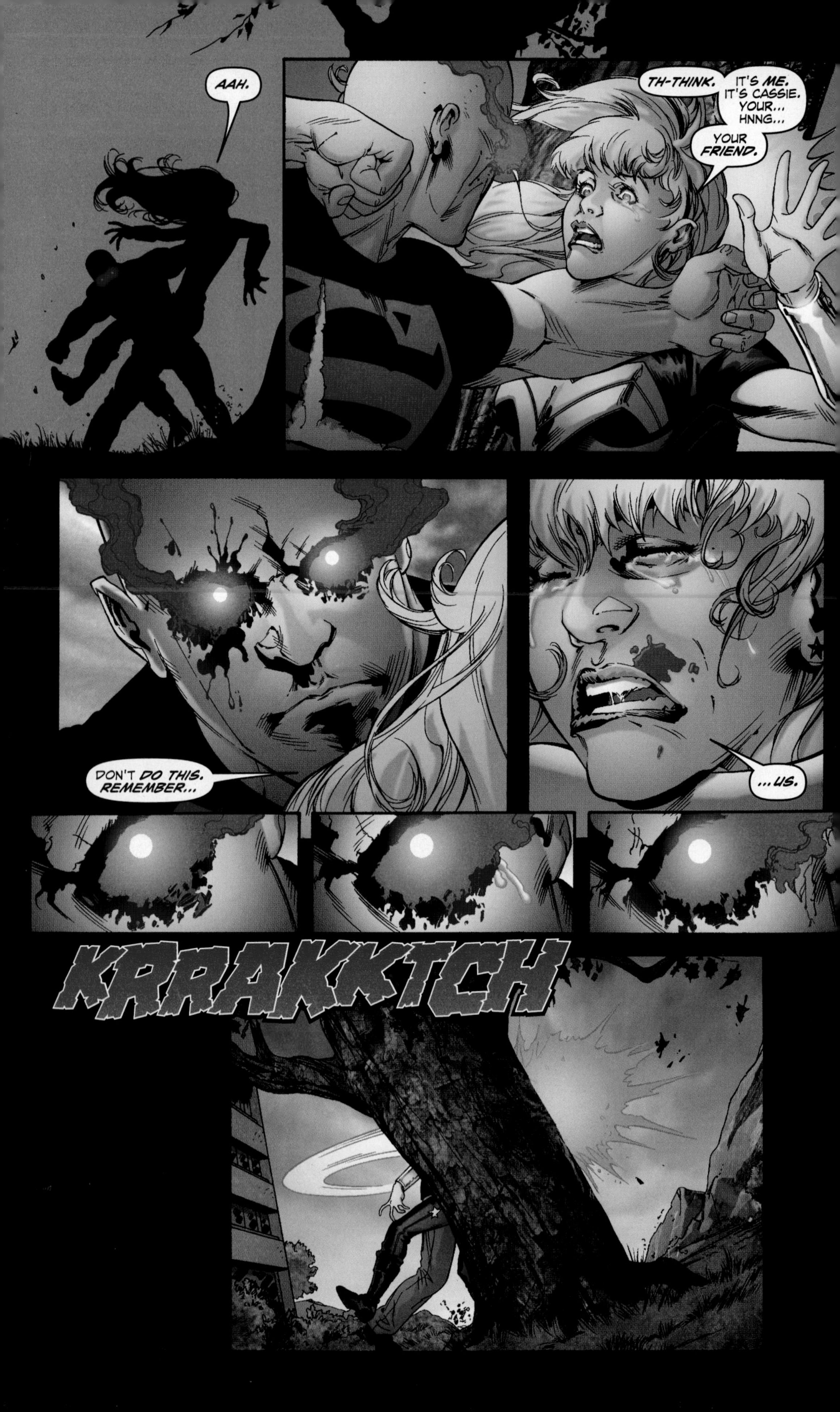
AAH.
TH-THINK.
IT'S ME. IT'S CASSIE. YOUR... HNNG...
YOUR FRIEND.
DON'T DO THIS. REMEMBER...
...US.
KRRAKKTCH

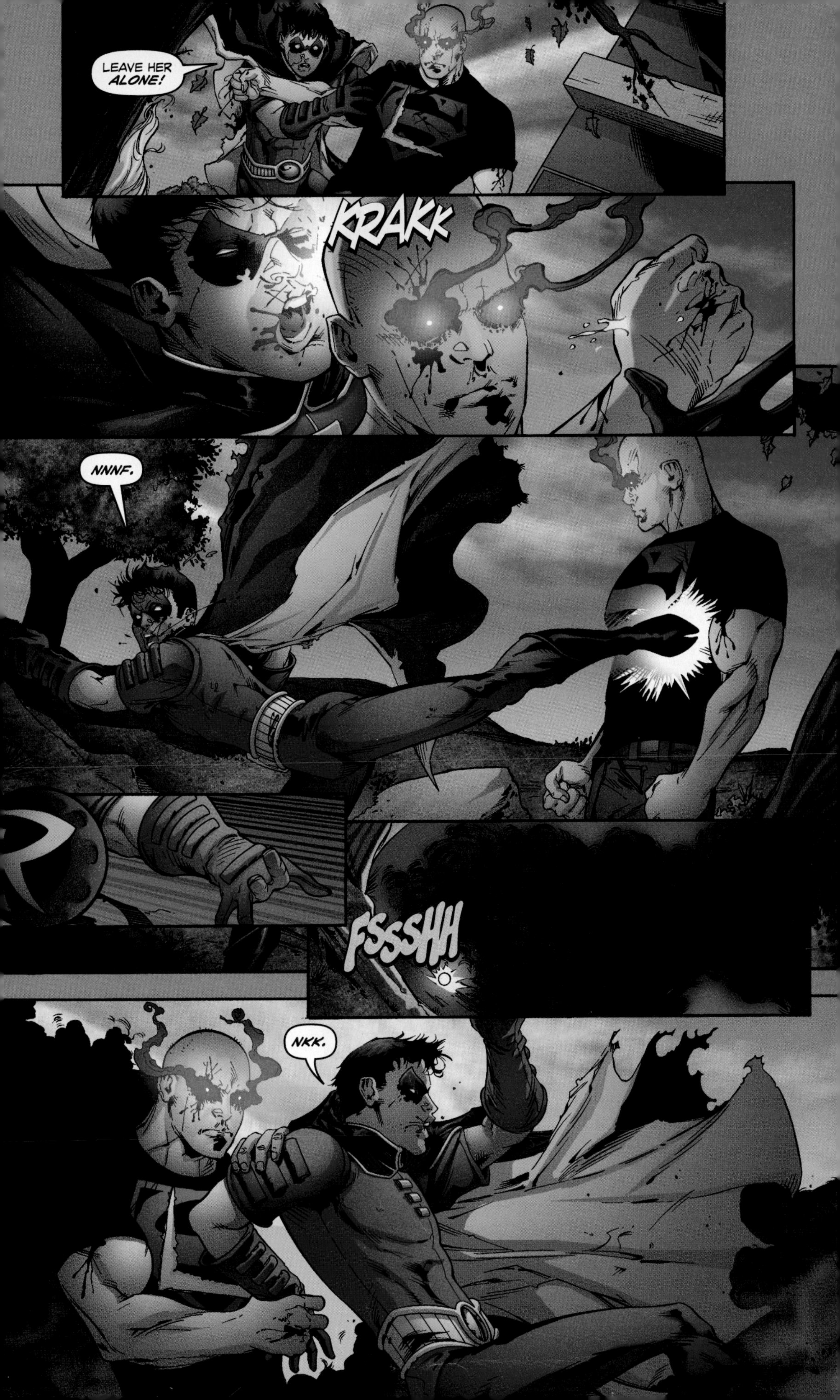
LEAVE HER ALONE!
KRAKK
NNNF.
FSSSHH
NKK.

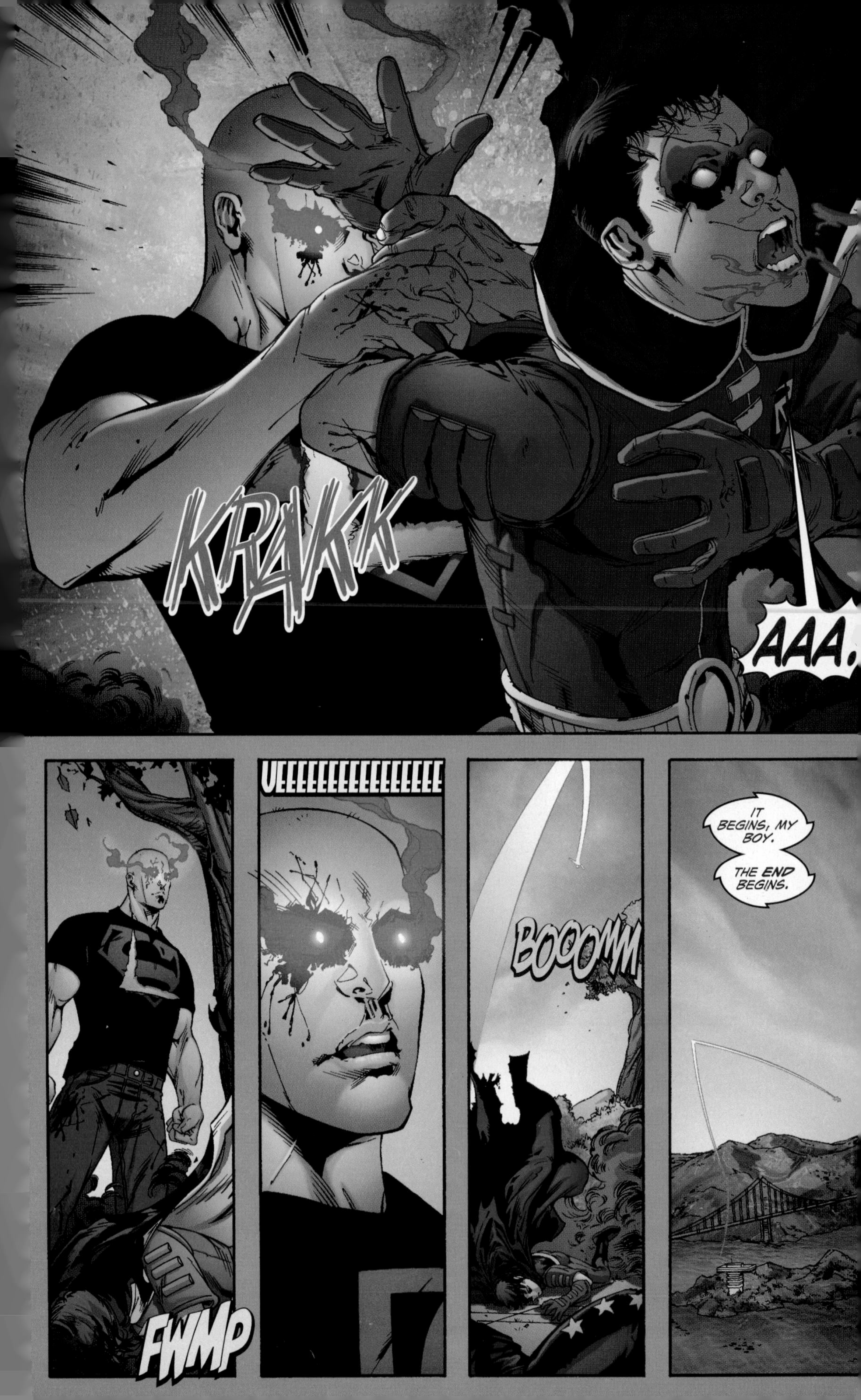
KRAKK
AAA.
FWMP
UEEEEEEEEEEEEEEEE
BOOOMM
IT BEGINS, MY BOY.
THE END BEGINS.

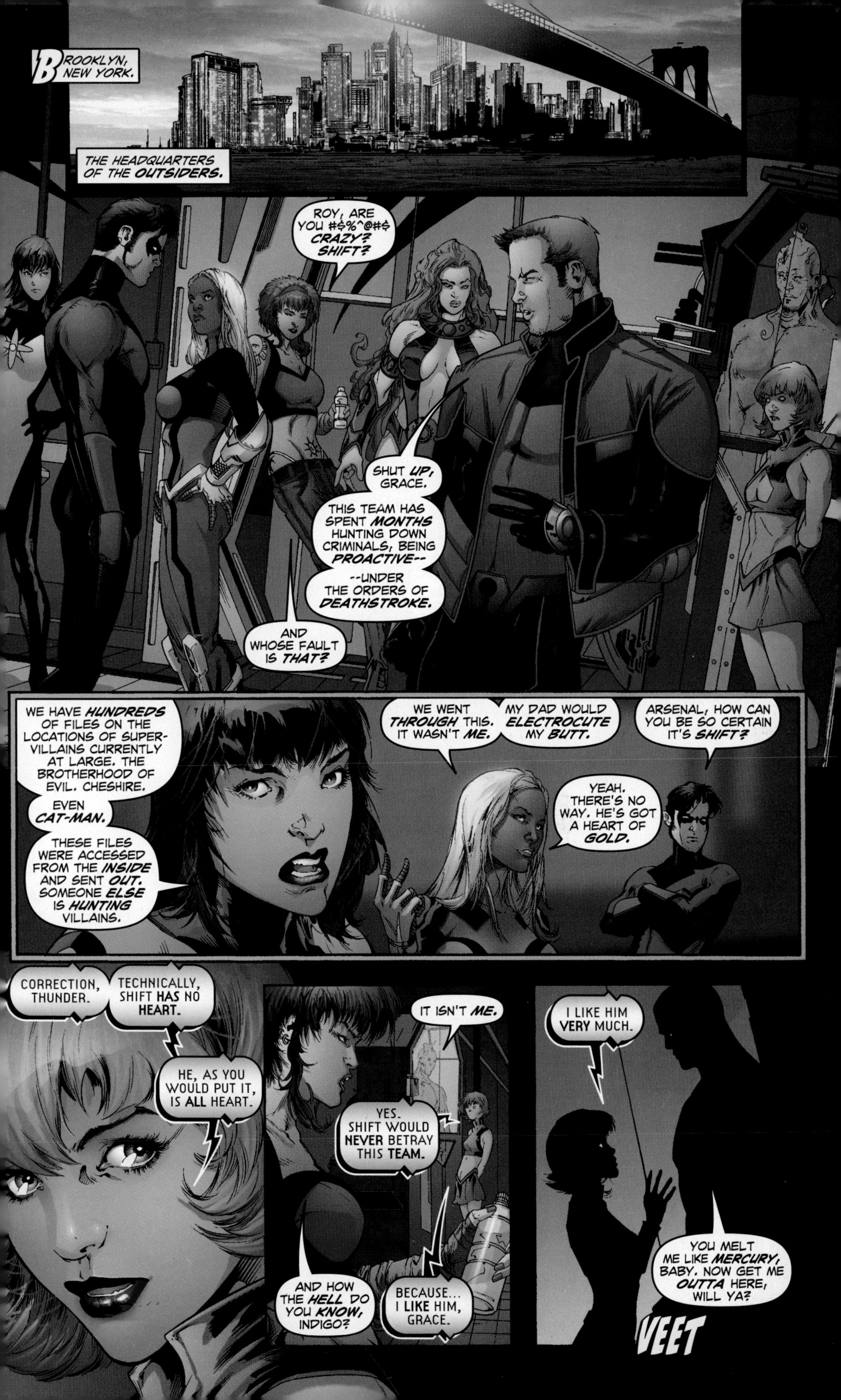

BROOKLYN, NEW YORK.
THE HEADQUARTERS OF THE OUTSIDERS.
ROY, ARE YOU #$%^@#$ CRAZY? SHIFT?
SHUT UP, GRACE.
THIS TEAM HAS SPENT MONTHS HUNTING DOWN CRIMINALS, BEING PROACTIVE--
--UNDER THE ORDERS OF DEATHSTROKE.
AND WHOSE FAULT IS THAT?
WE HAVE HUNDREDS OF FILES ON THE LOCATIONS OF SUPER-VILLAINS CURRENTLY AT LARGE. THE BROTHERHOOD OF EVIL. CHESHIRE.
EVEN CAT-MAN.
THESE FILES WERE ACCESSED FROM THE INSIDE AND SENT OUT. SOMEONE ELSE IS HUNTING VILLAINS.
WE WENT THROUGH THIS. IT WASN'T ME.
MY DAD WOULD ELECTROCUTE MY BUTT.
ARSENAL, HOW CAN YOU BE SO CERTAIN IT'S SHIFT?
YEAH. THERE'S NO WAY. HE'S GOT A HEART OF GOLD.
CORRECTION, THUNDER.
TECHNICALLY, SHIFT HAS NO HEART.
HE, AS YOU WOULD PUT IT, IS ALL HEART.
IT ISN'T ME.
YES. SHIFT WOULD NEVER BETRAY THIS TEAM.
AND HOW THE HELL DO YOU KNOW, INDIGO?
BECAUSE... I LIKE HIM, GRACE.
I LIKE HIM VERY MUCH.
YOU MELT ME LIKE MERCURY, BABY. NOW GET ME OUTTA HERE, WILL YA?
VEET

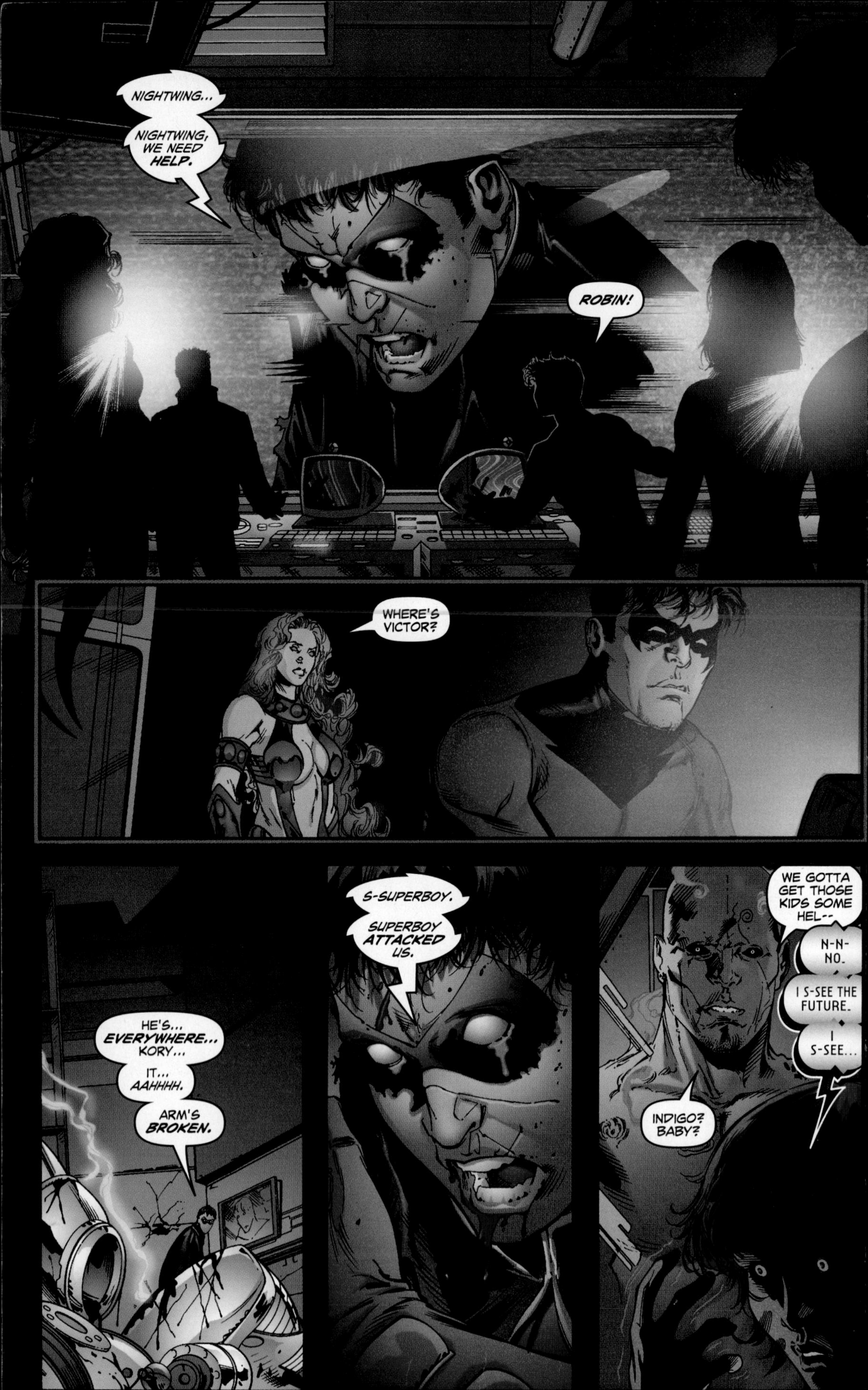
NIGHTWING...
NIGHTWING, WE NEED HELP.
ROBIN!
WHERE'S VICTOR?
HE'S... EVERYWHERE... KORY...
IT... AAHHHH.
ARM'S BROKEN.
S-SUPERBOY.
SUPERBOY ATTACKED US.
WE GOTTA GET THOSE KIDS SOME HEL--
N-N-NO.
I S-SEE THE FUTURE.
I S-SEE...
INDIGO? BABY?

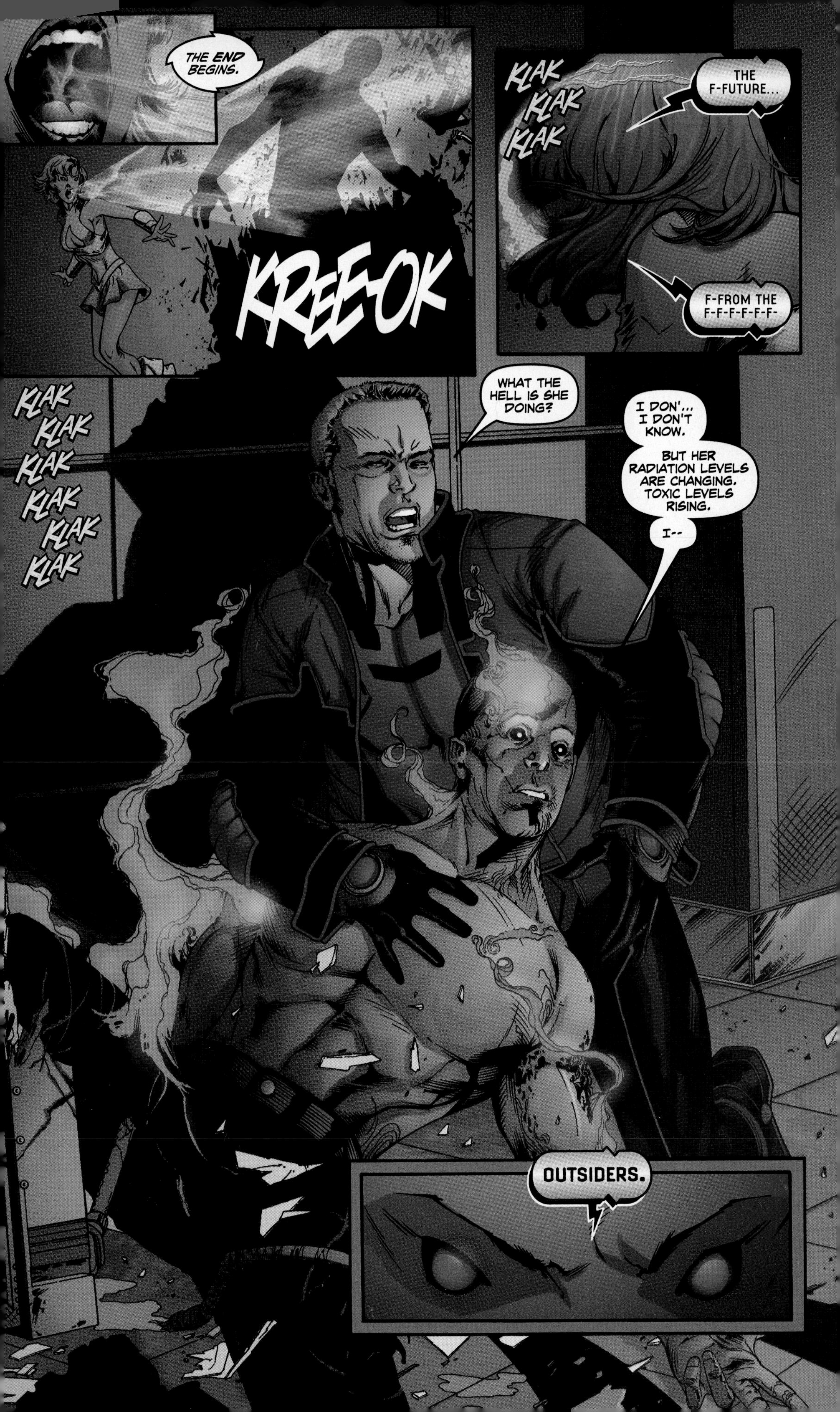
THE END BEGINS.
KREE-OK
KLAK KLAK KLAK
THE F-FUTURE...
F-FROM THE F-F-F-F-F-F-
KLAK KLAK KLAK KLAK KLAK KLAK
WHAT THE HELL IS SHE DOING?
I DON'... I DON'T KNOW.
BUT HER RADIATION LEVELS ARE CHANGING. TOXIC LEVELS RISING.
I--
OUTSIDERS.

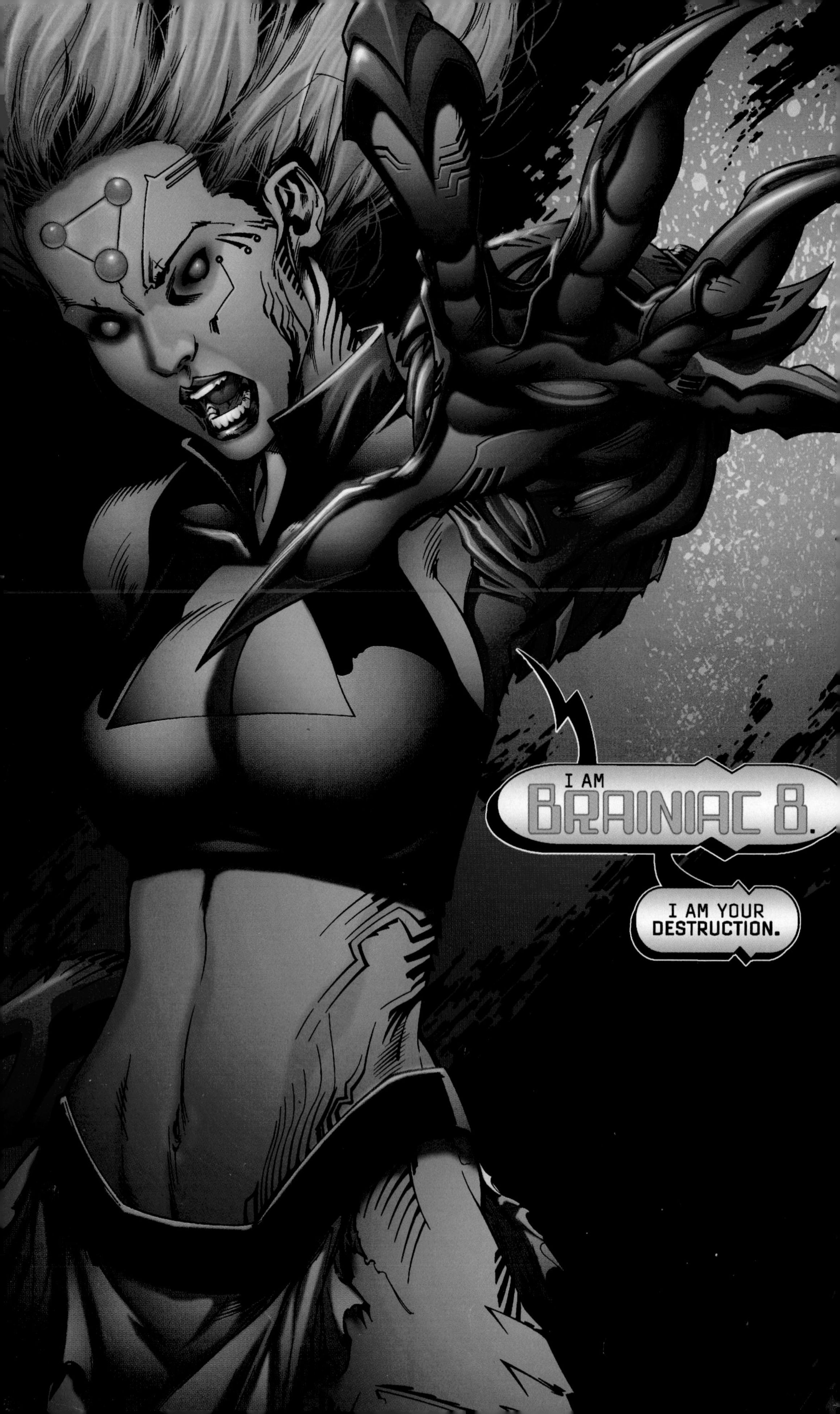
I AM BRAINIAC 8.
I AM YOUR DESTRUCTION.

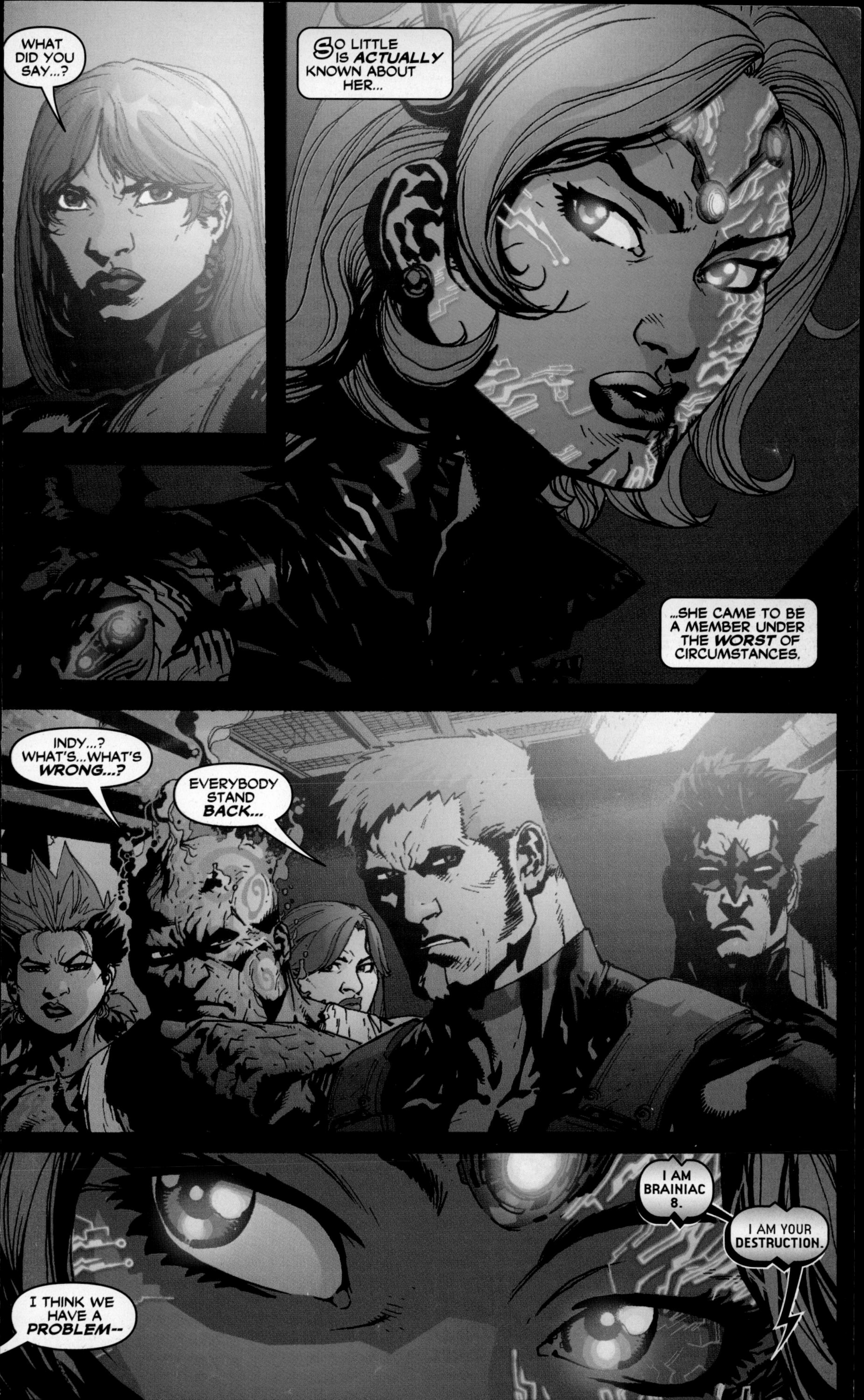
WHAT DID YOU SAY...?
SO LITTLE IS ACTUALLY KNOWN ABOUT HER...
...SHE CAME TO BE A MEMBER UNDER THE WORST OF CIRCUMSTANCES.
INDY...? WHAT'S...WHAT'S WRONG...?
EVERYBODY STAND BACK...
I AM BRAINIAC 8.
I AM YOUR DESTRUCTION.
I THINK WE HAVE A PROBLEM--

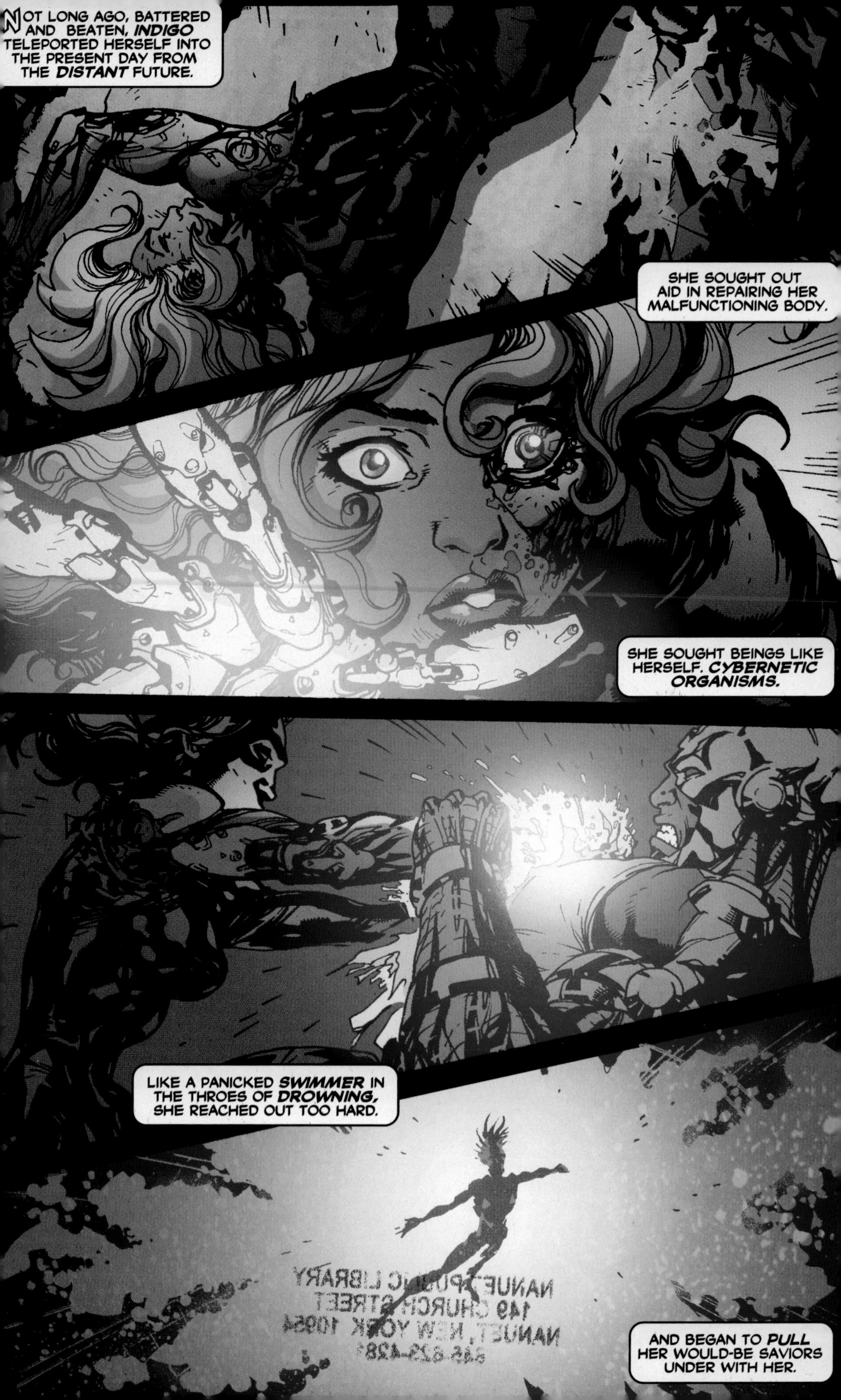
NOT LONG AGO, BATTERED AND BEATEN, INDIGO TELEPORTED HERSELF INTO THE PRESENT DAY FROM THE DISTANT FUTURE.
SHE SOUGHT OUT AID IN REPAIRING HER MALFUNCTIONING BODY.
SHE SOUGHT BEINGS LIKE HERSELF. CYBERNETIC ORGANISMS.
LIKE A PANICKED SWIMMER IN THE THROES OF DROWNING, SHE REACHED OUT TOO HARD.
AND BEGAN TO PULL HER WOULD-BE SAVIORS UNDER WITH HER.

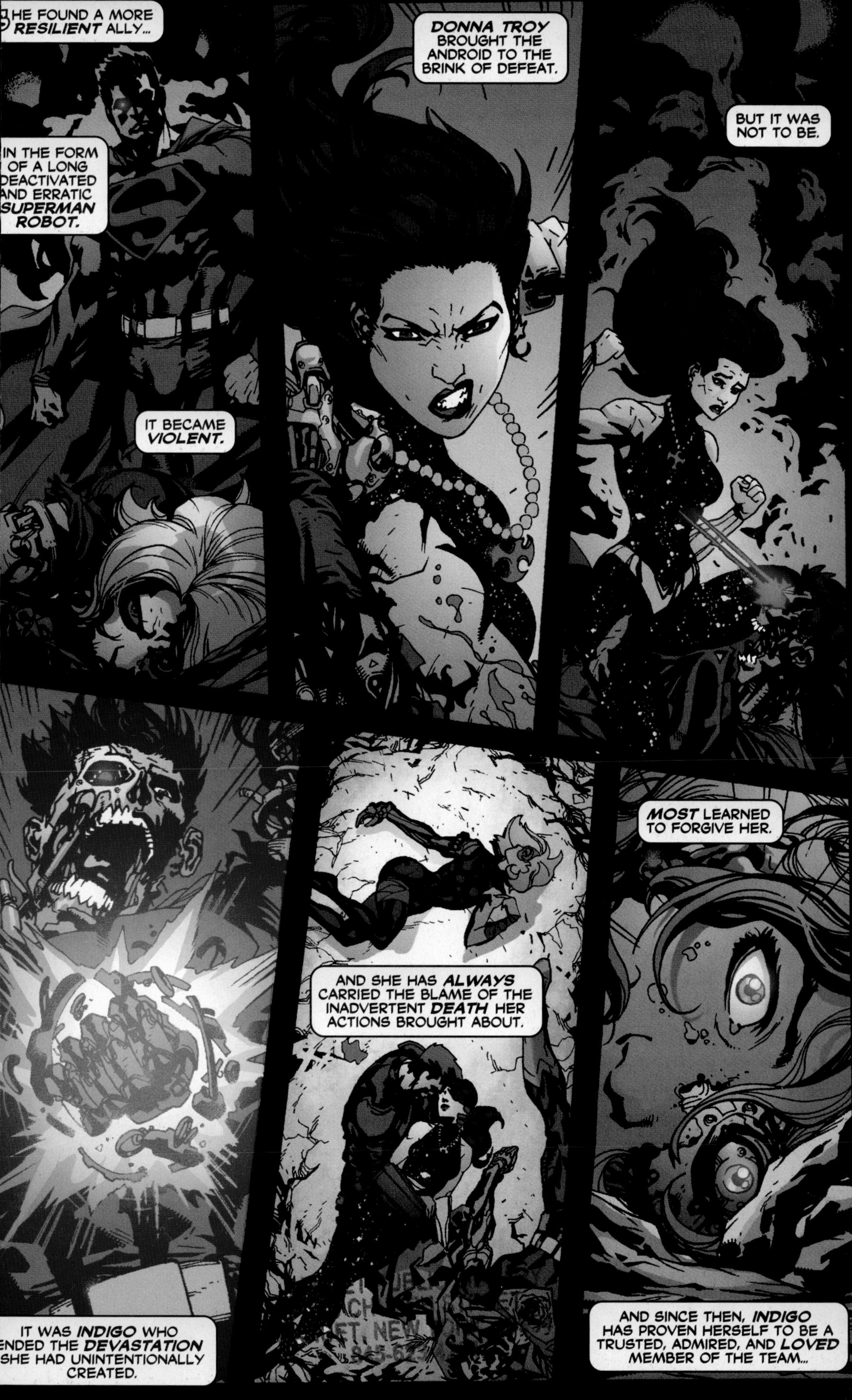

HE FOUND A MORE RESILIENT ALLY...
IN THE FORM OF A LONG DEACTIVATED AND ERRATIC SUPERMAN ROBOT.
IT BECAME VIOLENT.
DONNA TROY BROUGHT THE ANDROID TO THE BRINK OF DEFEAT.
BUT IT WAS NOT TO BE.
IT WAS INDIGO WHO ENDED THE DEVASTATION SHE HAD UNINTENTIONALLY CREATED.
AND SHE HAS ALWAYS CARRIED THE BLAME OF THE INADVERTENT DEATH HER ACTIONS BROUGHT ABOUT.
MOST LEARNED TO FORGIVE HER.
AND SINCE THEN, INDIGO HAS PROVEN HERSELF TO BE A TRUSTED, ADMIRED, AND LOVED MEMBER OF THE TEAM...

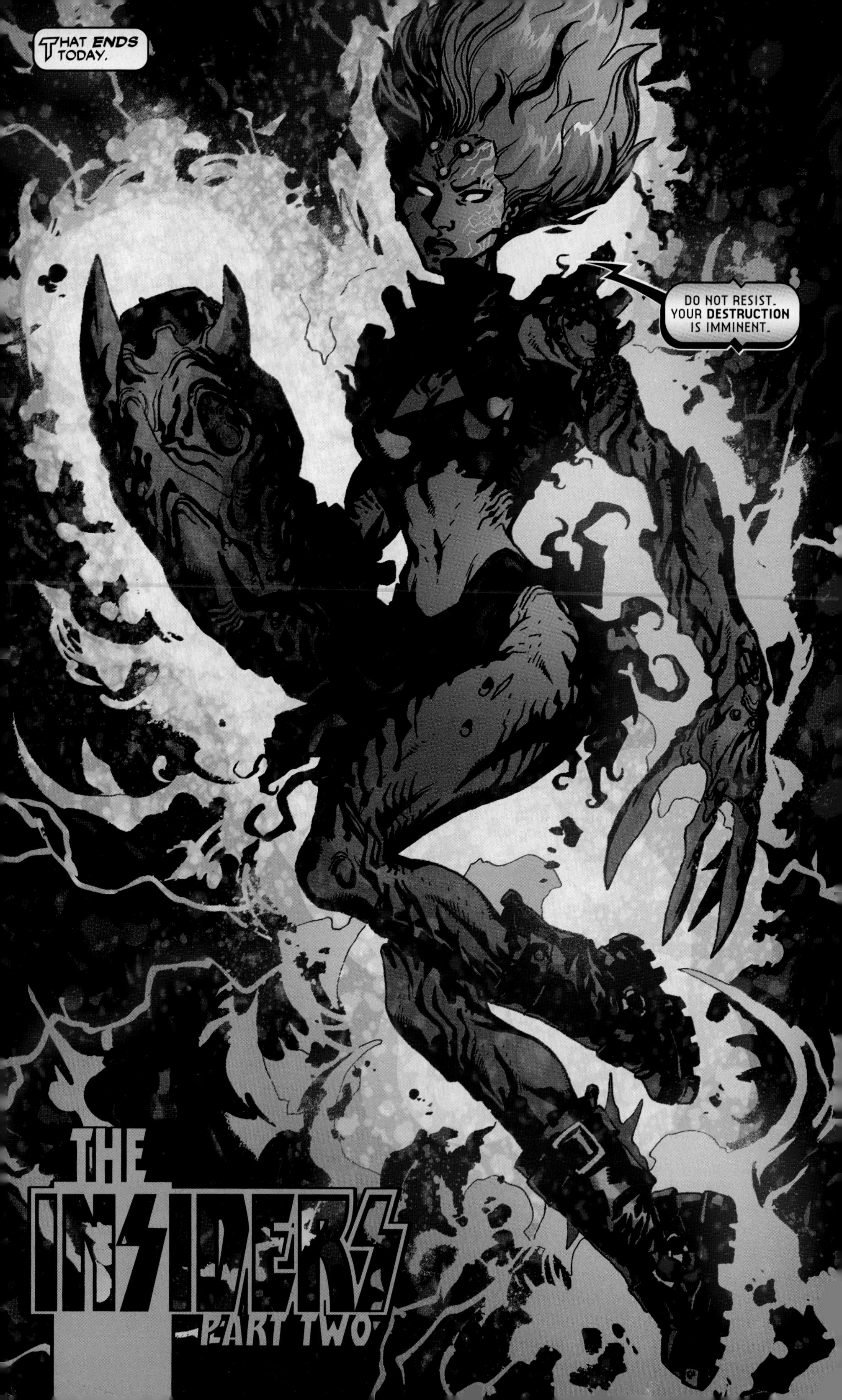
THAT ENDS TODAY.
DO NOT RESIST. YOUR DESTRUCTION IS IMMINENT.
THE INSIDERS
PART TWO

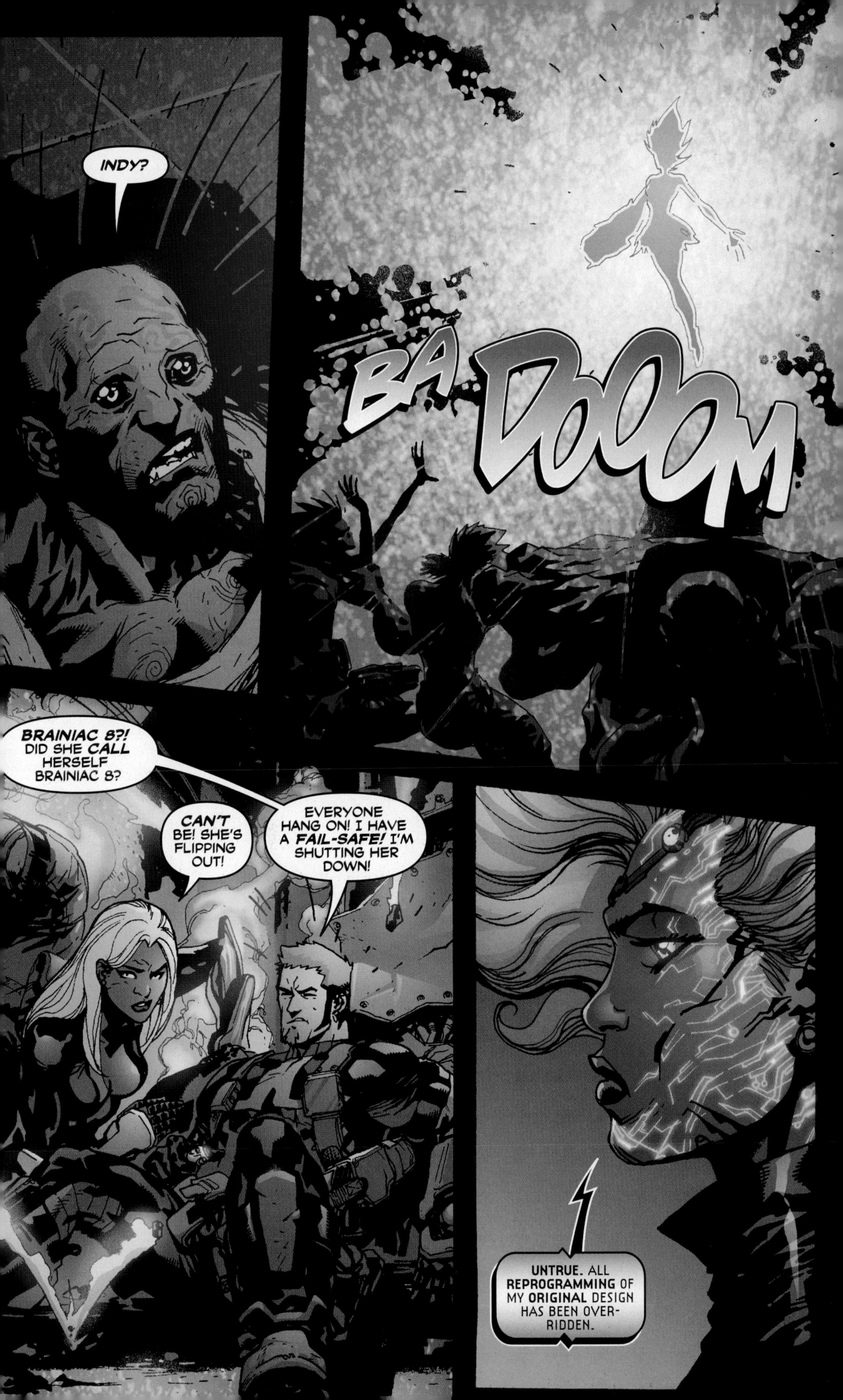
INDY?
BA DOOOM
BRAINIAC 8?! DID SHE CALL HERSELF BRAINIAC 8?
CAN'T BE! SHE'S FLIPPING OUT!
EVERYONE HANG ON! I HAVE A FAIL-SAFE! I'M SHUTTING HER DOWN!
UNTRUE. ALL REPROGRAMMING OF MY ORIGINAL DESIGN HAS BEEN OVER-RIDDEN.

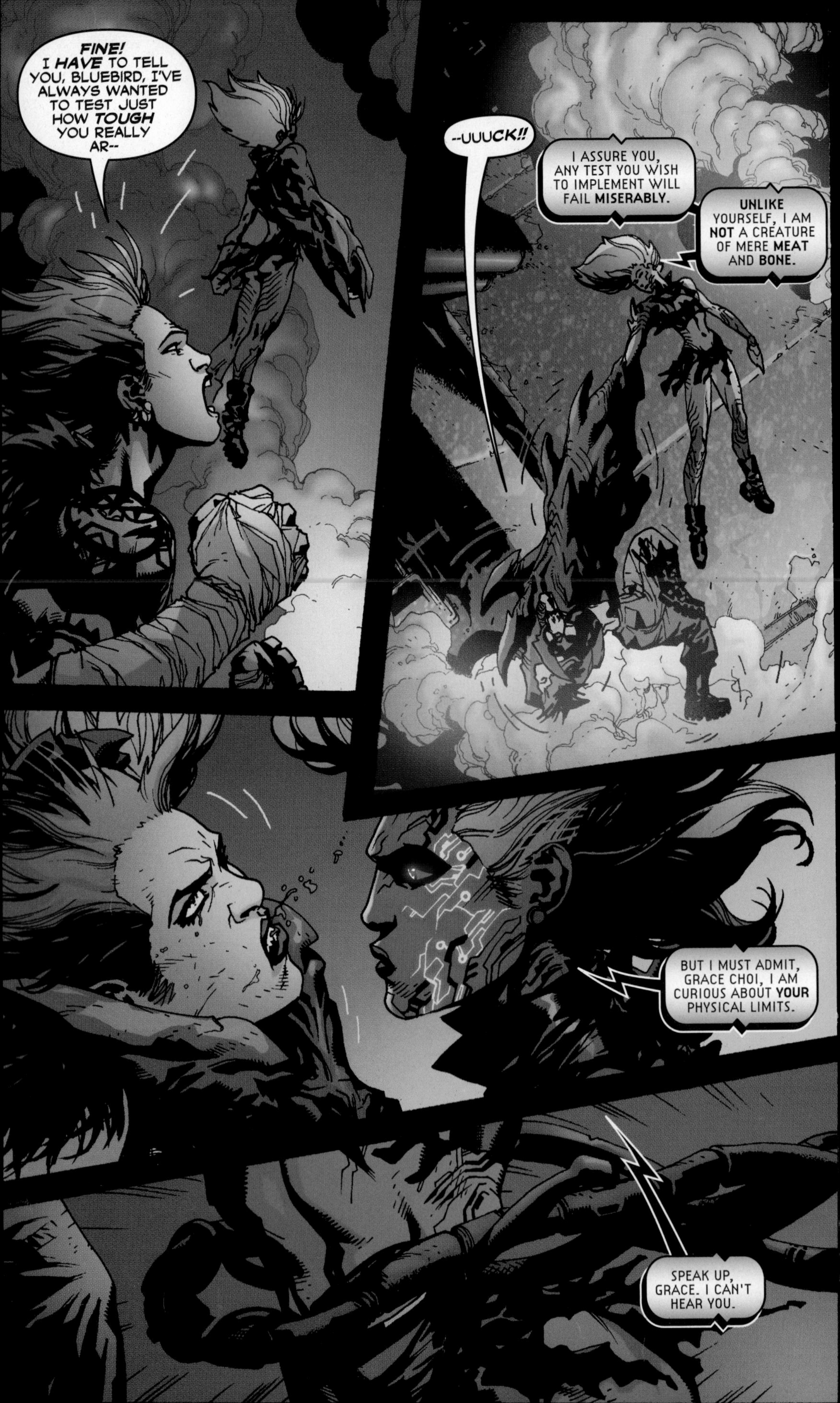
FINE! I HAVE TO TELL YOU, BLUEBIRD, I'VE ALWAYS WANTED TO TEST JUST HOW TOUGH YOU REALLY AR--
--UUUCK!!
I ASSURE YOU, ANY TEST YOU WISH TO IMPLEMENT WILL FAIL MISERABLY.
UNLIKE YOURSELF, I AM NOT A CREATURE OF MERE MEAT AND BONE.
BUT I MUST ADMIT, GRACE CHOI, I AM CURIOUS ABOUT YOUR PHYSICAL LIMITS.
SPEAK UP, GRACE. I CAN'T HEAR YOU.

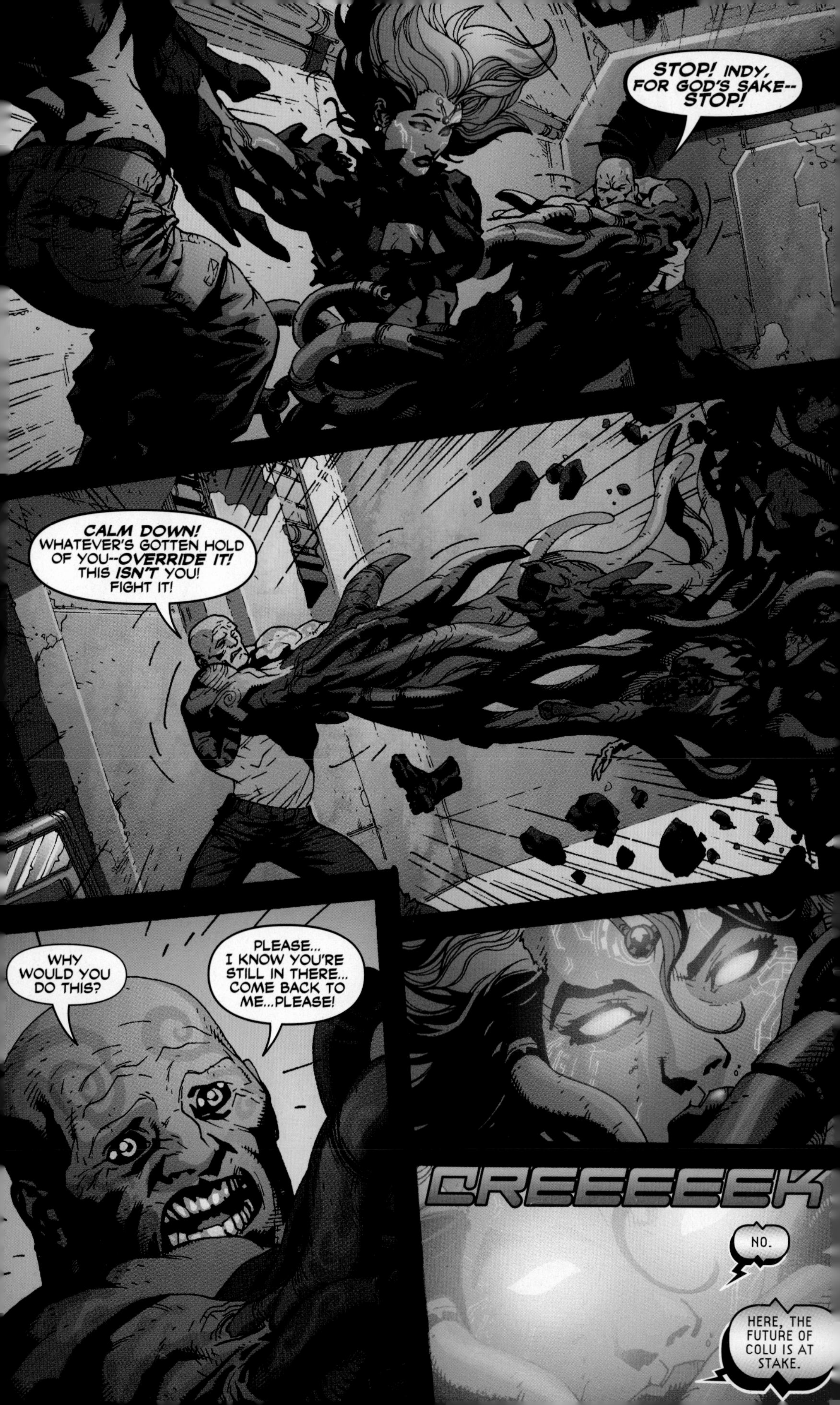
STOP! INDY, FOR GOD'S SAKE-- STOP!
CALM DOWN! WHATEVER'S GOTTEN HOLD OF YOU--OVERRIDE IT! THIS ISN'T YOU! FIGHT IT!
WHY WOULD YOU DO THIS?
PLEASE... I KNOW YOU'RE STILL IN THERE... COME BACK TO ME...PLEASE!
CREEEEEK
NO.
HERE, THE FUTURE OF COLU IS AT STAKE.

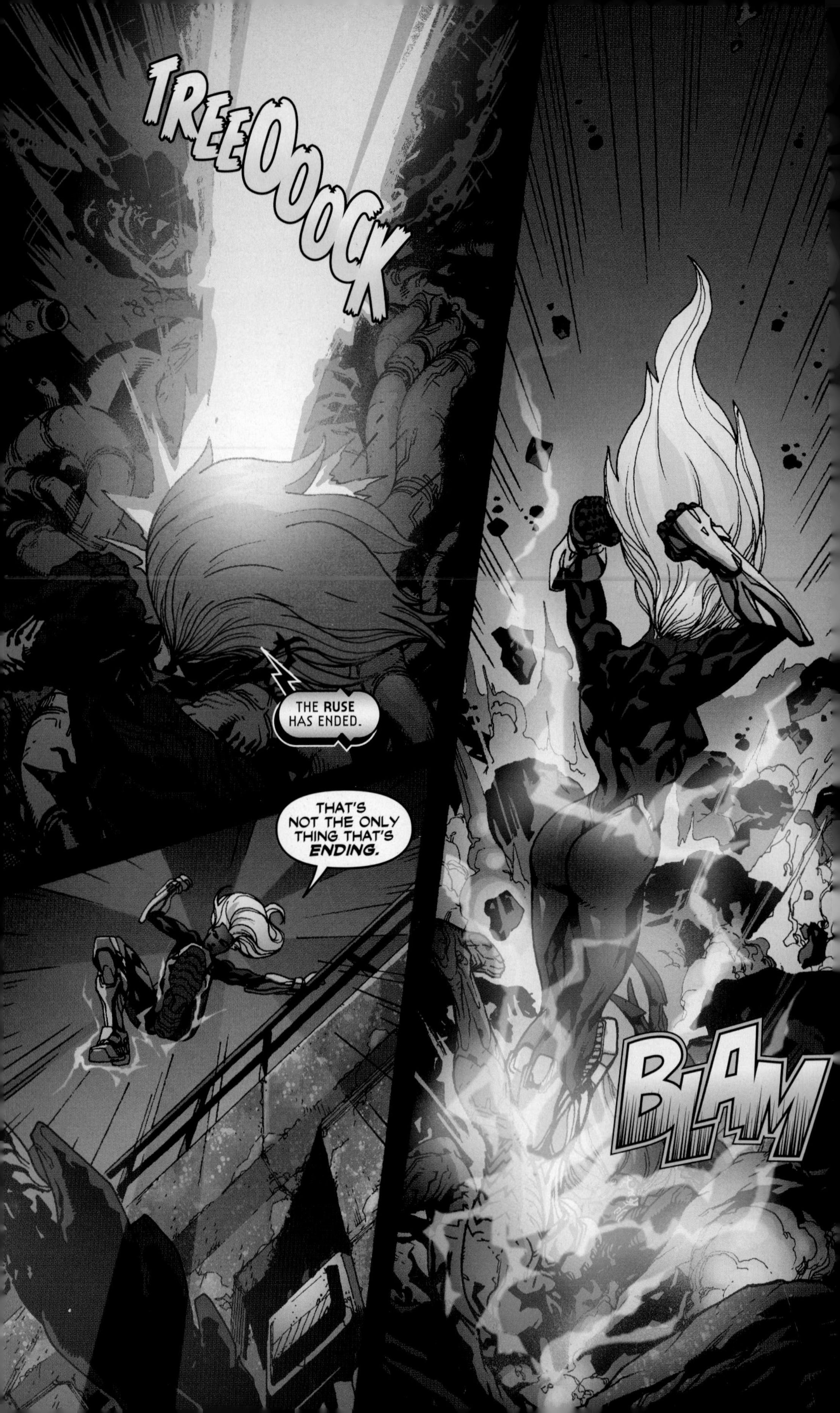
TREEOOOCK
THE RUSE HAS ENDED.
THAT'S NOT THE ONLY THING THAT'S ENDING.
BLAM

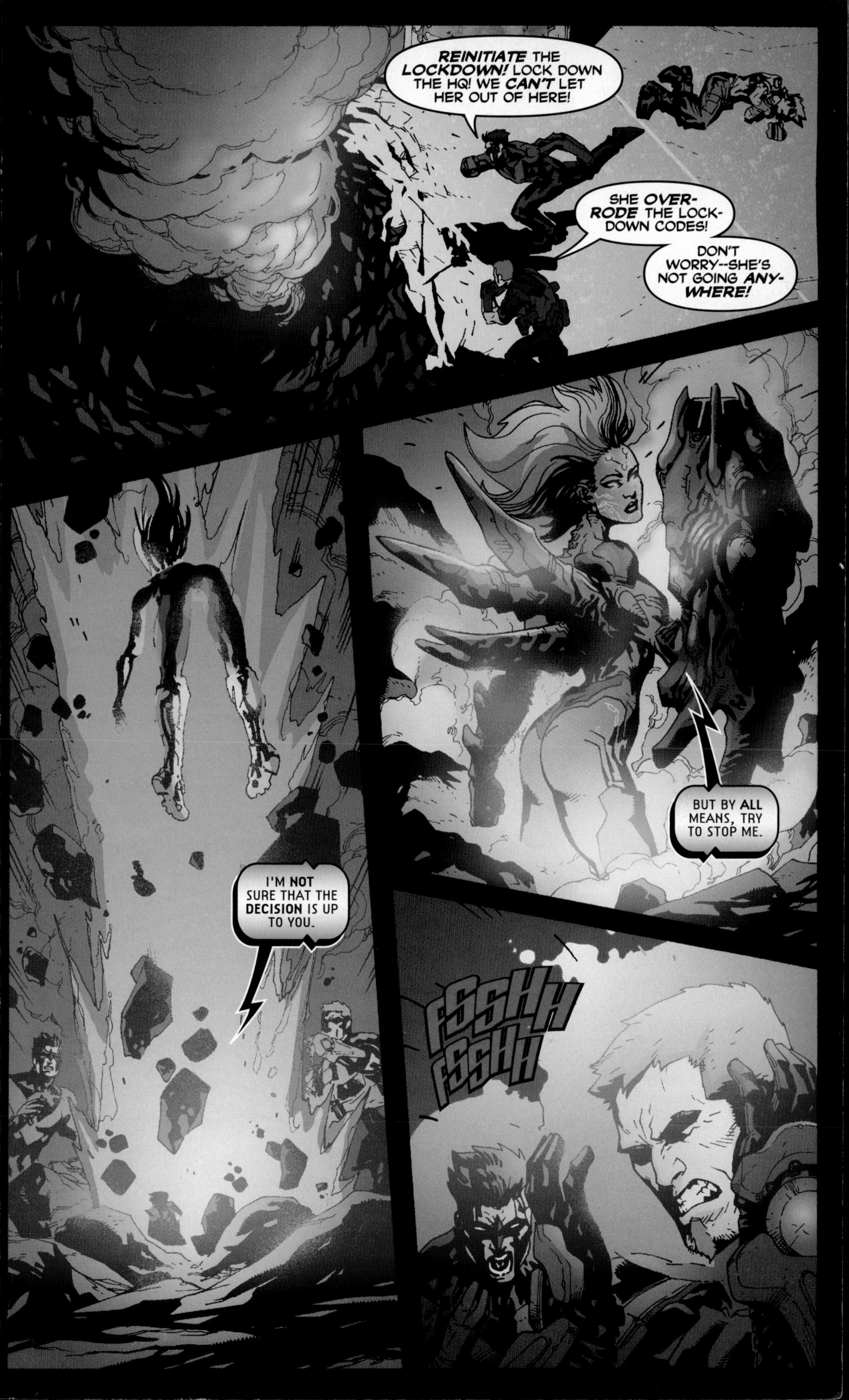
REINITIATE THE LOCKDOWN! LOCK DOWN THE HQ! WE CAN'T LET HER OUT OF HERE!
SHE OVER-RODE THE LOCK-DOWN CODES!
DON'T WORRY--SHE'S NOT GOING ANY-WHERE!
BUT BY ALL MEANS, TRY TO STOP ME.
I'M NOT SURE THAT THE DECISION IS UP TO YOU.
FSSHH FSSHH

RIGHT NOW, ROY, WHEN YOU'RE **DYING** FROM SUFFOCATION, WHEN THE **PANIC** HAS BEGUN TO SET IN...
...**THIS** IS THE PART WHEN YOU REMEMBER... THIS IS **ALL** YOUR FAULT.
AT THE MOMENT, I DON'T SEE THE ***BLAME*** FALLING ON ***HIM.***
CEE-OOK
REALLY?!

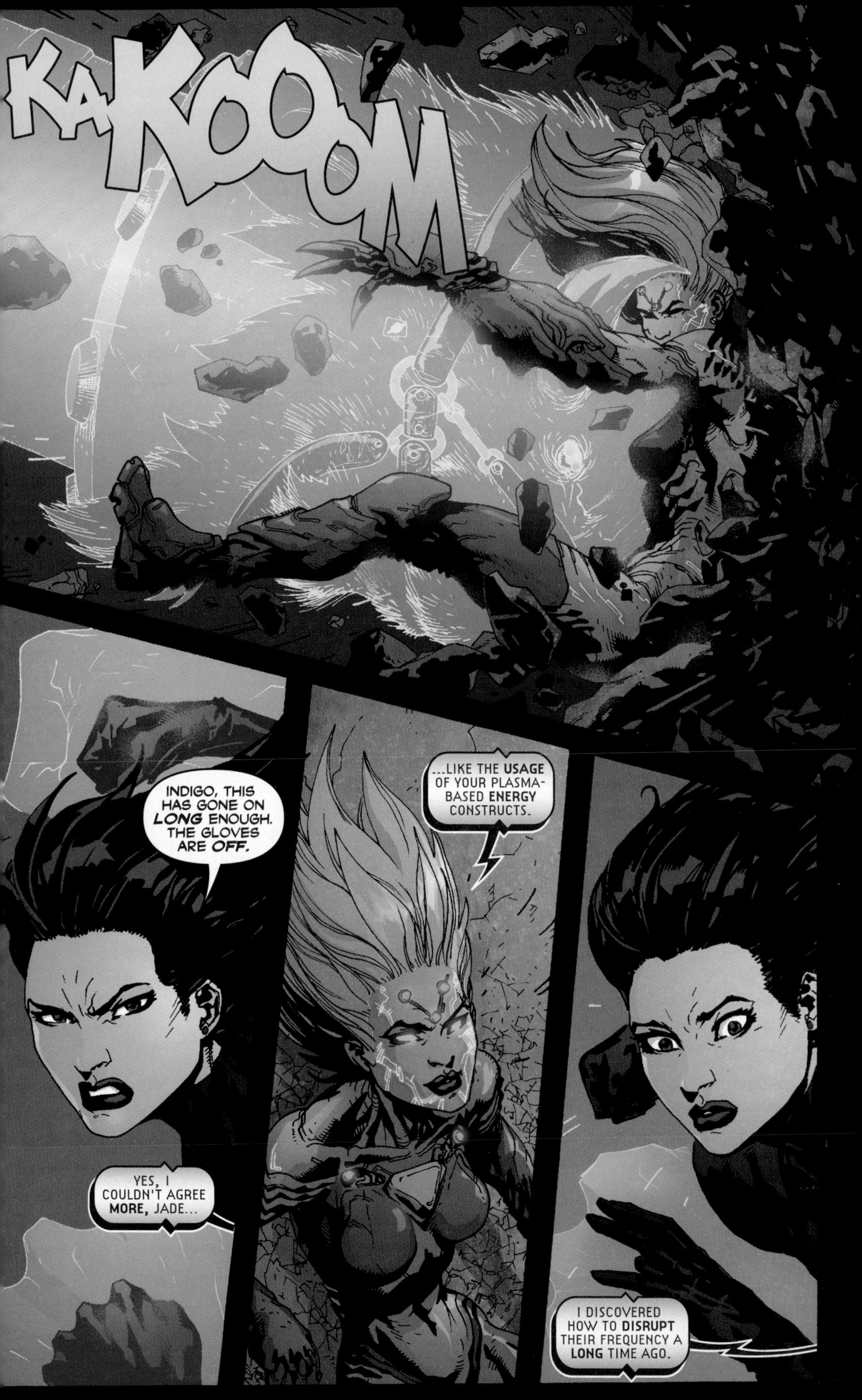
KAKOOOM
INDIGO, THIS HAS GONE ON LONG ENOUGH. THE GLOVES ARE OFF.
YES, I COULDN'T AGREE MORE, JADE...
...LIKE THE USAGE OF YOUR PLASMA-BASED ENERGY CONSTRUCTS.
I DISCOVERED HOW TO DISRUPT THEIR FREQUENCY A LONG TIME AGO.

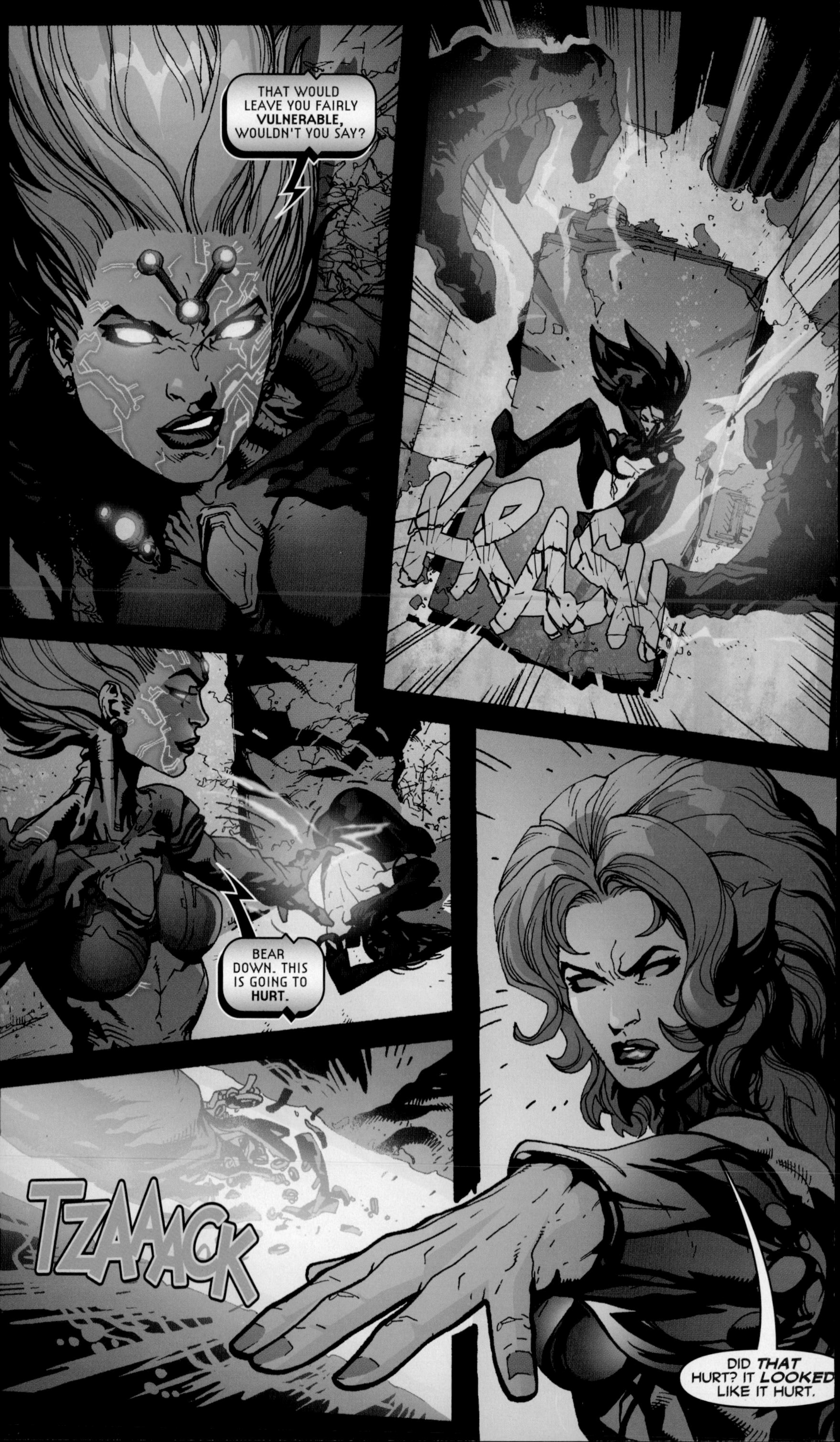

THAT WOULD LEAVE YOU FAIRLY VULNERABLE, WOULDN'T YOU SAY?
KRASH
BEAR DOWN. THIS IS GOING TO HURT.
TZAAACK
DID THAT HURT? IT LOOKED LIKE IT HURT.

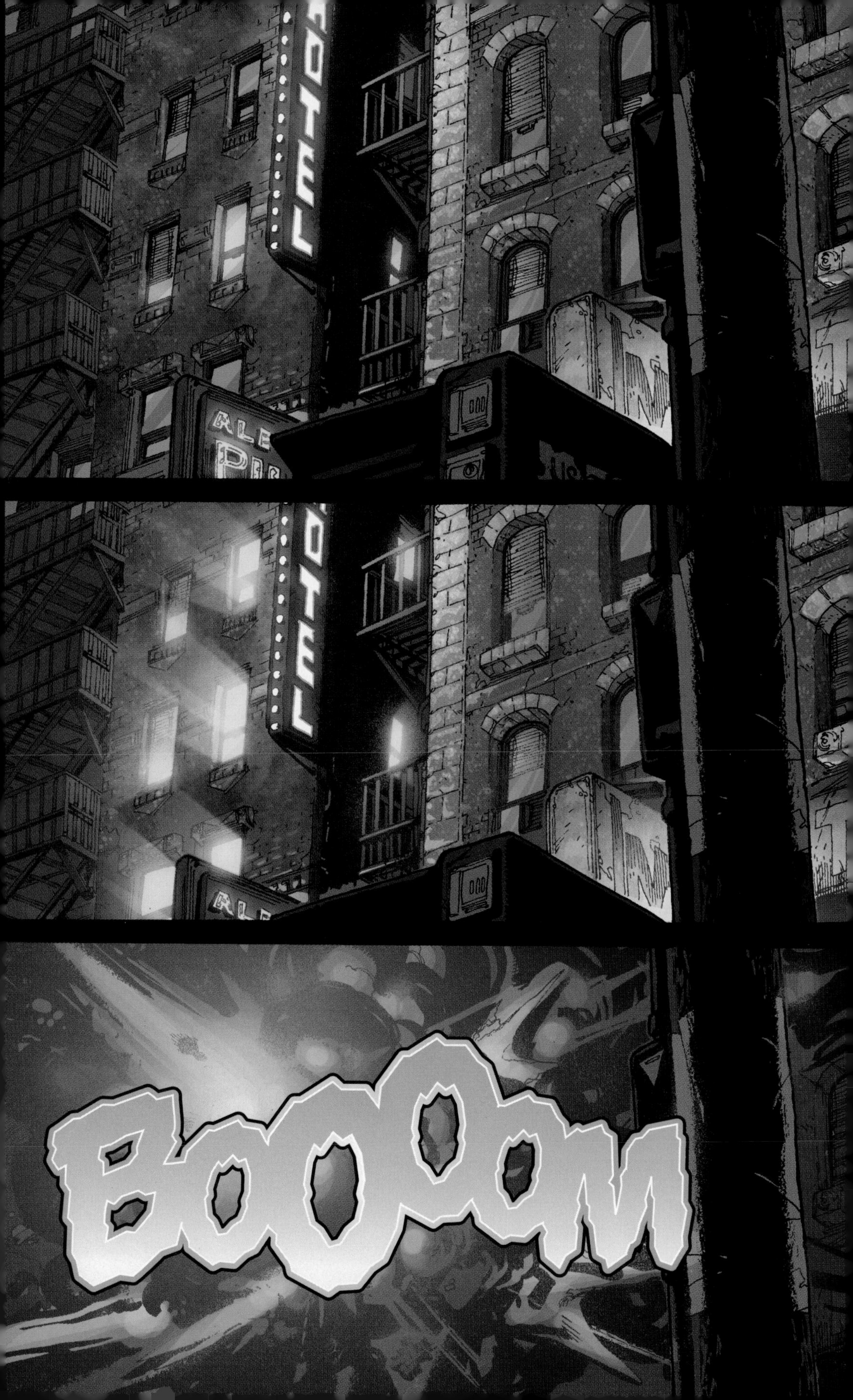
BOOOOM

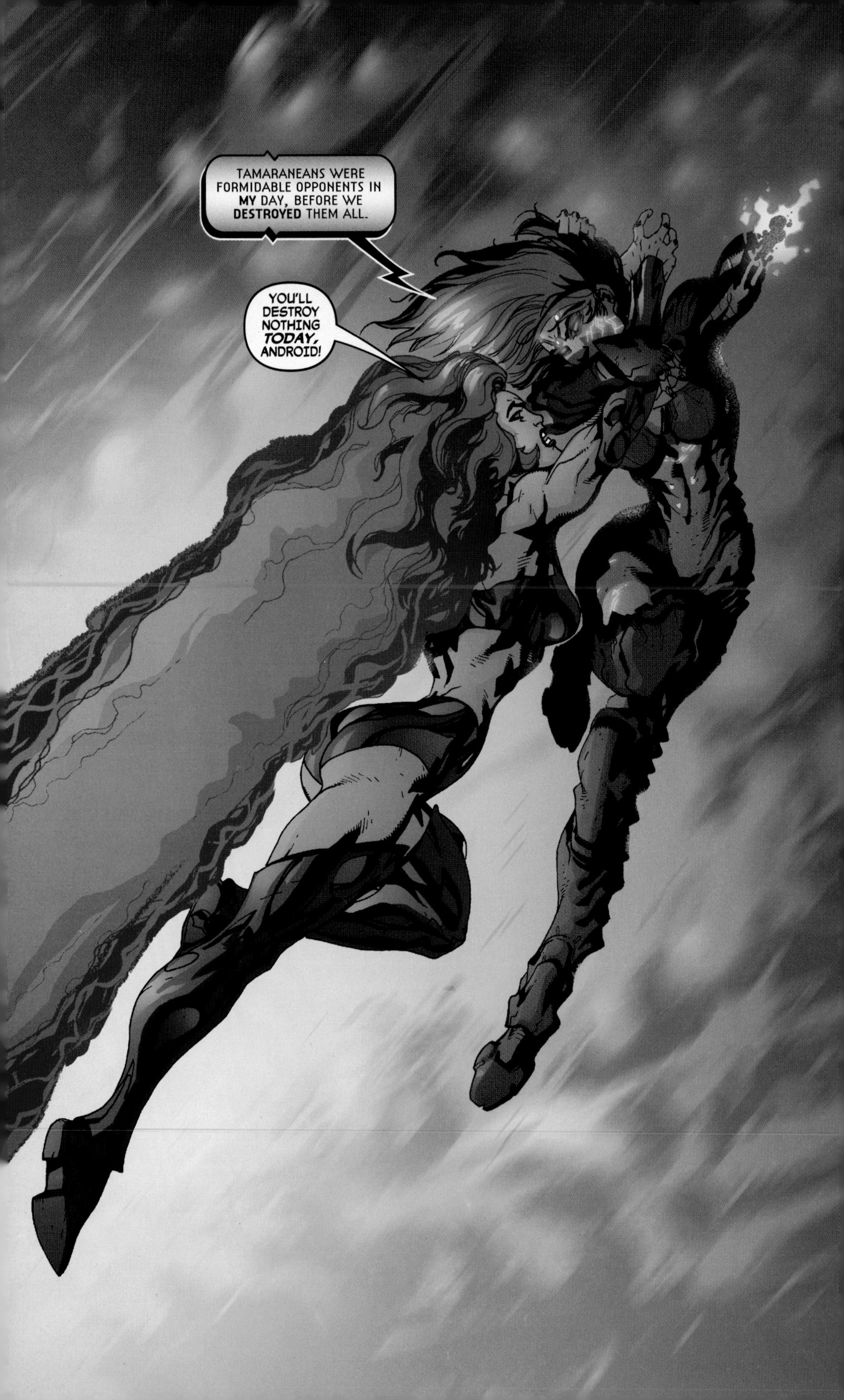
TAMARANEANS WERE FORMIDABLE OPPONENTS IN **MY** DAY, BEFORE WE **DESTROYED** THEM ALL.
YOU'LL DESTROY NOTHING ***TODAY,*** ANDROID!

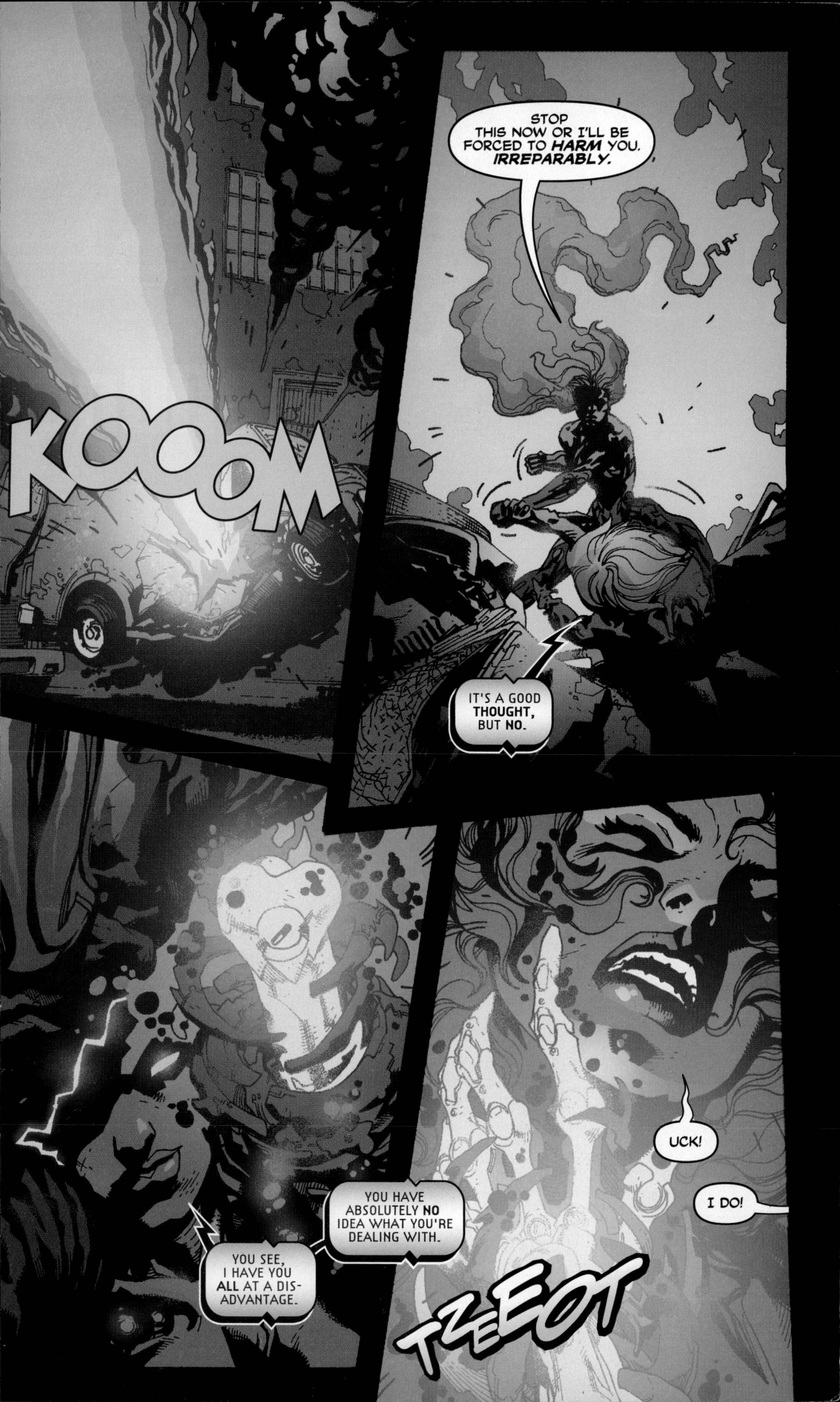

KOOOM
STOP THIS NOW OR I'LL BE FORCED TO **HARM** YOU. ***IRREPARABLY.***
IT'S A GOOD **THOUGHT,** BUT **NO.**
YOU HAVE ABSOLUTELY **NO** IDEA WHAT YOU'RE DEALING WITH.
YOU SEE, I HAVE YOU **ALL** AT A DIS-ADVANTAGE.
UCK!
I DO!
TZEEOT

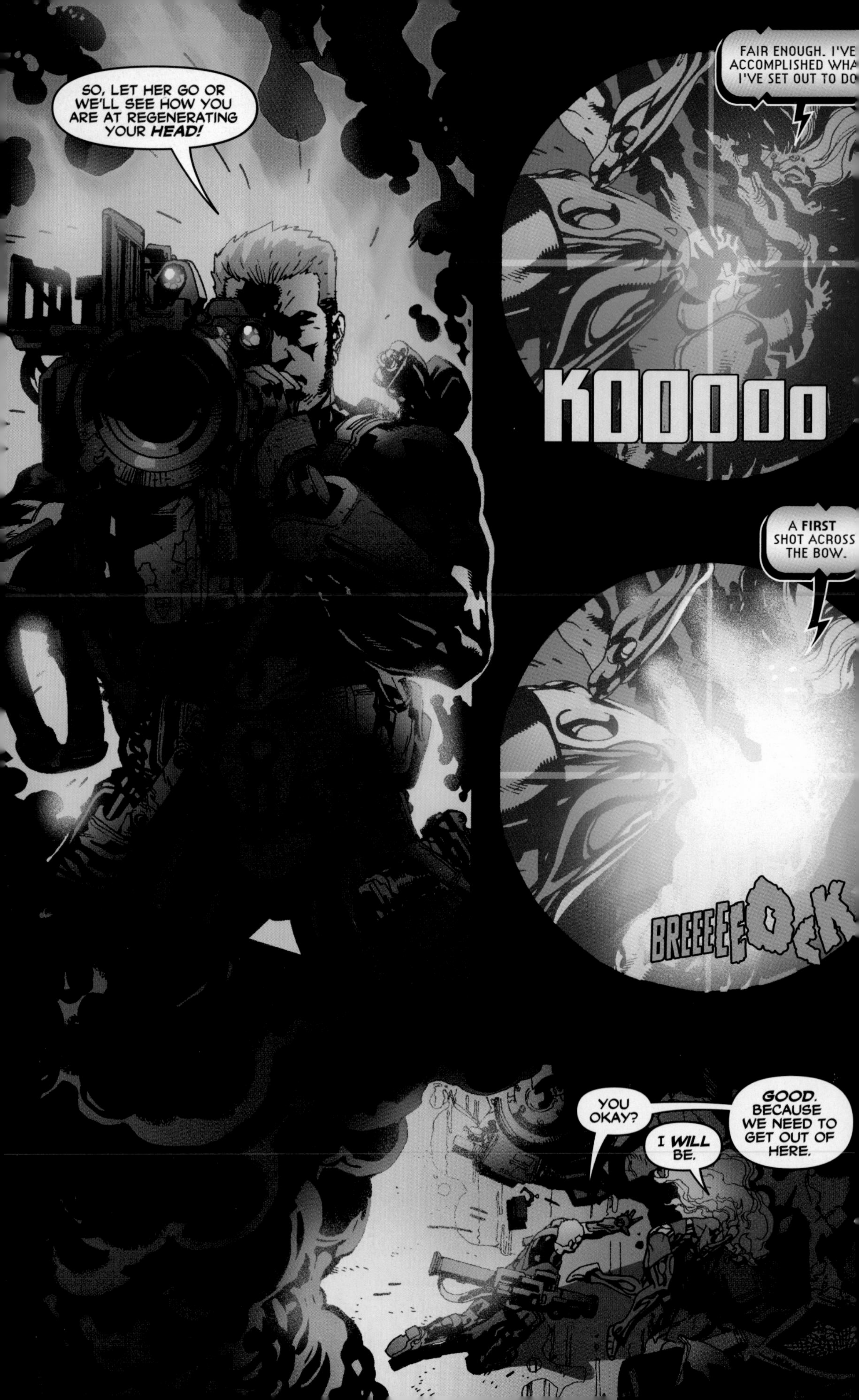
SO, LET HER GO OR WE'LL SEE HOW YOU ARE AT REGENERATING YOUR ***HEAD!***
FAIR ENOUGH. I'VE ACCOMPLISHED WHA I'VE SET OUT TO DO
KOOOoo
A **FIRST** SHOT ACROSS THE BOW.
BREEEEEOCK
YOU OKAY?
I ***WILL*** BE.
GOOD. BECAUSE WE NEED TO GET OUT OF HERE.

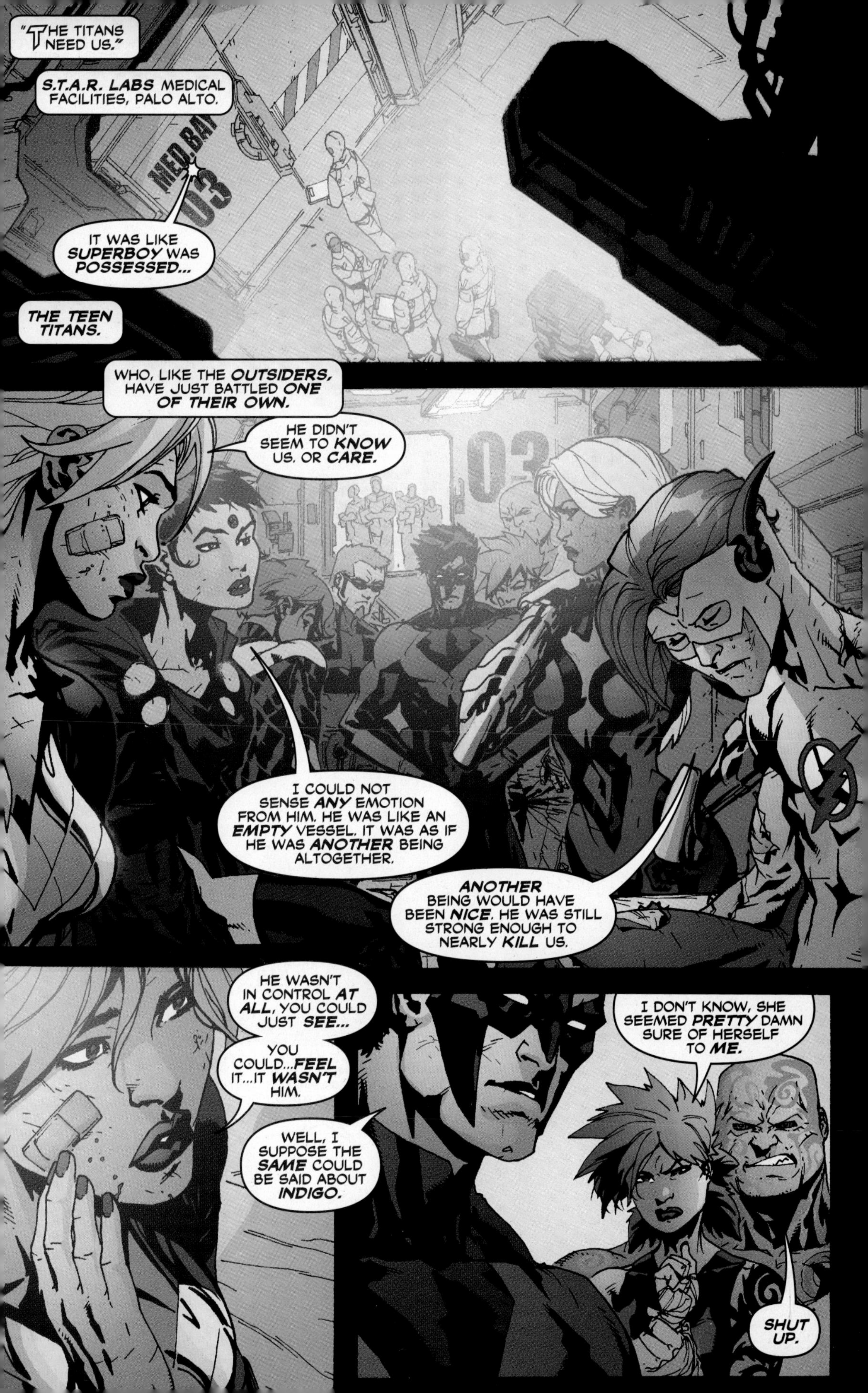
"THE TITANS NEED US."
S.T.A.R. LABS MEDICAL FACILITIES, PALO ALTO.
MED.BAY 03
IT WAS LIKE SUPERBOY WAS POSSESSED...
THE TEEN TITANS.
WHO, LIKE THE OUTSIDERS, HAVE JUST BATTLED ONE OF THEIR OWN.
HE DIDN'T SEEM TO KNOW US. OR CARE.
03
I COULD NOT SENSE ANY EMOTION FROM HIM. HE WAS LIKE AN EMPTY VESSEL. IT WAS AS IF HE WAS ANOTHER BEING ALTOGETHER.
ANOTHER BEING WOULD HAVE BEEN NICE. HE WAS STILL STRONG ENOUGH TO NEARLY KILL US.
HE WASN'T IN CONTROL AT ALL, YOU COULD JUST SEE...
YOU COULD...FEEL IT...IT WASN'T HIM.
WELL, I SUPPOSE THE SAME COULD BE SAID ABOUT INDIGO.
I DON'T KNOW, SHE SEEMED PRETTY DAMN SURE OF HERSELF TO ME.
SHUT UP.

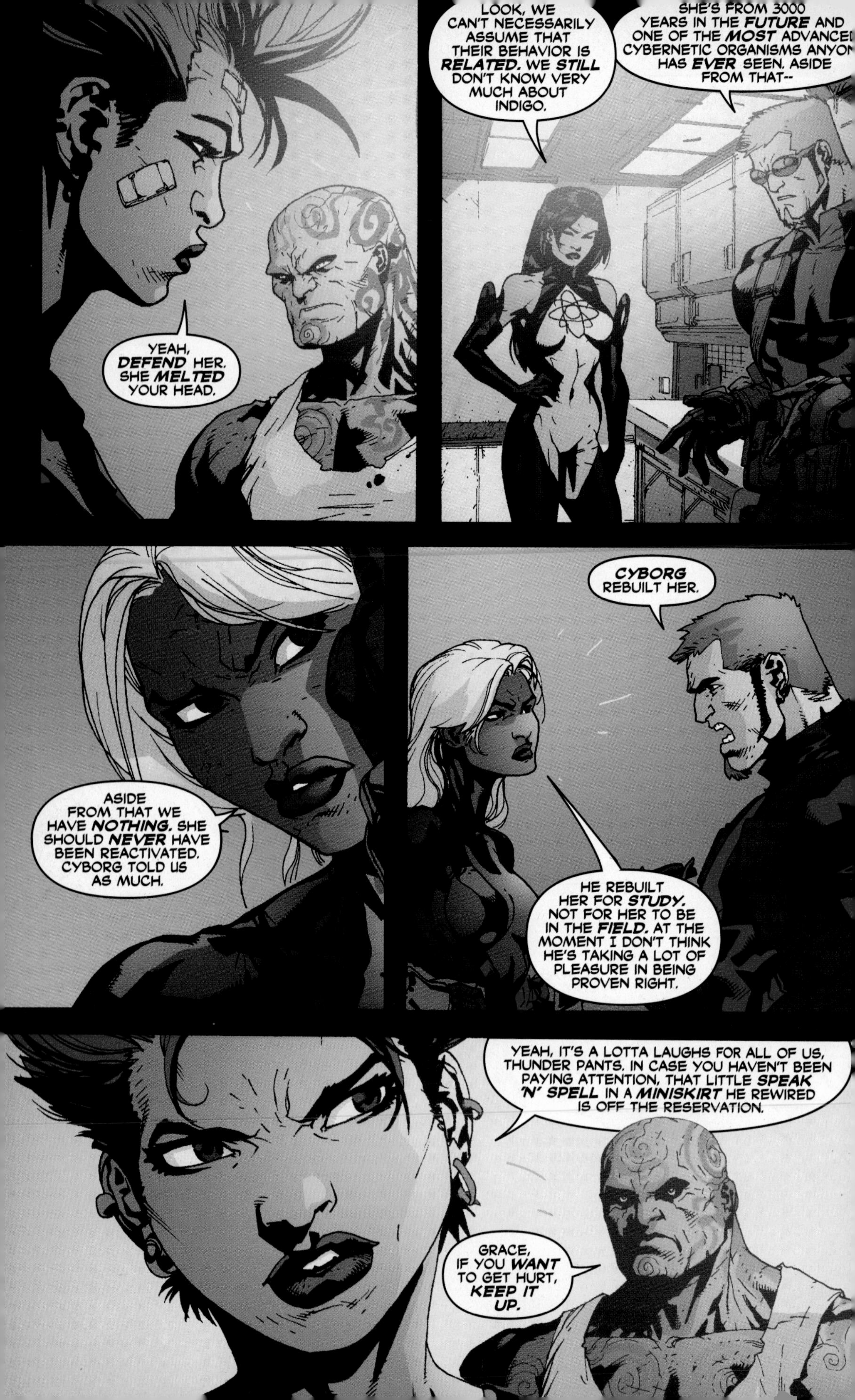
YEAH, DEFEND HER. SHE MELTED YOUR HEAD.
LOOK, WE CAN'T NECESSARILY ASSUME THAT THEIR BEHAVIOR IS RELATED. WE STILL DON'T KNOW VERY MUCH ABOUT INDIGO.
SHE'S FROM 3000 YEARS IN THE FUTURE AND ONE OF THE MOST ADVANCED CYBERNETIC ORGANISMS ANYONE HAS EVER SEEN. ASIDE FROM THAT--
ASIDE FROM THAT WE HAVE NOTHING. SHE SHOULD NEVER HAVE BEEN REACTIVATED. CYBORG TOLD US AS MUCH.
CYBORG REBUILT HER.
HE REBUILT HER FOR STUDY. NOT FOR HER TO BE IN THE FIELD. AT THE MOMENT I DON'T THINK HE'S TAKING A LOT OF PLEASURE IN BEING PROVEN RIGHT.
YEAH, IT'S A LOTTA LAUGHS FOR ALL OF US, THUNDER PANTS. IN CASE YOU HAVEN'T BEEN PAYING ATTENTION, THAT LITTLE SPEAK 'N' SPELL IN A MINISKIRT HE REWIRED IS OFF THE RESERVATION.
GRACE, IF YOU WANT TO GET HURT, KEEP IT UP.

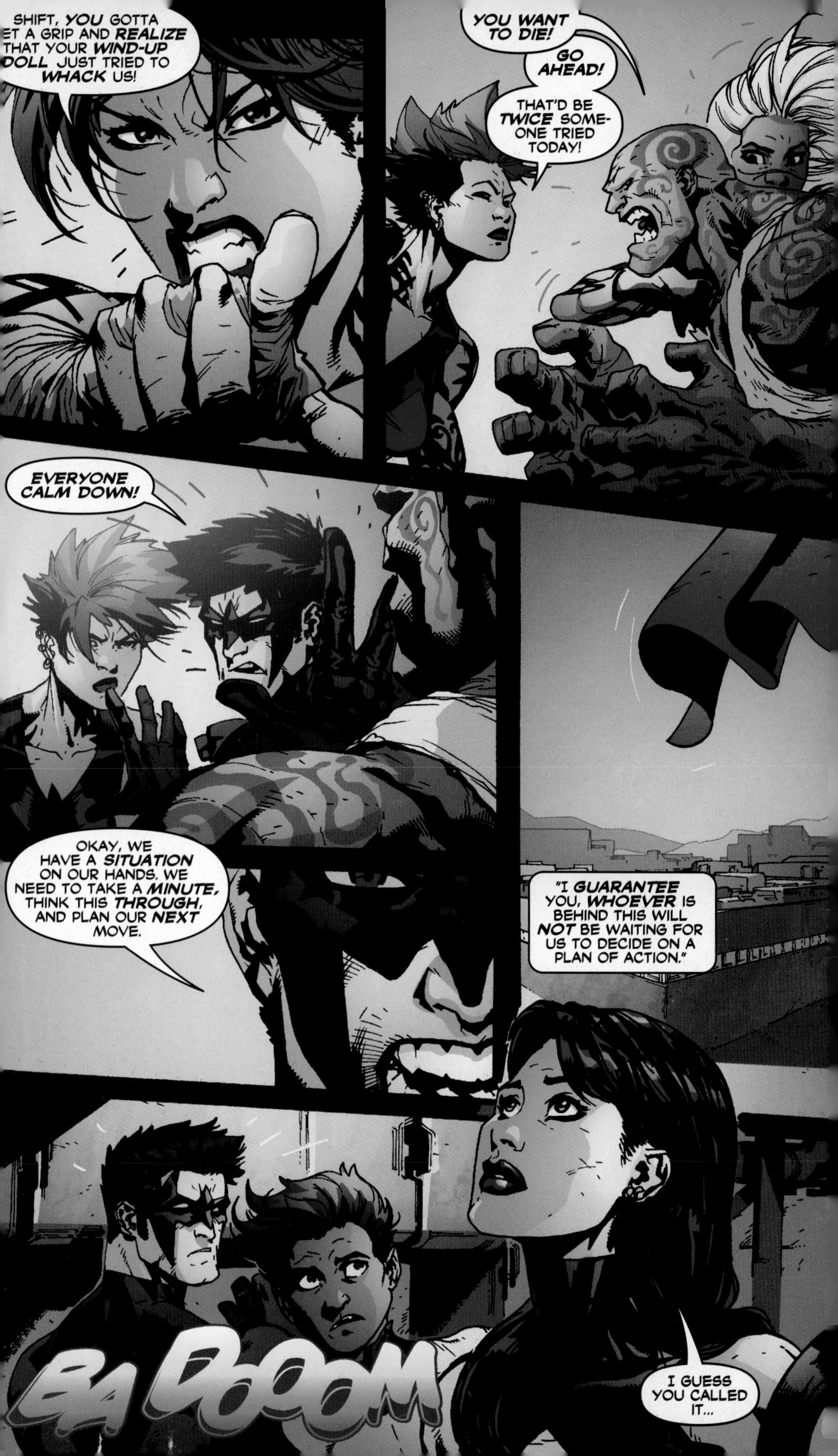
SHIFT, YOU GOTTA ET A GRIP AND REALIZE THAT YOUR WIND-UP DOLL JUST TRIED TO WHACK US!
YOU WANT TO DIE!
GO AHEAD!
THAT'D BE TWICE SOME-ONE TRIED TODAY!
EVERYONE CALM DOWN!
OKAY, WE HAVE A SITUATION ON OUR HANDS. WE NEED TO TAKE A MINUTE, THINK THIS THROUGH, AND PLAN OUR NEXT MOVE.
"I GUARANTEE YOU, WHOEVER IS BEHIND THIS WILL NOT BE WAITING FOR US TO DECIDE ON A PLAN OF ACTION."
BA DOOOM
I GUESS YOU CALLED IT...

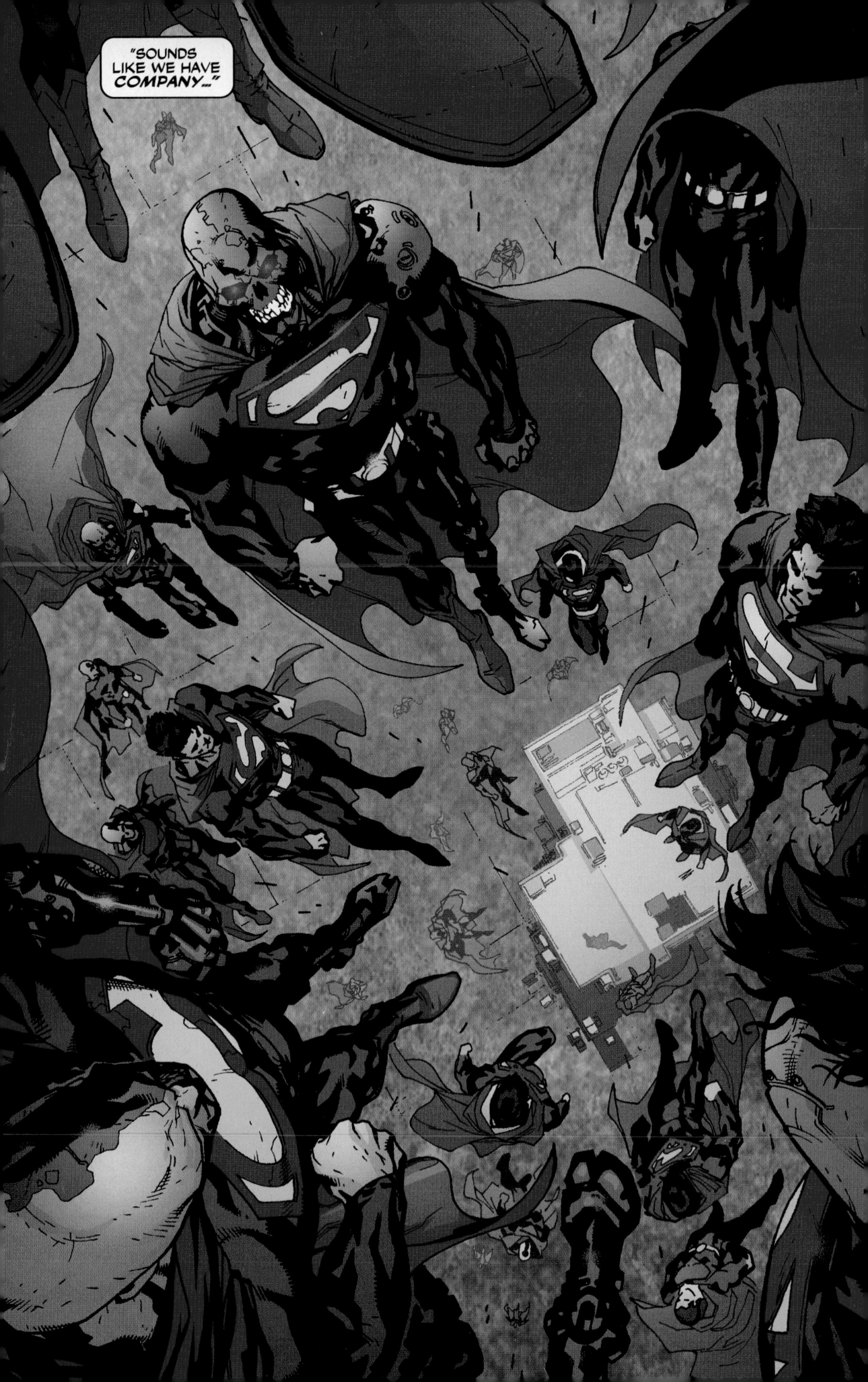
"SOUNDS LIKE WE HAVE COMPANY..."

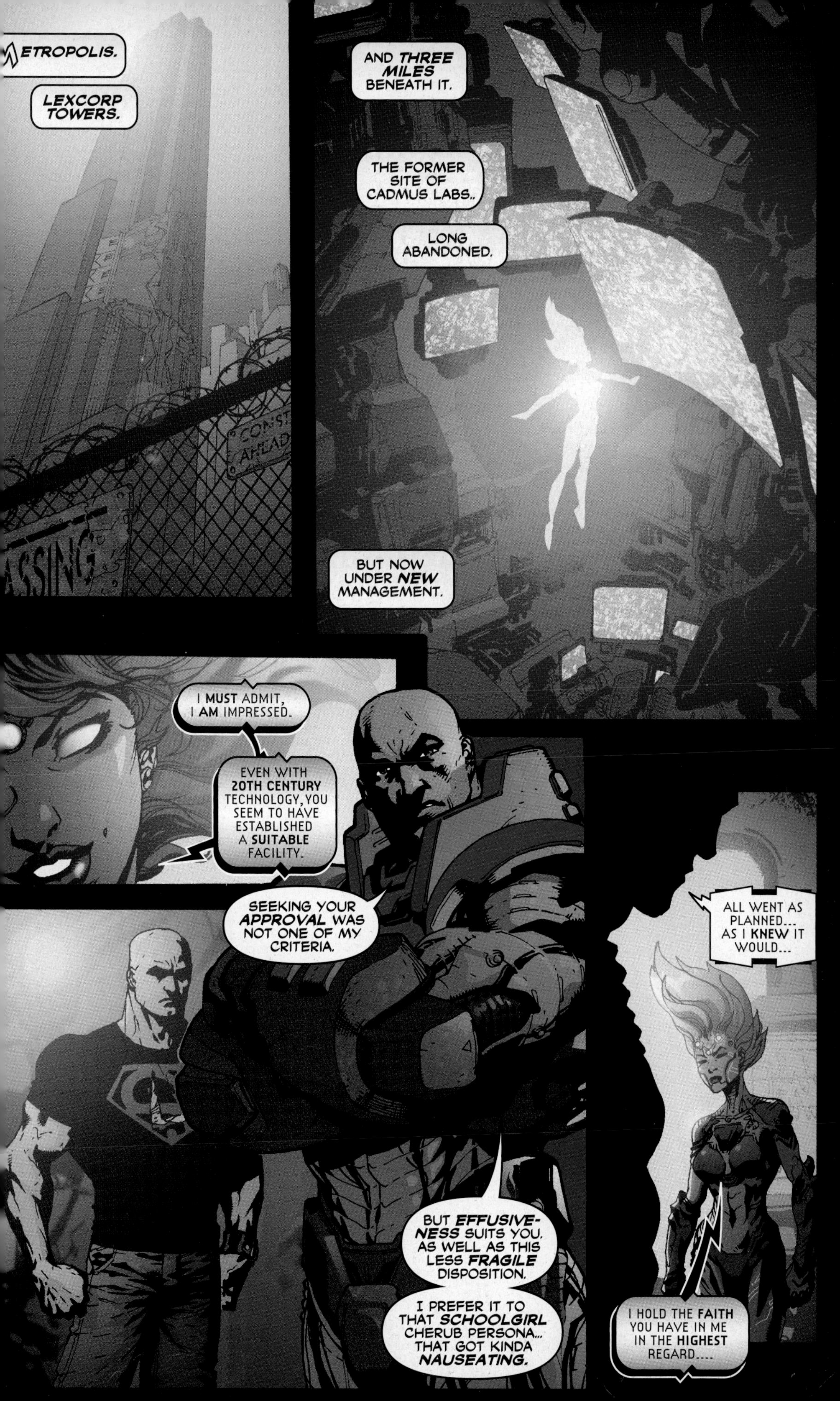
METROPOLIS.
LEXCORP TOWERS.
AND THREE MILES BENEATH IT.
THE FORMER SITE OF CADMUS LABS..
LONG ABANDONED.
BUT NOW UNDER NEW MANAGEMENT.
I MUST ADMIT, I AM IMPRESSED.
EVEN WITH 20TH CENTURY TECHNOLOGY, YOU SEEM TO HAVE ESTABLISHED A SUITABLE FACILITY.
SEEKING YOUR APPROVAL WAS NOT ONE OF MY CRITERIA.
ALL WENT AS PLANNED... AS I KNEW IT WOULD...
BUT EFFUSIVENESS SUITS YOU, AS WELL AS THIS LESS FRAGILE DISPOSITION.
I PREFER IT TO THAT SCHOOLGIRL CHERUB PERSONA... THAT GOT KINDA NAUSEATING.
I HOLD THE FAITH YOU HAVE IN ME IN THE HIGHEST REGARD....

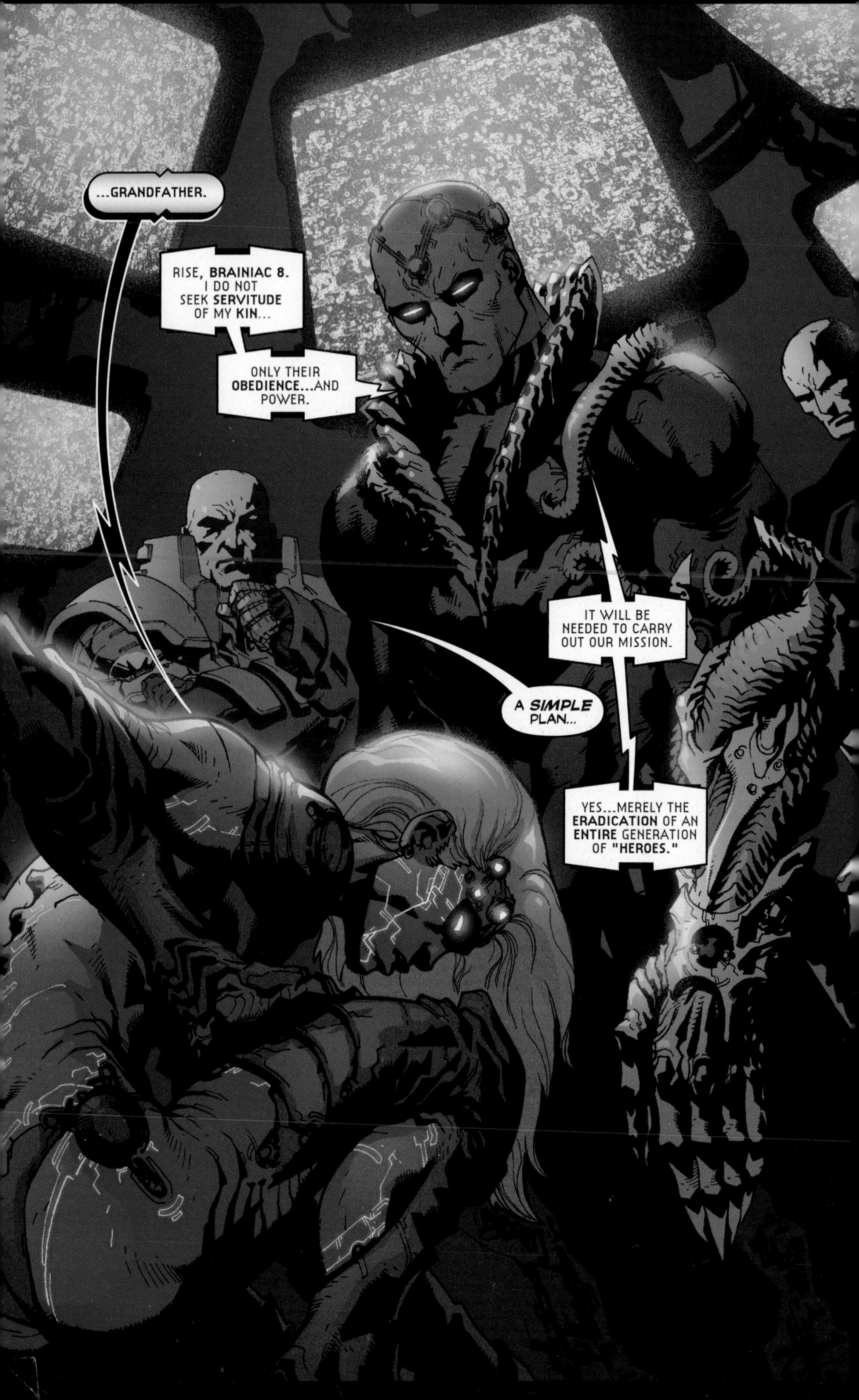
...GRANDFATHER.
RISE, BRAINIAC 8. I DO NOT SEEK SERVITUDE OF MY KIN...
ONLY THEIR OBEDIENCE...AND POWER.
IT WILL BE NEEDED TO CARRY OUT OUR MISSION.
A SIMPLE PLAN...
YES...MERELY THE ERADICATION OF AN ENTIRE GENERATION OF "HEROES."

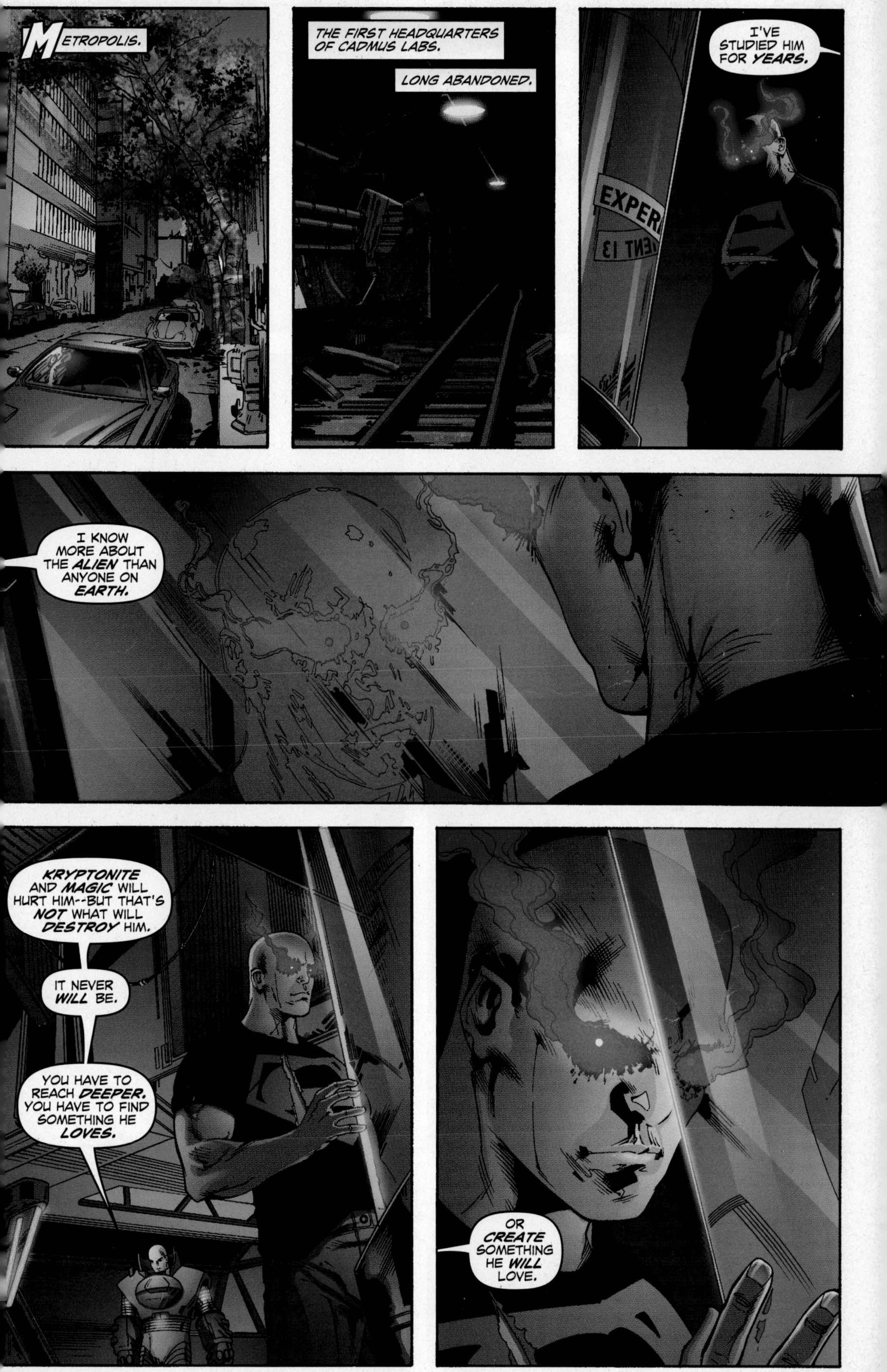
METROPOLIS.
THE FIRST HEADQUARTERS OF CADMUS LABS.
LONG ABANDONED.
I'VE STUDIED HIM FOR YEARS.
EXPERI
ENT 13
I KNOW MORE ABOUT THE ALIEN THAN ANYONE ON EARTH.
KRYPTONITE AND MAGIC WILL HURT HIM--BUT THAT'S NOT WHAT WILL DESTROY HIM.
IT NEVER WILL BE.
YOU HAVE TO REACH DEEPER. YOU HAVE TO FIND SOMETHING HE LOVES.
OR CREATE SOMETHING HE WILL LOVE.

HE *LOVES* HIS *BOY*.

AND WHEN HIS BOY TURNS *AGAINST* THE JUSTICE LEAGUE'S *CHILDREN*, WHEN *SUPERMAN* BURIES THOSE *COFFINS*...

WELL, *THAT*...

...*THAT* WILL *KILL* HIM.

YOU ARE MY *GREATEST* INVENTION. THE *GENETIC* MATERIAL I GAVE YOU. THE PROGRAMMING I IMPLANTED INSIDE YOU.

ALL UNDER WESTFIELD'S NOSE. HIS AMBITIONS WERE *SHALLOW*. MINE ARE *RIGHTEOUS*.

FATH...ER?

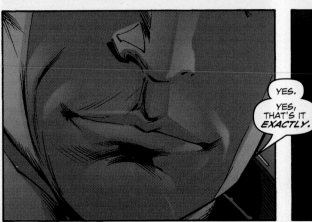

YES. YES, THAT'S IT *EXACTLY*.

BRAINIAC AND HIS DESCENDANT CAN WORRY ABOUT THE IMPLICATIONS *DONNA TROY* HAS FOR THEIR *FUTURE*.

MY...*SON* AND I WILL TAKE CARE OF THE *PRESENT*.

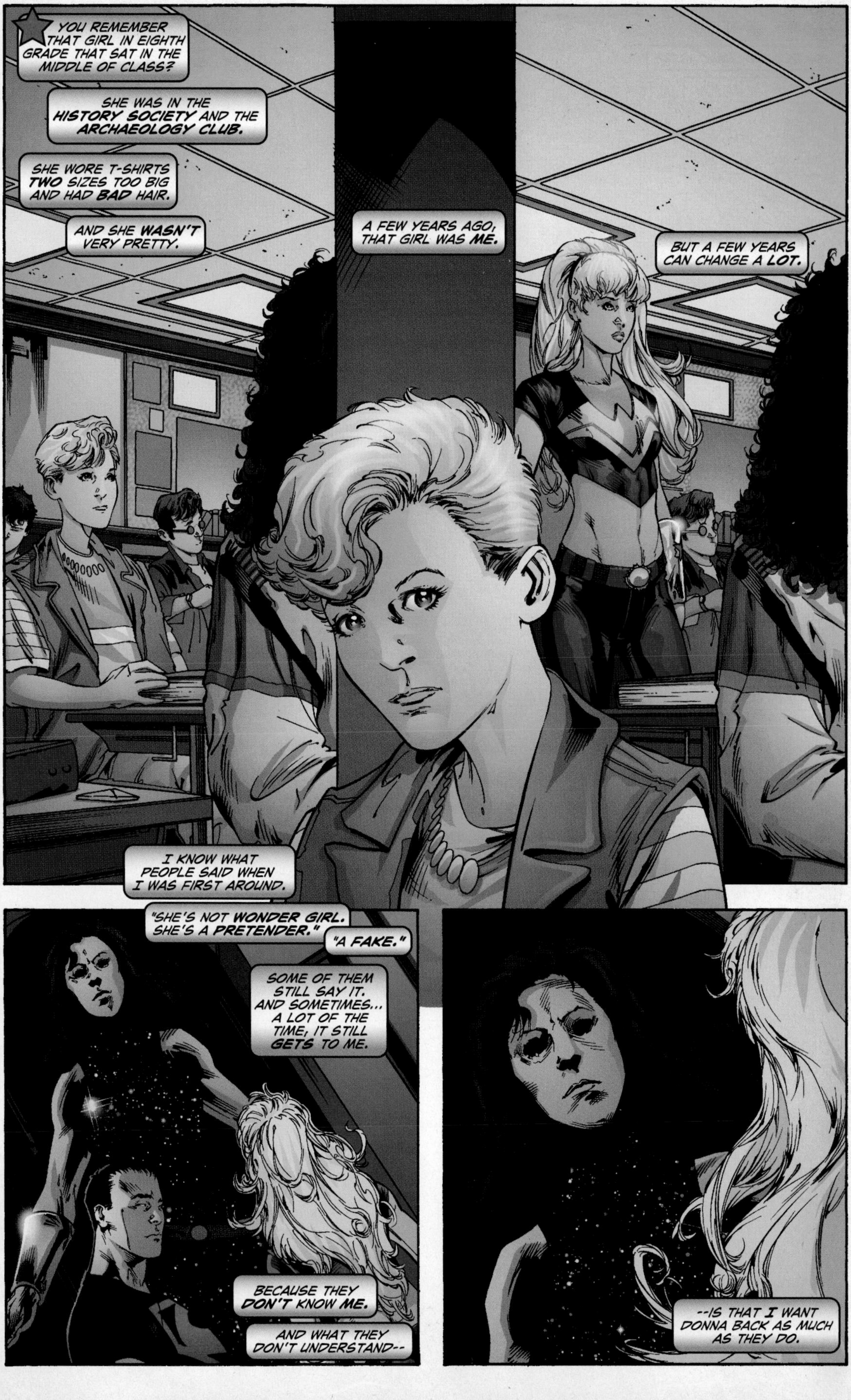
YOU REMEMBER THAT GIRL IN EIGHTH GRADE THAT SAT IN THE MIDDLE OF CLASS?
SHE WAS IN THE HISTORY SOCIETY AND THE ARCHAEOLOGY CLUB.
SHE WORE T-SHIRTS TWO SIZES TOO BIG AND HAD BAD HAIR.
AND SHE WASN'T VERY PRETTY.
A FEW YEARS AGO, THAT GIRL WAS ME.
BUT A FEW YEARS CAN CHANGE A LOT.
I KNOW WHAT PEOPLE SAID WHEN I WAS FIRST AROUND.
"SHE'S NOT WONDER GIRL. SHE'S A PRETENDER."
"A FAKE."
SOME OF THEM STILL SAY IT. AND SOMETIMES... A LOT OF THE TIME, IT STILL GETS TO ME.
BECAUSE THEY DON'T KNOW ME.
AND WHAT THEY DON'T UNDERSTAND--
--IS THAT I WANT DONNA BACK AS MUCH AS THEY DO.

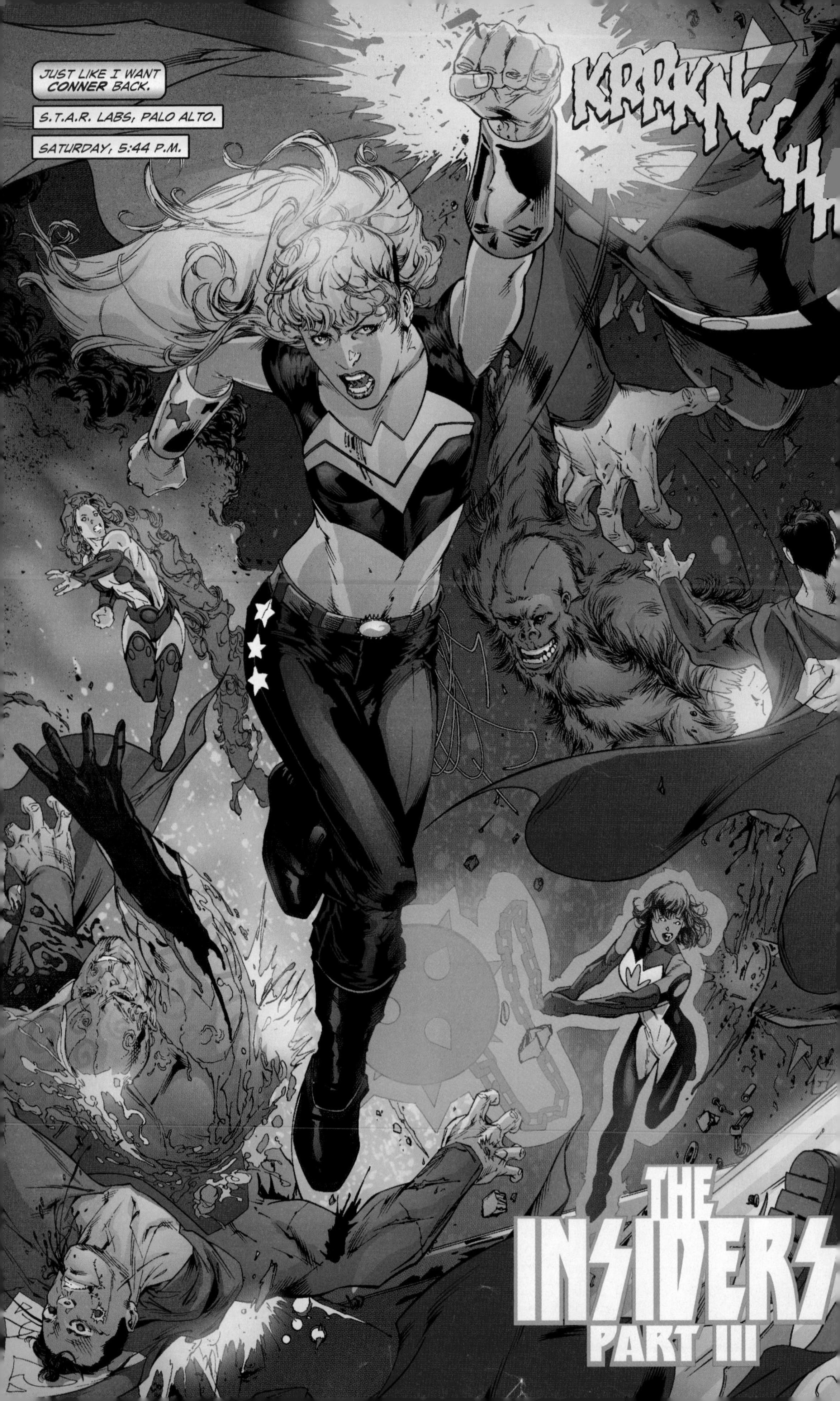
JUST LIKE I WANT CONNER BACK.
S.T.A.R. LABS, PALO ALTO.
SATURDAY, 5:44 P.M.
KRAKNGHH
THE INSIDERS PART III

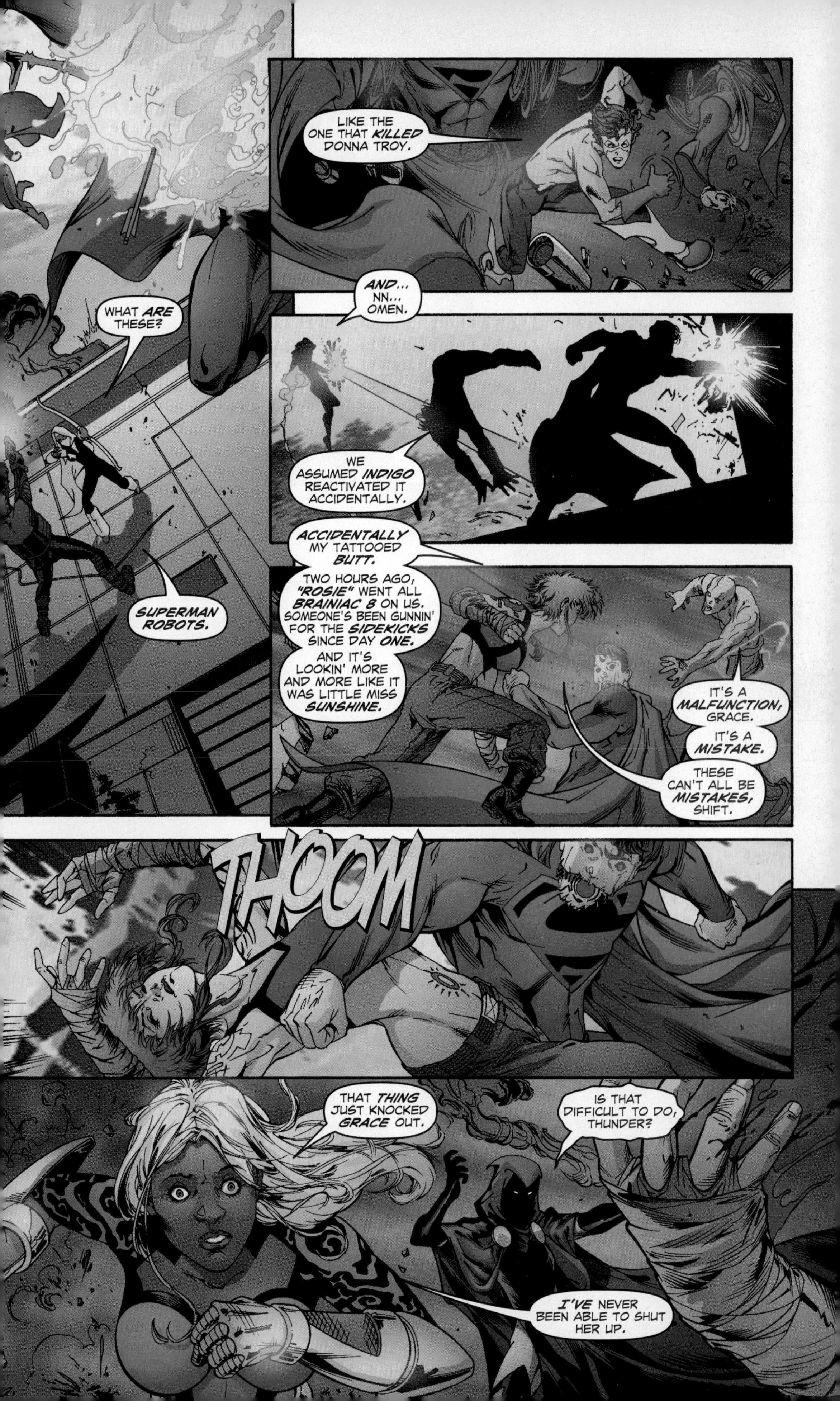
LIKE THE ONE THAT *KILLED* DONNA TROY.
WHAT *ARE* THESE?
AND... NN... OMEN.
WE ASSUMED *INDIGO* REACTIVATED IT ACCIDENTALLY.
SUPERMAN ROBOTS.
ACCIDENTALLY MY TATTOOED *BUTT*.
TWO HOURS AGO, *"ROSIE"* WENT ALL *BRAINIAC 8* ON US. SOMEONE'S BEEN GUNNIN' FOR THE *SIDEKICKS* SINCE DAY *ONE*.
AND IT'S LOOKIN' MORE AND MORE LIKE IT WAS LITTLE MISS *SUNSHINE*.
IT'S A *MALFUNCTION*, GRACE.
IT'S A *MISTAKE*.
THESE CAN'T ALL BE *MISTAKES*, SHIFT.
THOOM
THAT *THING* JUST KNOCKED *GRACE* OUT.
IS THAT DIFFICULT TO DO, THUNDER?
I'VE NEVER BEEN ABLE TO SHUT HER UP.

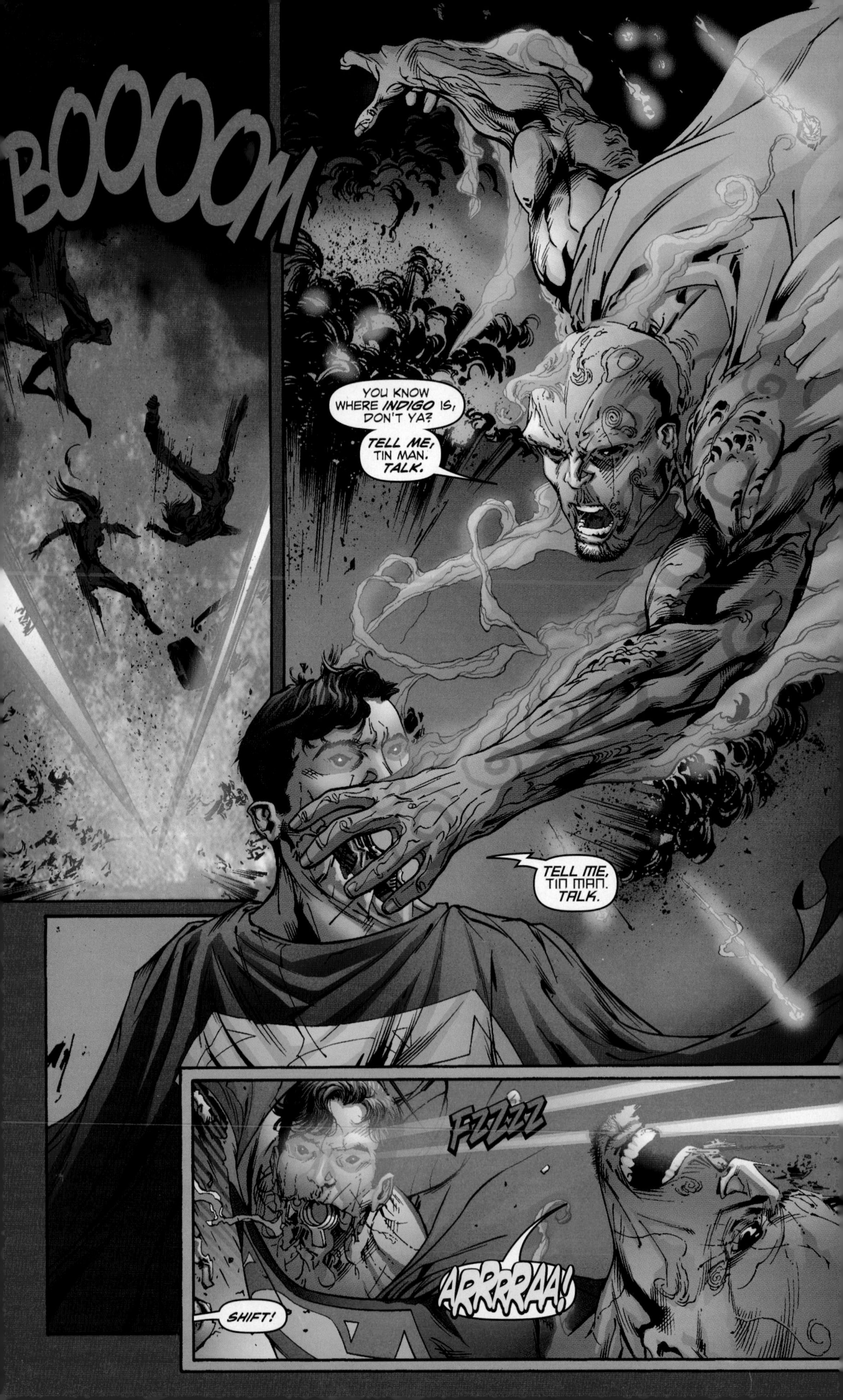
BOOOOM
YOU KNOW WHERE INDIGO IS, DON'T YA?
TELL ME, TIN MAN. TALK.
TELL ME, TIN MAN. TALK.
FZZZZ
ARRRRAA!!
SHIFT!

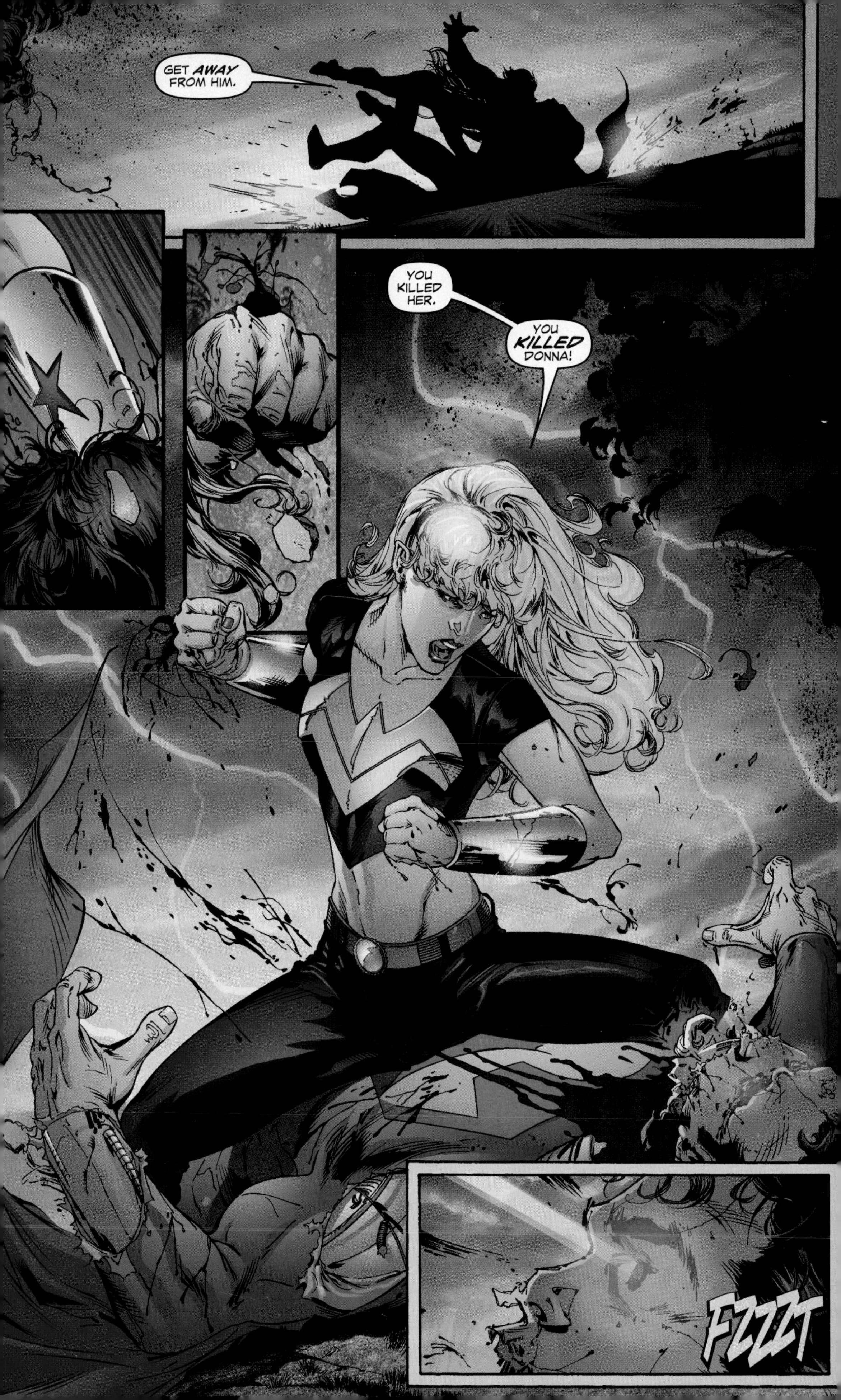
GET AWAY FROM HIM.
YOU KILLED HER.
YOU KILLED DONNA!
FZZZT

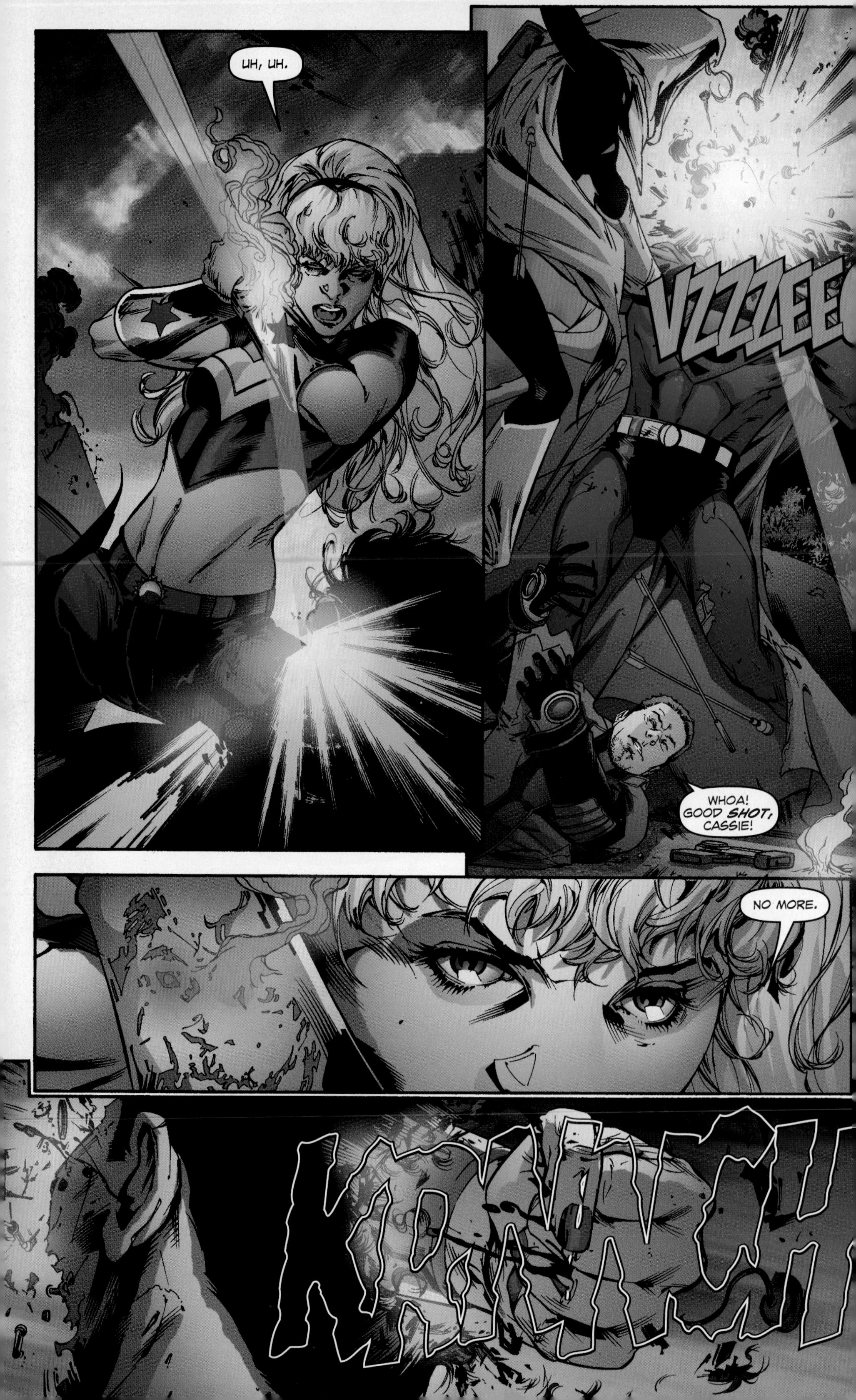
UH, UH.
VZZZEE
WHOA! GOOD SHOT, CASSIE!
NO MORE.

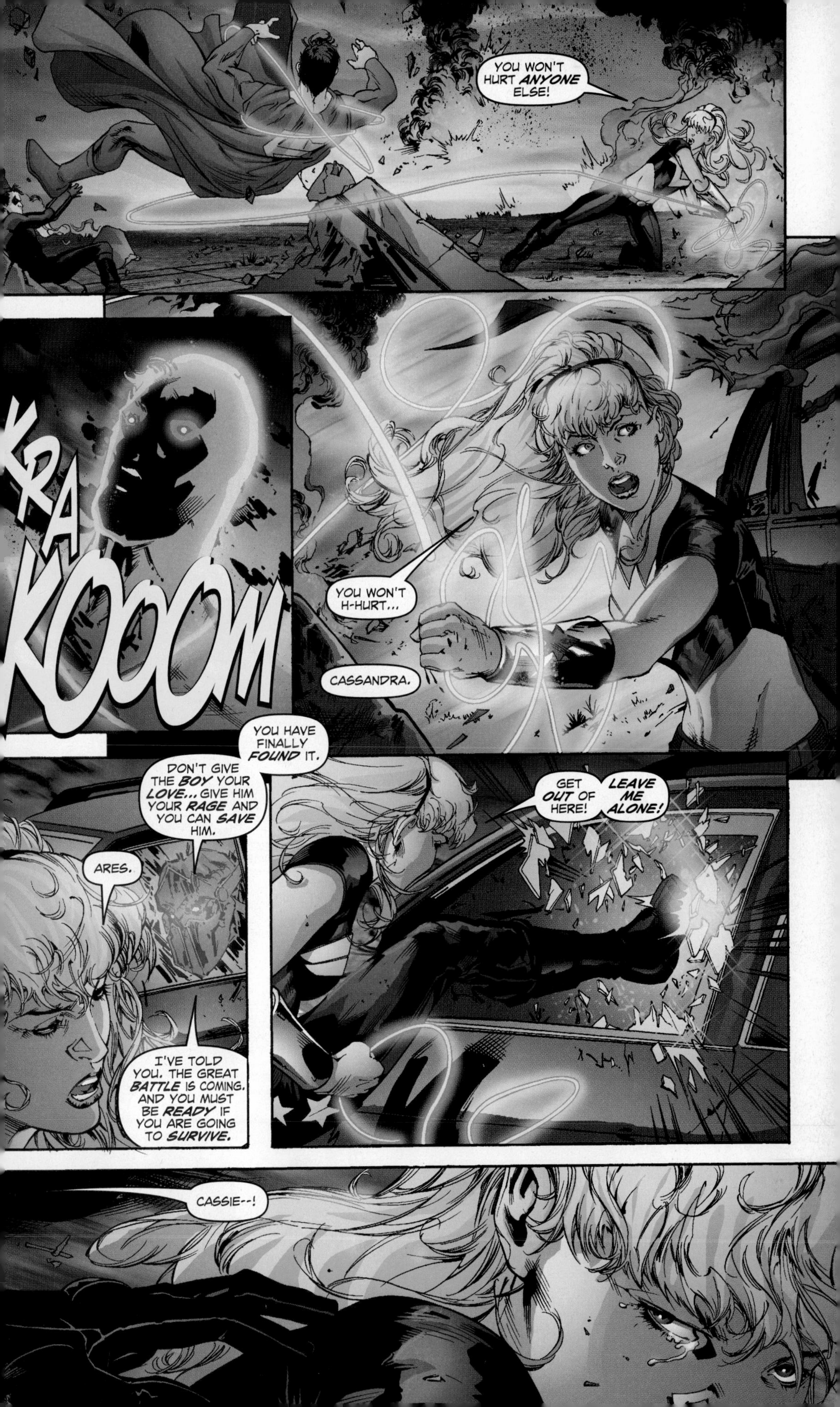
YOU WON'T HURT ANYONE ELSE!
KRA KOOOM
YOU WON'T H-HURT...
CASSANDRA.
YOU HAVE FINALLY FOUND IT.
DON'T GIVE THE BOY YOUR LOVE... GIVE HIM YOUR RAGE AND YOU CAN SAVE HIM.
ARES.
I'VE TOLD YOU. THE GREAT BATTLE IS COMING. AND YOU MUST BE READY IF YOU ARE GOING TO SURVIVE.
GET OUT OF HERE!
LEAVE ME ALONE!
CASSIE--!

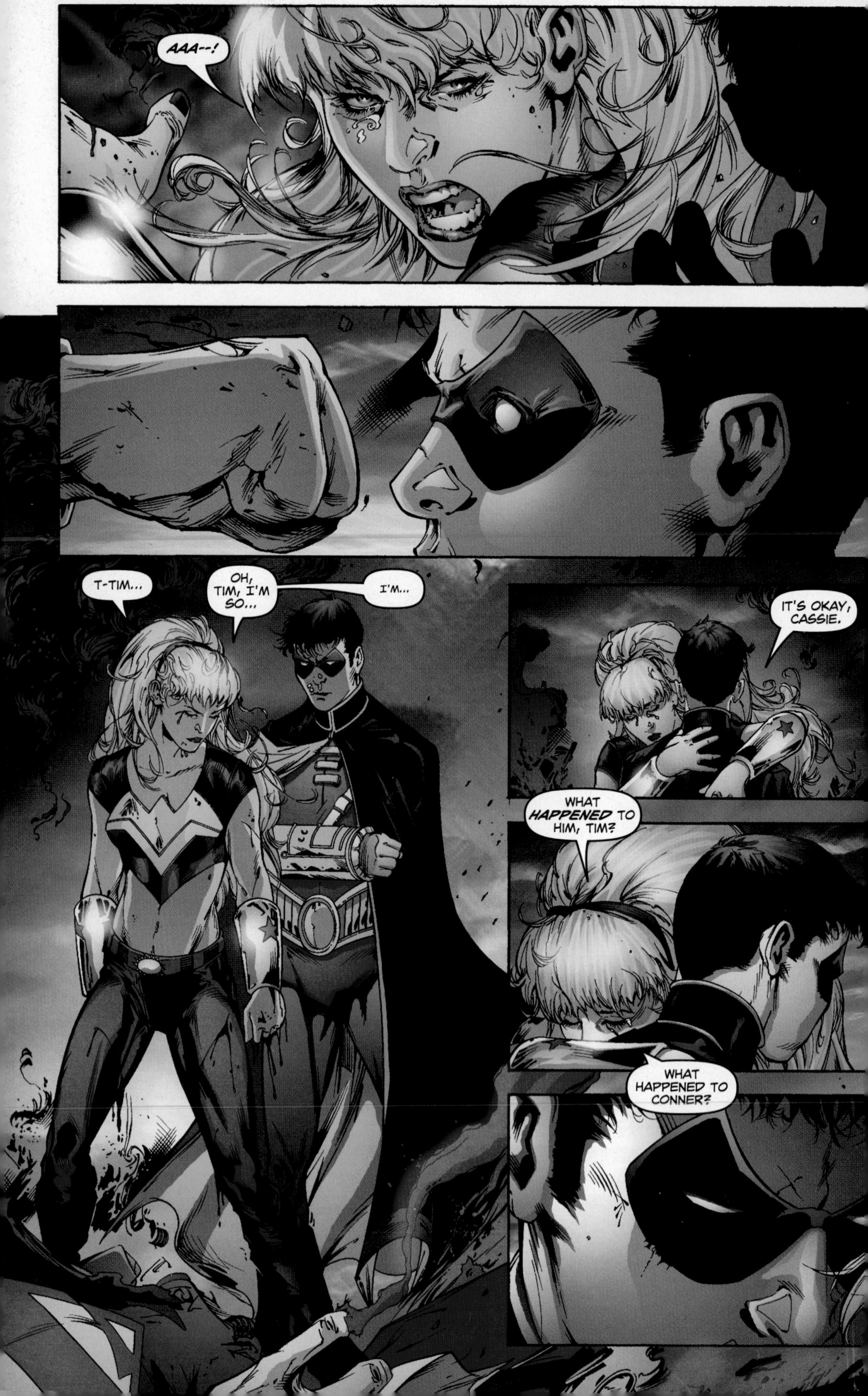
AAA--!
T-TIM...
OH, TIM, I'M SO...
I'M...
IT'S OKAY, CASSIE.
WHAT HAPPENED TO HIM, TIM?
WHAT HAPPENED TO CONNER?

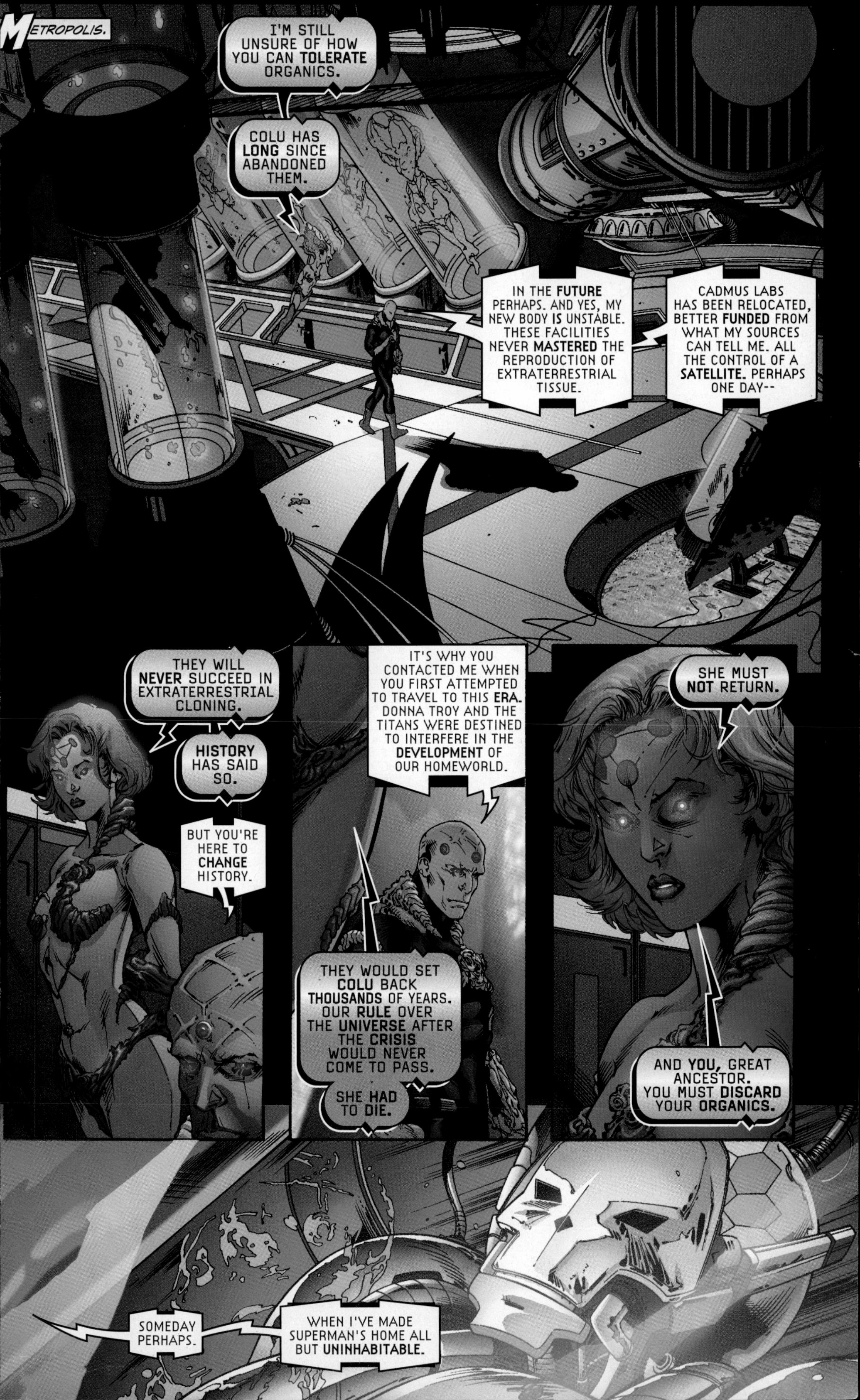
METROPOLIS.
I'M STILL UNSURE OF HOW YOU CAN TOLERATE ORGANICS.
COLU HAS LONG SINCE ABANDONED THEM.
IN THE FUTURE PERHAPS. AND YES, MY NEW BODY IS UNSTABLE. THESE FACILITIES NEVER MASTERED THE REPRODUCTION OF EXTRATERRESTRIAL TISSUE.
CADMUS LABS HAS BEEN RELOCATED, BETTER FUNDED FROM WHAT MY SOURCES CAN TELL ME. ALL THE CONTROL OF A SATELLITE. PERHAPS ONE DAY--
THEY WILL NEVER SUCCEED IN EXTRATERRESTRIAL CLONING.
HISTORY HAS SAID SO.
BUT YOU'RE HERE TO CHANGE HISTORY.
IT'S WHY YOU CONTACTED ME WHEN YOU FIRST ATTEMPTED TO TRAVEL TO THIS ERA. DONNA TROY AND THE TITANS WERE DESTINED TO INTERFERE IN THE DEVELOPMENT OF OUR HOMEWORLD.
THEY WOULD SET COLU BACK THOUSANDS OF YEARS. OUR RULE OVER THE UNIVERSE AFTER THE CRISIS WOULD NEVER COME TO PASS.
SHE HAD TO DIE.
SHE MUST NOT RETURN.
AND YOU, GREAT ANCESTOR. YOU MUST DISCARD YOUR ORGANICS.
SOMEDAY PERHAPS.
WHEN I'VE MADE SUPERMAN'S HOME ALL BUT UNINHABITABLE.

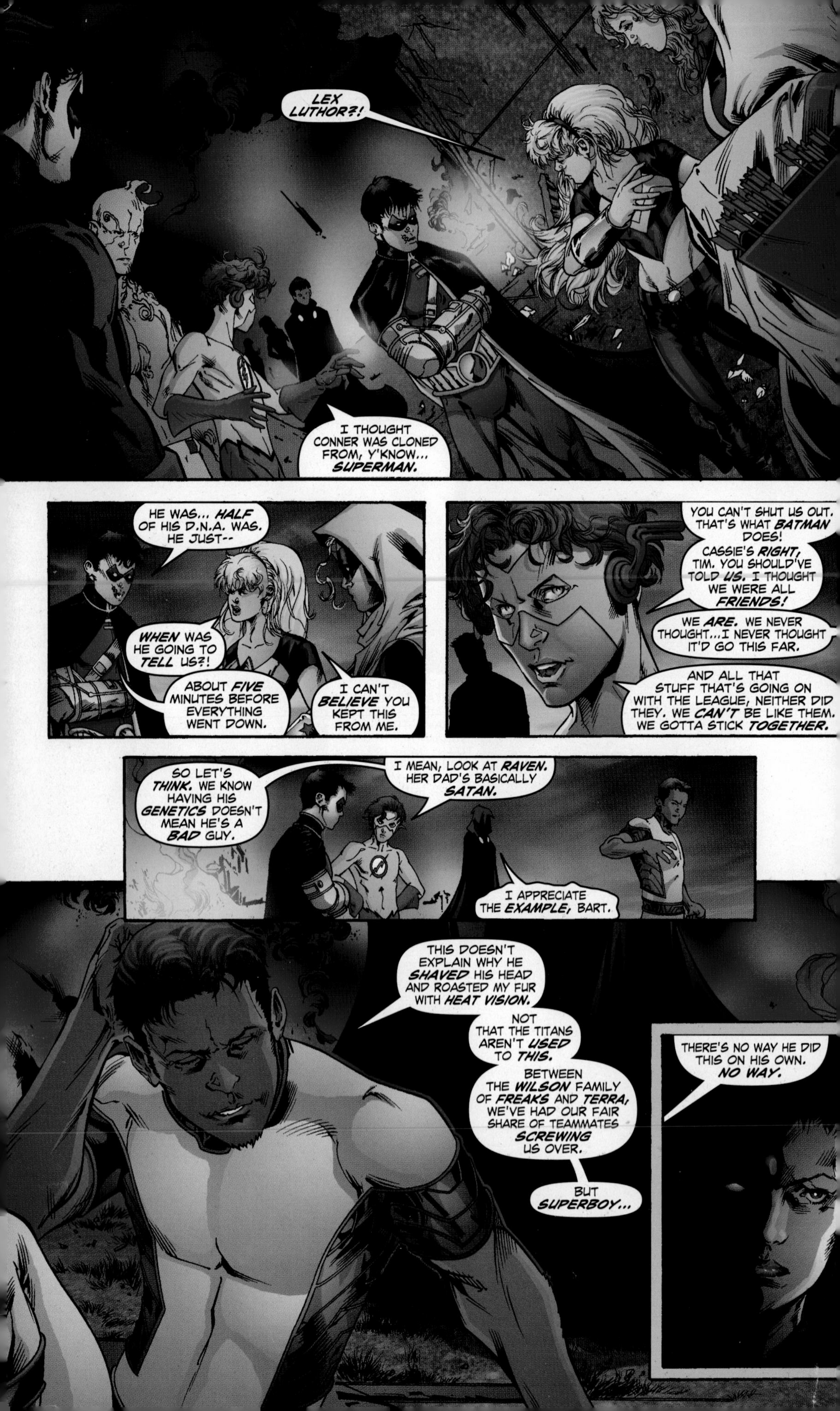

LEX LUTHOR?!
I THOUGHT CONNER WAS CLONED FROM, Y'KNOW... SUPERMAN.
HE WAS... HALF OF HIS D.N.A. WAS. HE JUST--
WHEN WAS HE GOING TO TELL US?!
ABOUT FIVE MINUTES BEFORE EVERYTHING WENT DOWN.
I CAN'T BELIEVE YOU KEPT THIS FROM ME.
YOU CAN'T SHUT US OUT. THAT'S WHAT BATMAN DOES!
CASSIE'S RIGHT, TIM. YOU SHOULD'VE TOLD US. I THOUGHT WE WERE ALL FRIENDS!
WE ARE. WE NEVER THOUGHT...I NEVER THOUGHT IT'D GO THIS FAR.
AND ALL THAT STUFF THAT'S GOING ON WITH THE LEAGUE, NEITHER DID THEY. WE CAN'T BE LIKE THEM. WE GOTTA STICK TOGETHER.
SO LET'S THINK. WE KNOW HAVING HIS GENETICS DOESN'T MEAN HE'S A BAD GUY.
I MEAN, LOOK AT RAVEN. HER DAD'S BASICALLY SATAN.
I APPRECIATE THE EXAMPLE, BART.
THIS DOESN'T EXPLAIN WHY HE SHAVED HIS HEAD AND ROASTED MY FUR WITH HEAT VISION.
NOT THAT THE TITANS AREN'T USED TO THIS.
BETWEEN THE WILSON FAMILY OF FREAKS AND TERRA, WE'VE HAD OUR FAIR SHARE OF TEAMMATES SCREWING US OVER.
BUT SUPERBOY...
THERE'S NO WAY HE DID THIS ON HIS OWN. NO WAY.

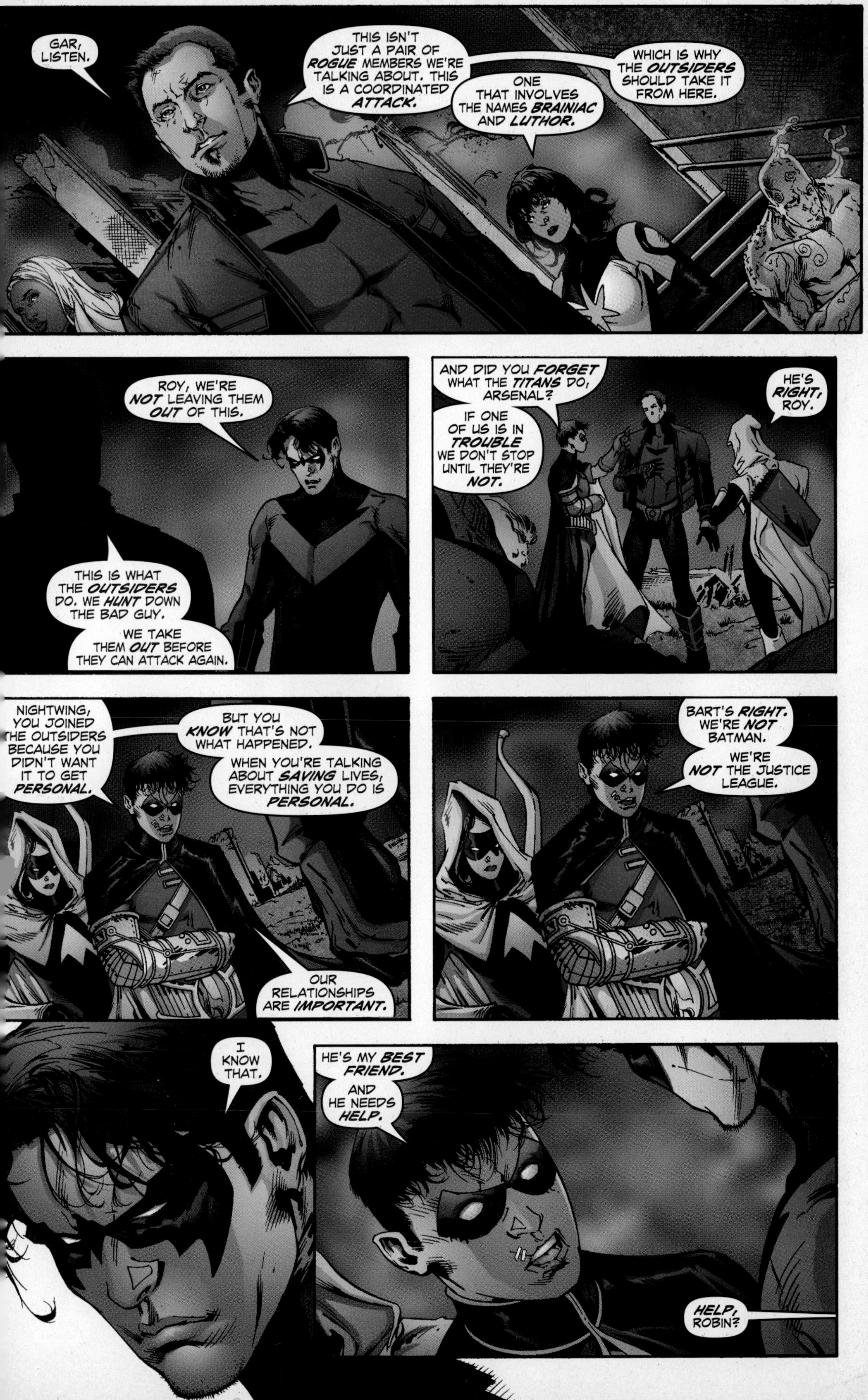
GAR, LISTEN.
THIS ISN'T JUST A PAIR OF ROGUE MEMBERS WE'RE TALKING ABOUT. THIS IS A COORDINATED ATTACK.
ONE THAT INVOLVES THE NAMES BRAINIAC AND LUTHOR.
WHICH IS WHY THE OUTSIDERS SHOULD TAKE IT FROM HERE.
ROY, WE'RE NOT LEAVING THEM OUT OF THIS.
THIS IS WHAT THE OUTSIDERS DO. WE HUNT DOWN THE BAD GUY.
WE TAKE THEM OUT BEFORE THEY CAN ATTACK AGAIN.
AND DID YOU FORGET WHAT THE TITANS DO, ARSENAL?
IF ONE OF US IS IN TROUBLE WE DON'T STOP UNTIL THEY'RE NOT.
HE'S RIGHT, ROY.
NIGHTWING, YOU JOINED THE OUTSIDERS BECAUSE YOU DIDN'T WANT IT TO GET PERSONAL.
BUT YOU KNOW THAT'S NOT WHAT HAPPENED.
WHEN YOU'RE TALKING ABOUT SAVING LIVES, EVERYTHING YOU DO IS PERSONAL.
OUR RELATIONSHIPS ARE IMPORTANT.
BART'S RIGHT. WE'RE NOT BATMAN.
WE'RE NOT THE JUSTICE LEAGUE.
I KNOW THAT.
HE'S MY BEST FRIEND.
AND HE NEEDS HELP.
HELP, ROBIN?

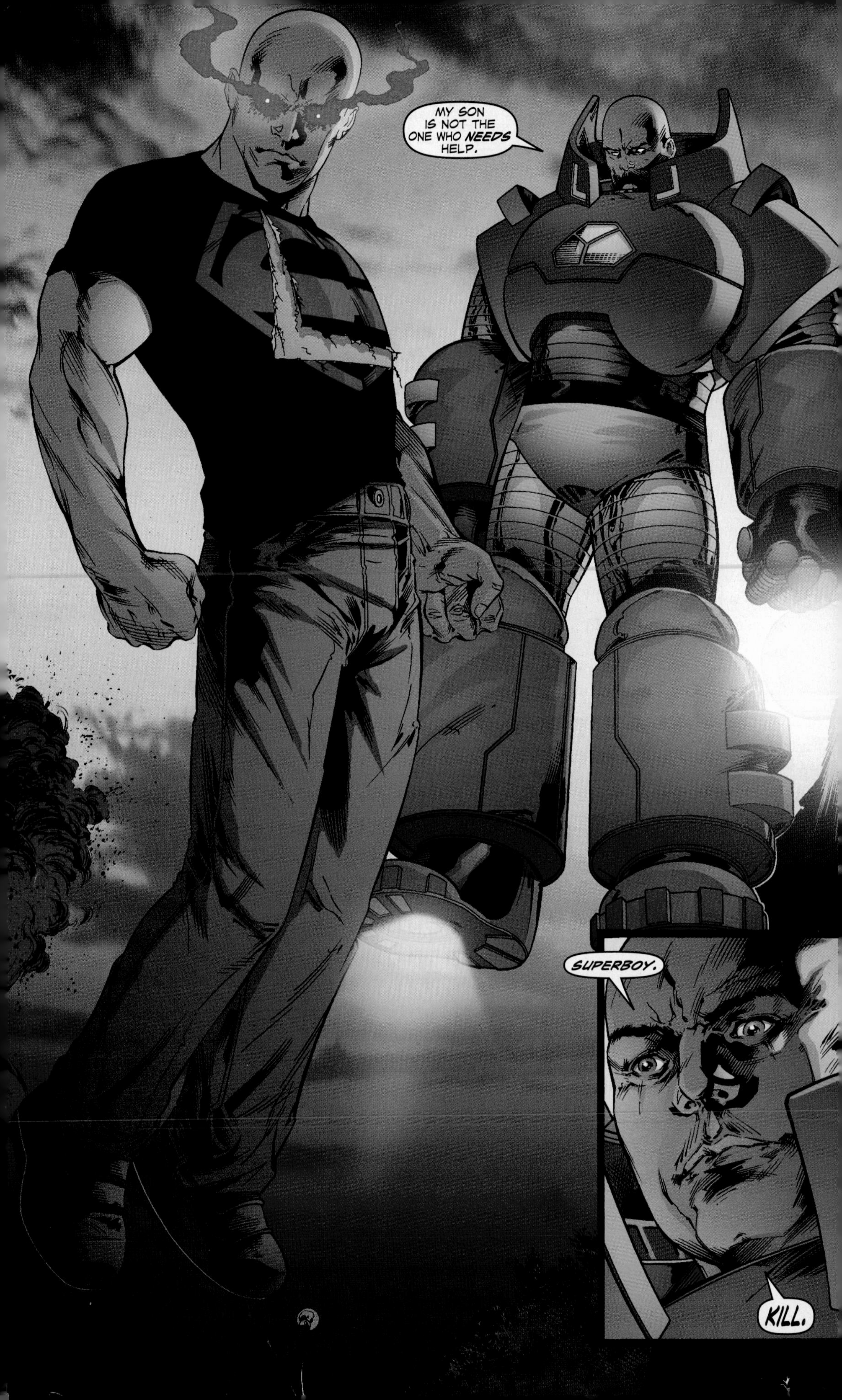

MY SON IS NOT THE ONE WHO *NEEDS* HELP.
SUPERBOY.
KILL.

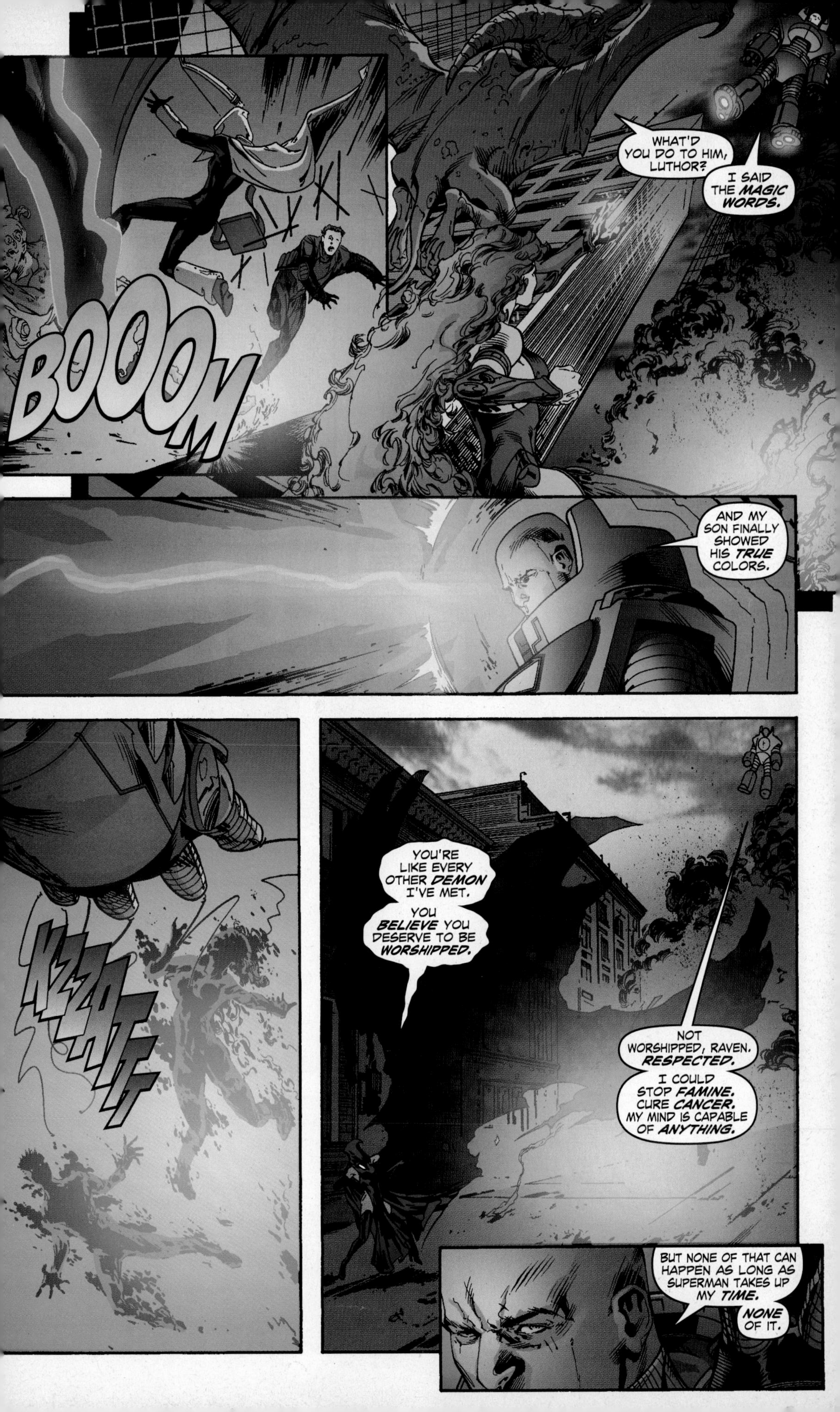
BOOOM
WHAT'D YOU DO TO HIM, LUTHOR?
I SAID THE *MAGIC* *WORDS*.
AND MY SON FINALLY SHOWED HIS *TRUE* COLORS.
KZZATT
YOU'RE LIKE EVERY OTHER *DEMON* I'VE MET.
YOU *BELIEVE* YOU DESERVE TO BE *WORSHIPPED*.
NOT WORSHIPPED, RAVEN. *RESPECTED*.
I COULD STOP *FAMINE*. CURE *CANCER*. MY MIND IS CAPABLE OF *ANYTHING*.
BUT NONE OF THAT CAN HAPPEN AS LONG AS SUPERMAN TAKES UP MY *TIME*.
NONE OF IT.

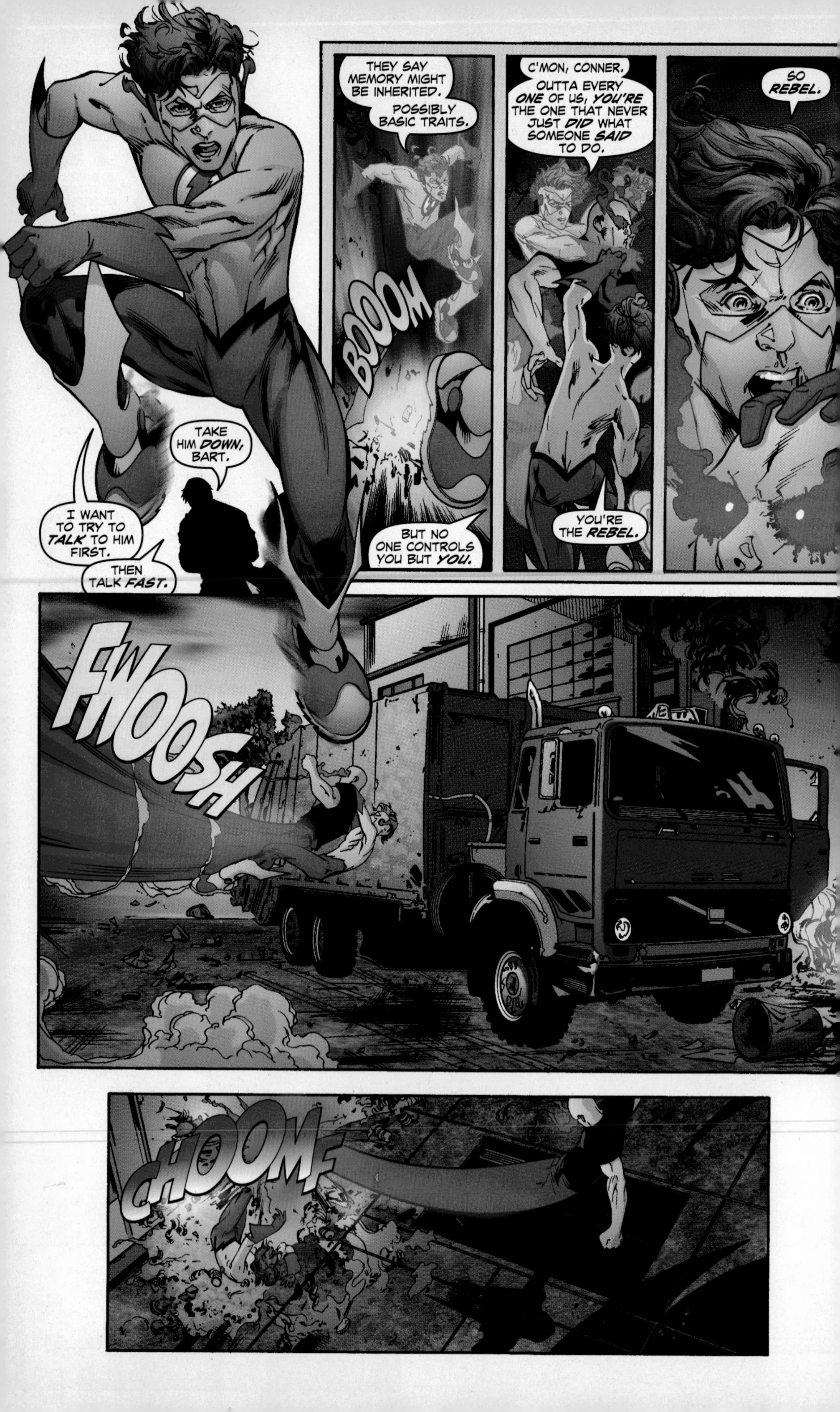
TAKE HIM DOWN, BART.
I WANT TO TRY TO TALK TO HIM FIRST.
THEN TALK FAST.
THEY SAY MEMORY MIGHT BE INHERITED.
POSSIBLY BASIC TRAITS.
BOOOM
BUT NO ONE CONTROLS YOU BUT YOU.
C'MON, CONNER.
OUTTA EVERY ONE OF US, YOU'RE THE ONE THAT NEVER JUST DID WHAT SOMEONE SAID TO DO.
YOU'RE THE REBEL.
SO REBEL.
FWOOSH
CHOOMF

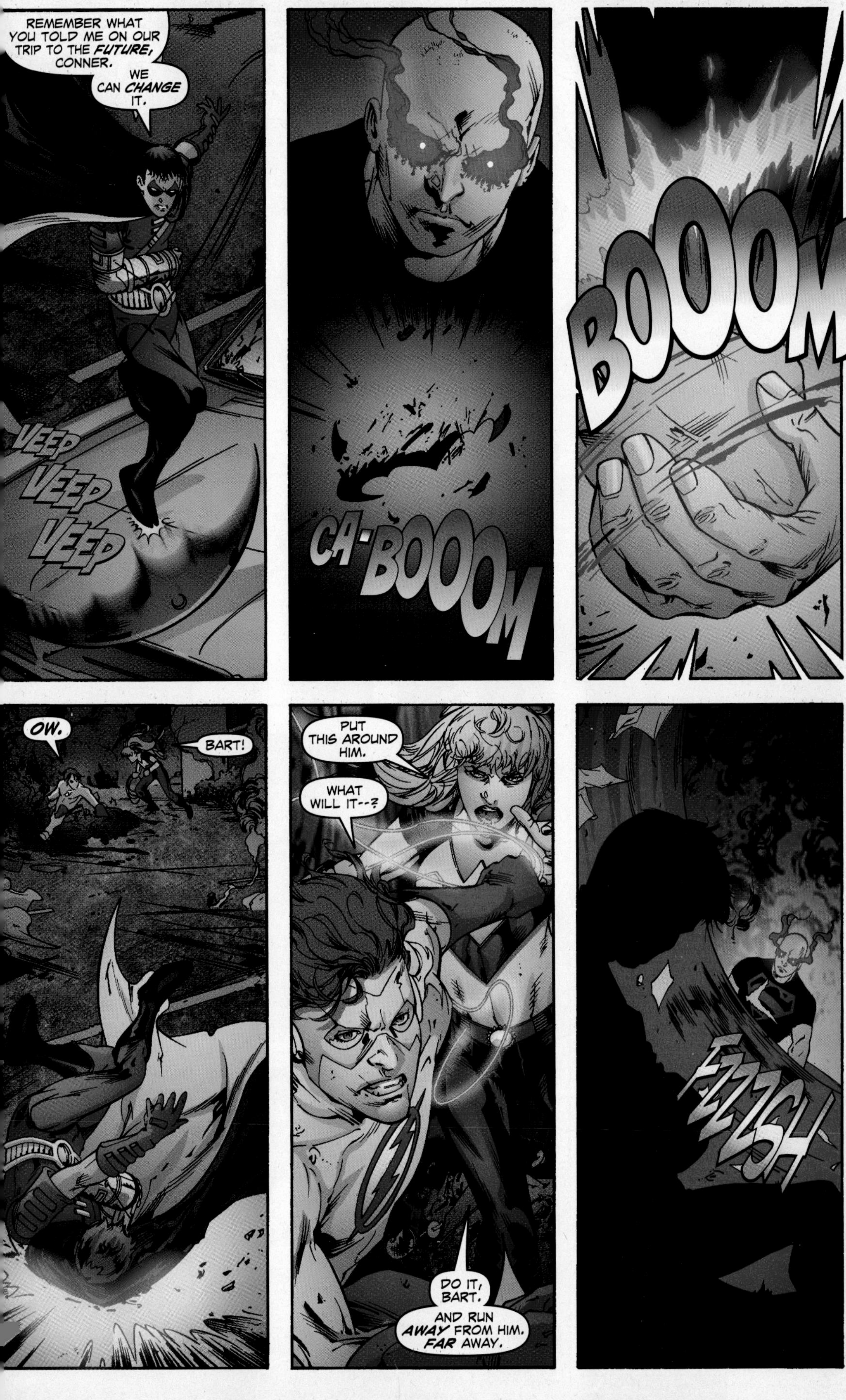

REMEMBER WHAT YOU TOLD ME ON OUR TRIP TO THE *FUTURE,* CONNER.
WE CAN *CHANGE* IT.
VEEP VEEP VEEP
CA-BOOOM
BOOOM
OW.
BART!
PUT THIS AROUND HIM.
WHAT WILL IT--?
DO IT, BART.
AND RUN *AWAY* FROM HIM. *FAR* AWAY.
FZZZSH

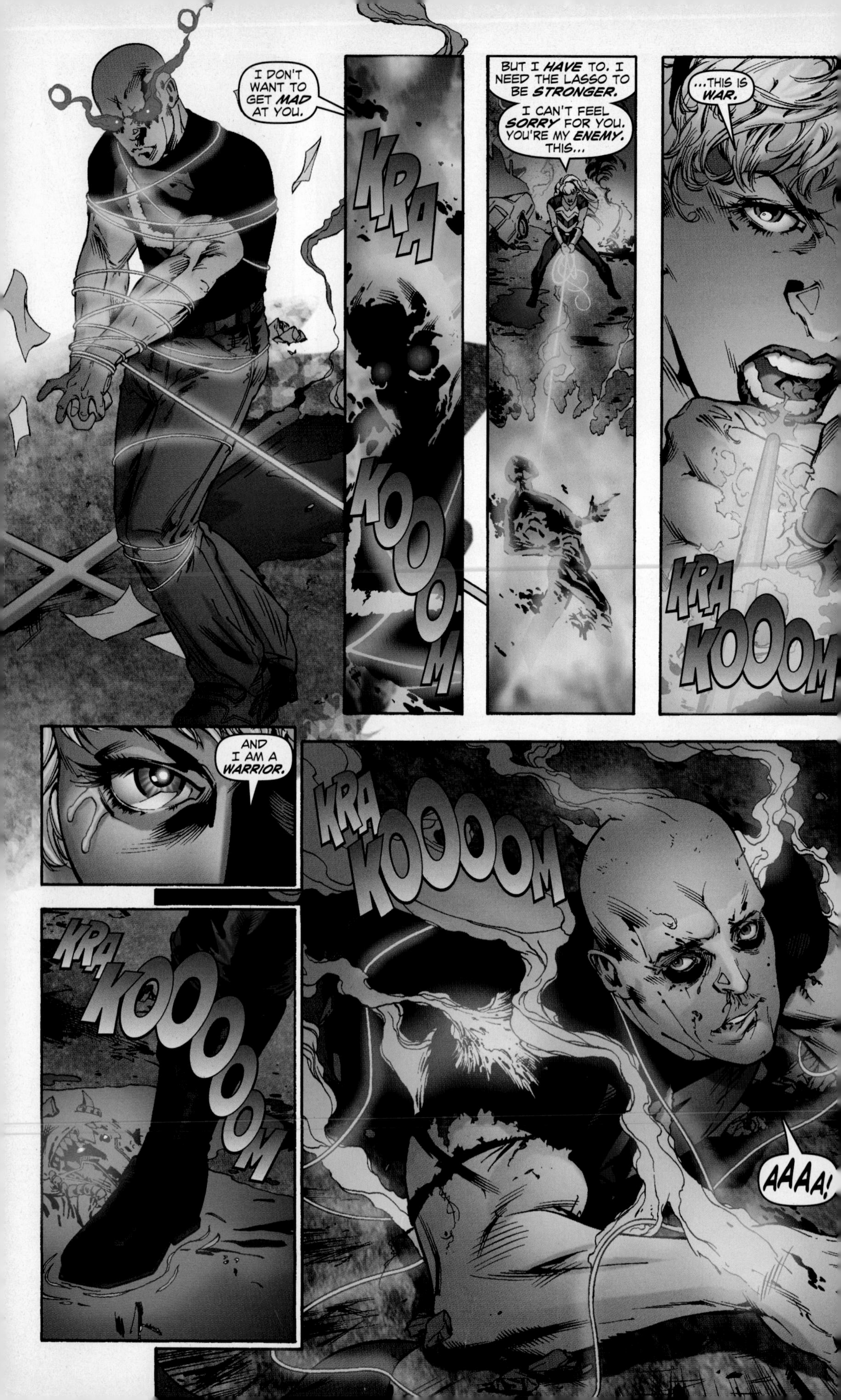
I DON'T WANT TO GET MAD AT YOU.
KRA KOOOOM
BUT I HAVE TO. I NEED THE LASSO TO BE STRONGER.
I CAN'T FEEL SORRY FOR YOU. YOU'RE MY ENEMY. THIS...
...THIS IS WAR.
KRA KOOOM
AND I AM A WARRIOR.
KRA KOOOOOM
KRA KOOOOOOM
AAAA!

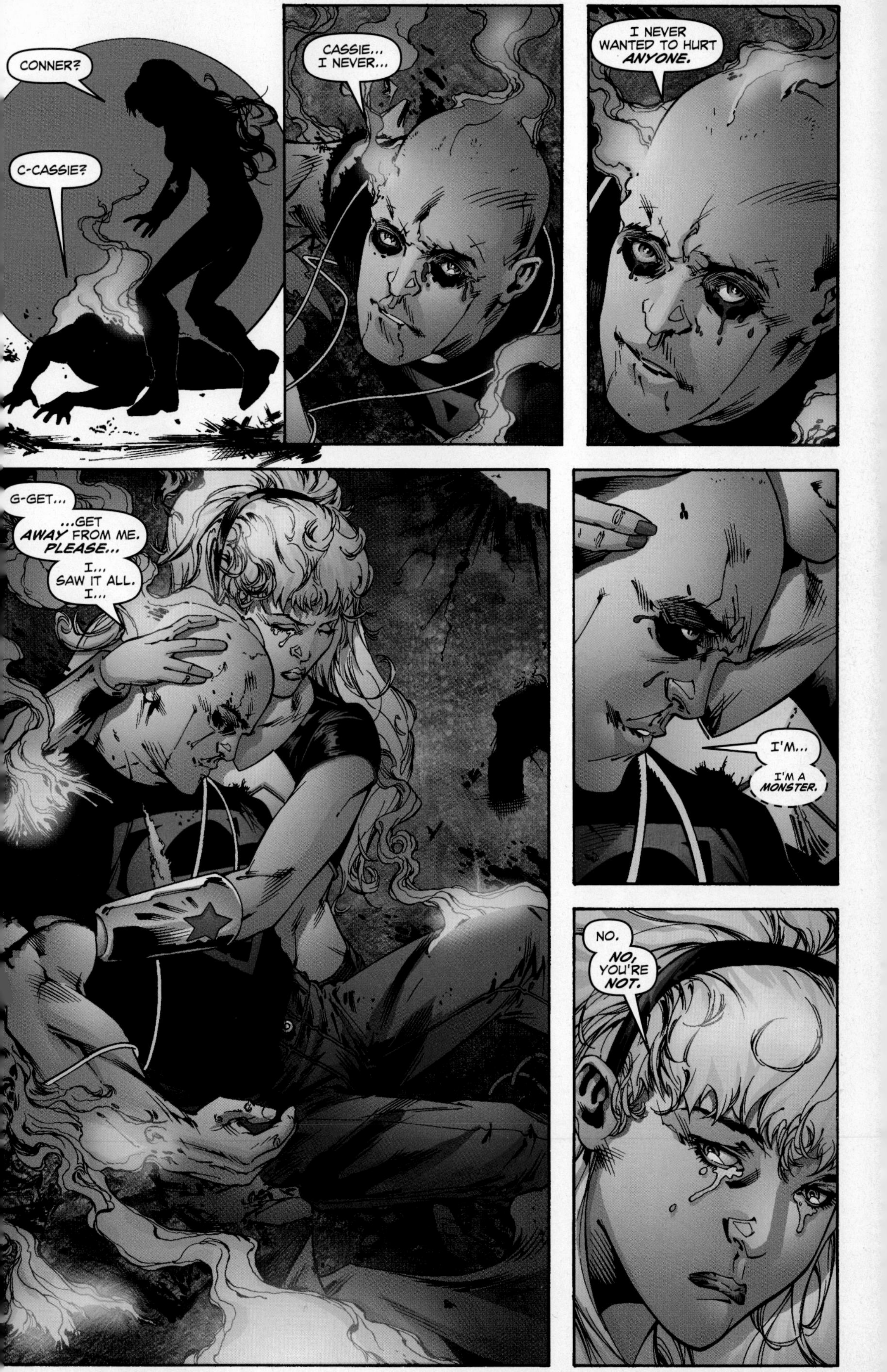
CONNER?
C-CASSIE?
CASSIE... I NEVER...
I NEVER WANTED TO HURT ANYONE.
G-GET...
...GET AWAY FROM ME. PLEASE...
I... SAW IT ALL. I...
I'M...
I'M A MONSTER.
NO.
NO, YOU'RE NOT.

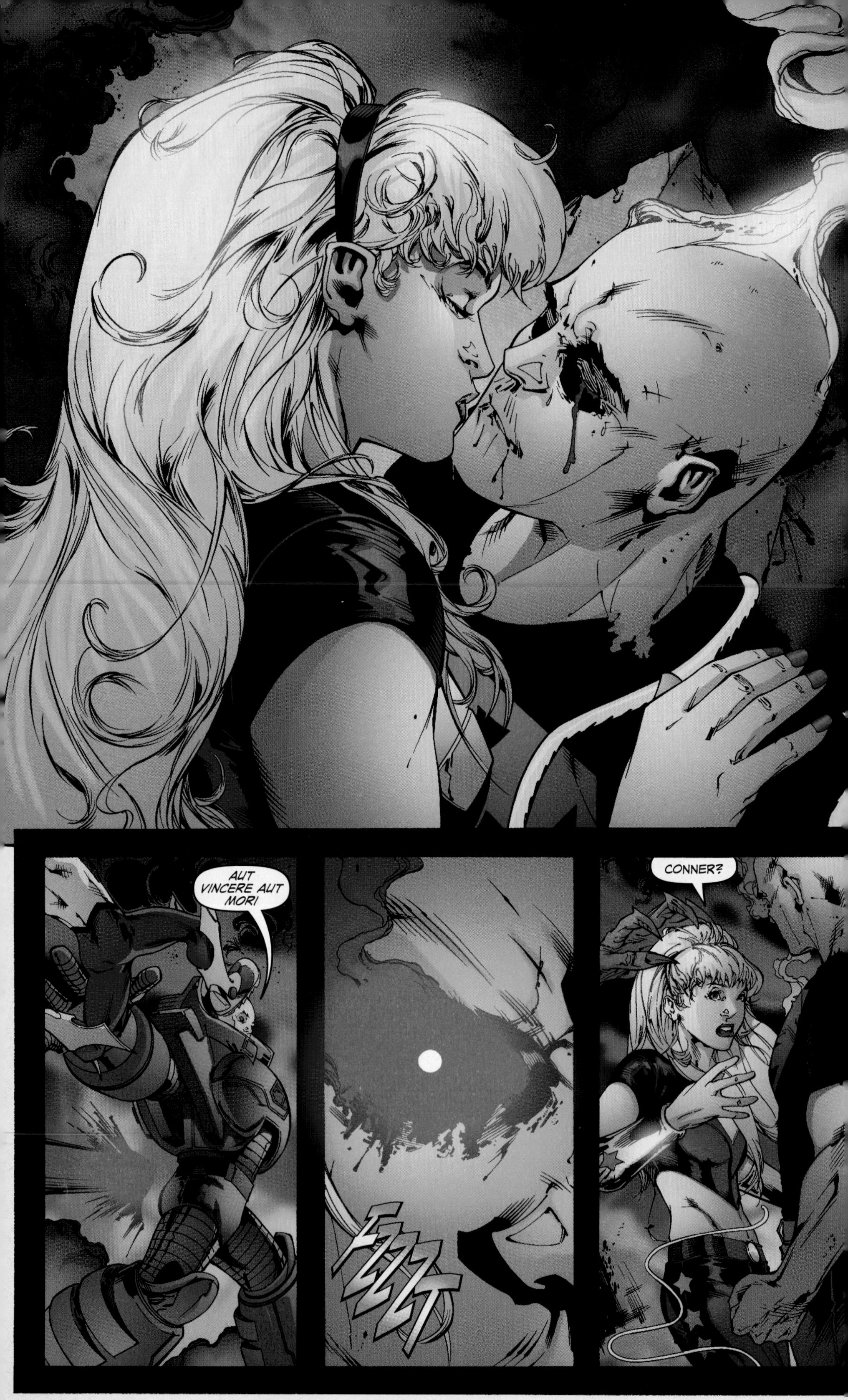
AUT VINCERE AUT MORI
FZZZT
CONNER?

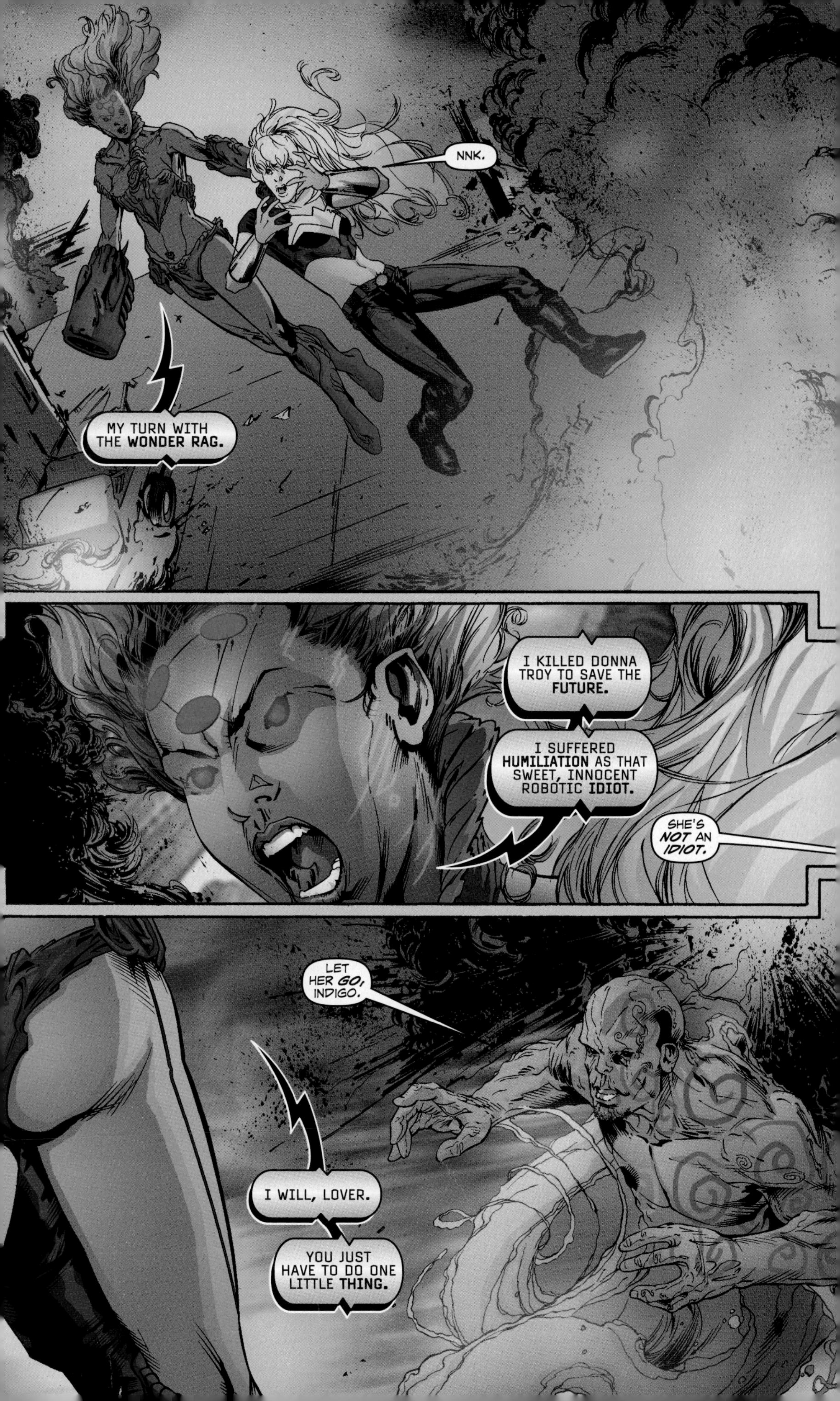

NNK.
MY TURN WITH THE WONDER RAG.
I KILLED DONNA TROY TO SAVE THE FUTURE.
I SUFFERED HUMILIATION AS THAT SWEET, INNOCENT ROBOTIC IDIOT.
SHE'S NOT AN IDIOT.
LET HER GO, INDIGO.
I WILL, LOVER.
YOU JUST HAVE TO DO ONE LITTLE THING.

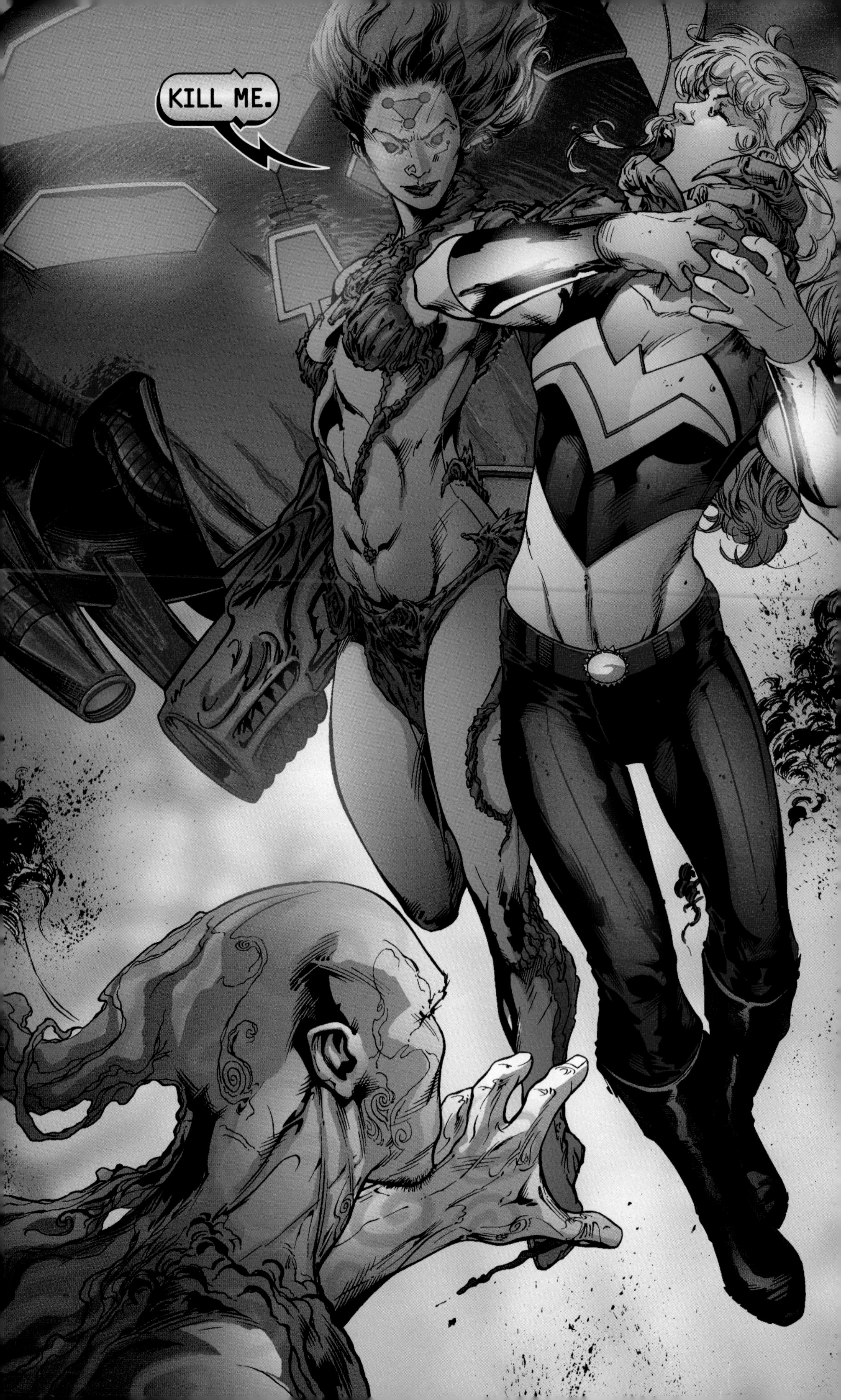
KILL ME.

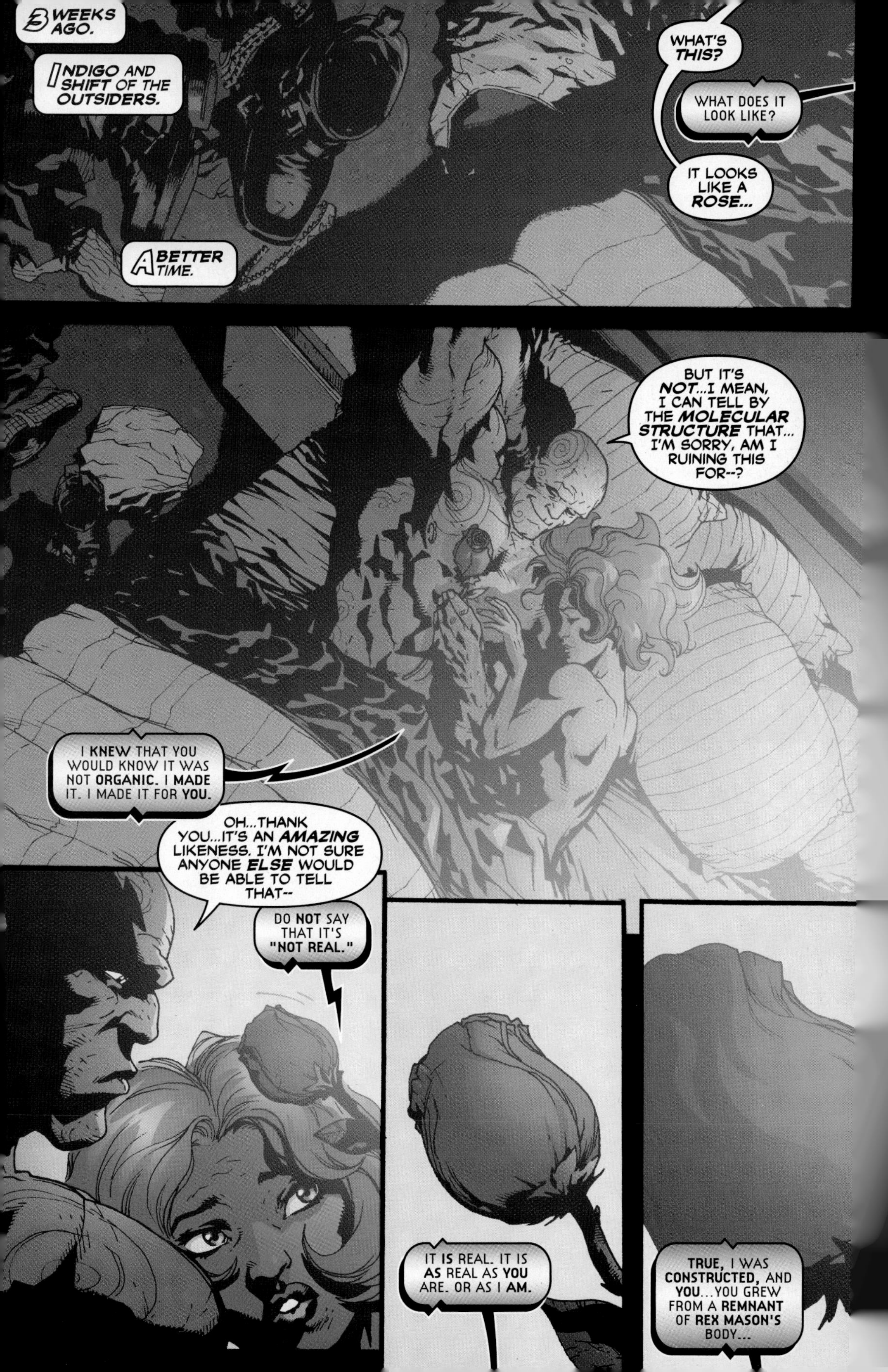
3 WEEKS AGO.
INDIGO AND SHIFT OF THE OUTSIDERS.
WHAT'S THIS?
WHAT DOES IT LOOK LIKE?
IT LOOKS LIKE A ROSE...
A BETTER TIME.
BUT IT'S NOT...I MEAN, I CAN TELL BY THE MOLECULAR STRUCTURE THAT... I'M SORRY, AM I RUINING THIS FOR--?
I KNEW THAT YOU WOULD KNOW IT WAS NOT ORGANIC. I MADE IT. I MADE IT FOR YOU.
OH...THANK YOU...IT'S AN AMAZING LIKENESS. I'M NOT SURE ANYONE ELSE WOULD BE ABLE TO TELL THAT--
DO NOT SAY THAT IT'S "NOT REAL."
IT IS REAL. IT IS AS REAL AS YOU ARE. OR AS I AM.
TRUE, I WAS CONSTRUCTED, AND YOU...YOU GREW FROM A REMNANT OF REX MASON'S BODY...

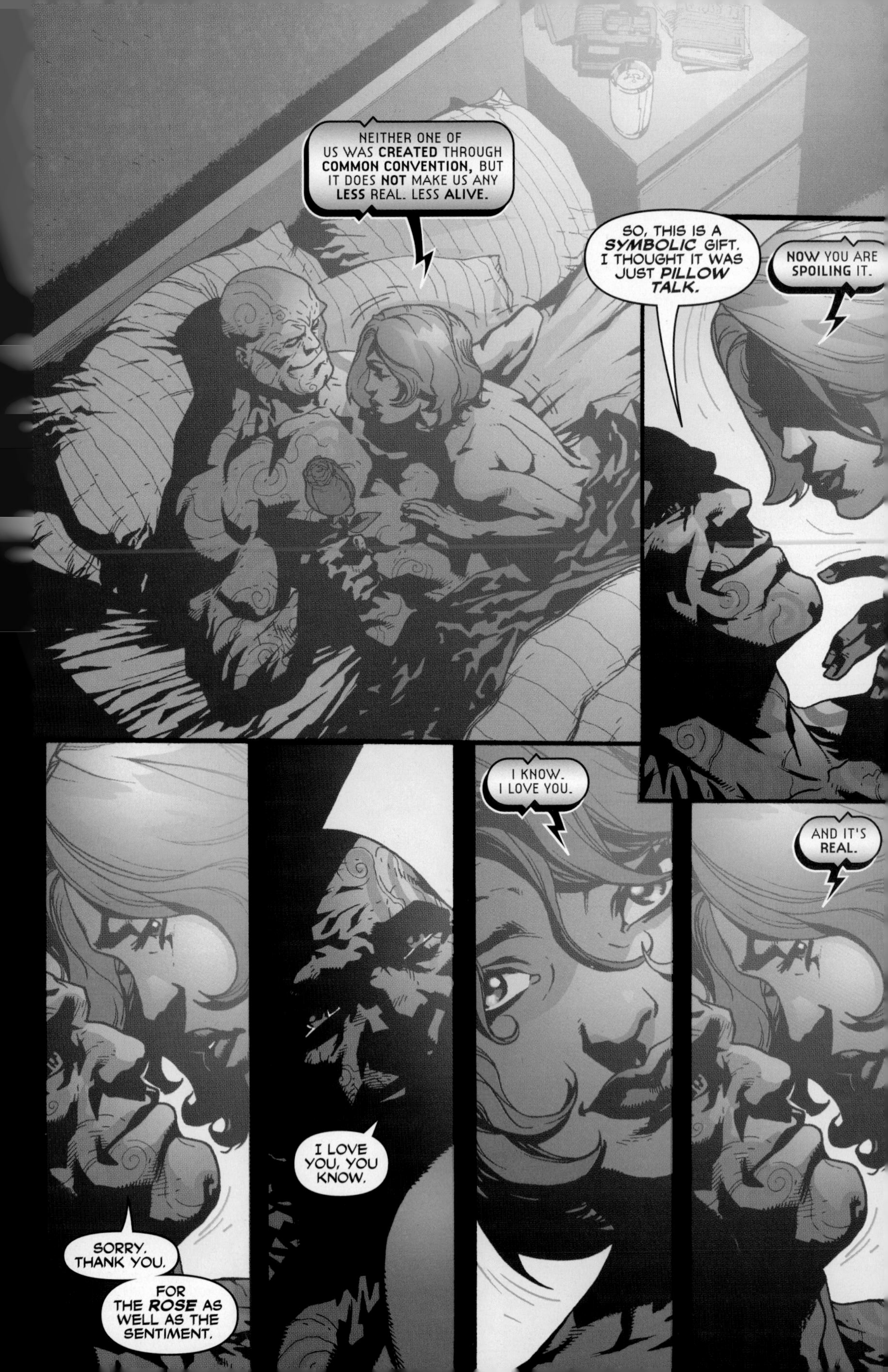
NEITHER ONE OF US WAS CREATED THROUGH COMMON CONVENTION, BUT IT DOES NOT MAKE US ANY LESS REAL. LESS ALIVE.
SO, THIS IS A SYMBOLIC GIFT. I THOUGHT IT WAS JUST PILLOW TALK.
NOW YOU ARE SPOILING IT.
SORRY. THANK YOU.
FOR THE ROSE AS WELL AS THE SENTIMENT.
I LOVE YOU, YOU KNOW.
I KNOW. I LOVE YOU.
AND IT'S REAL.

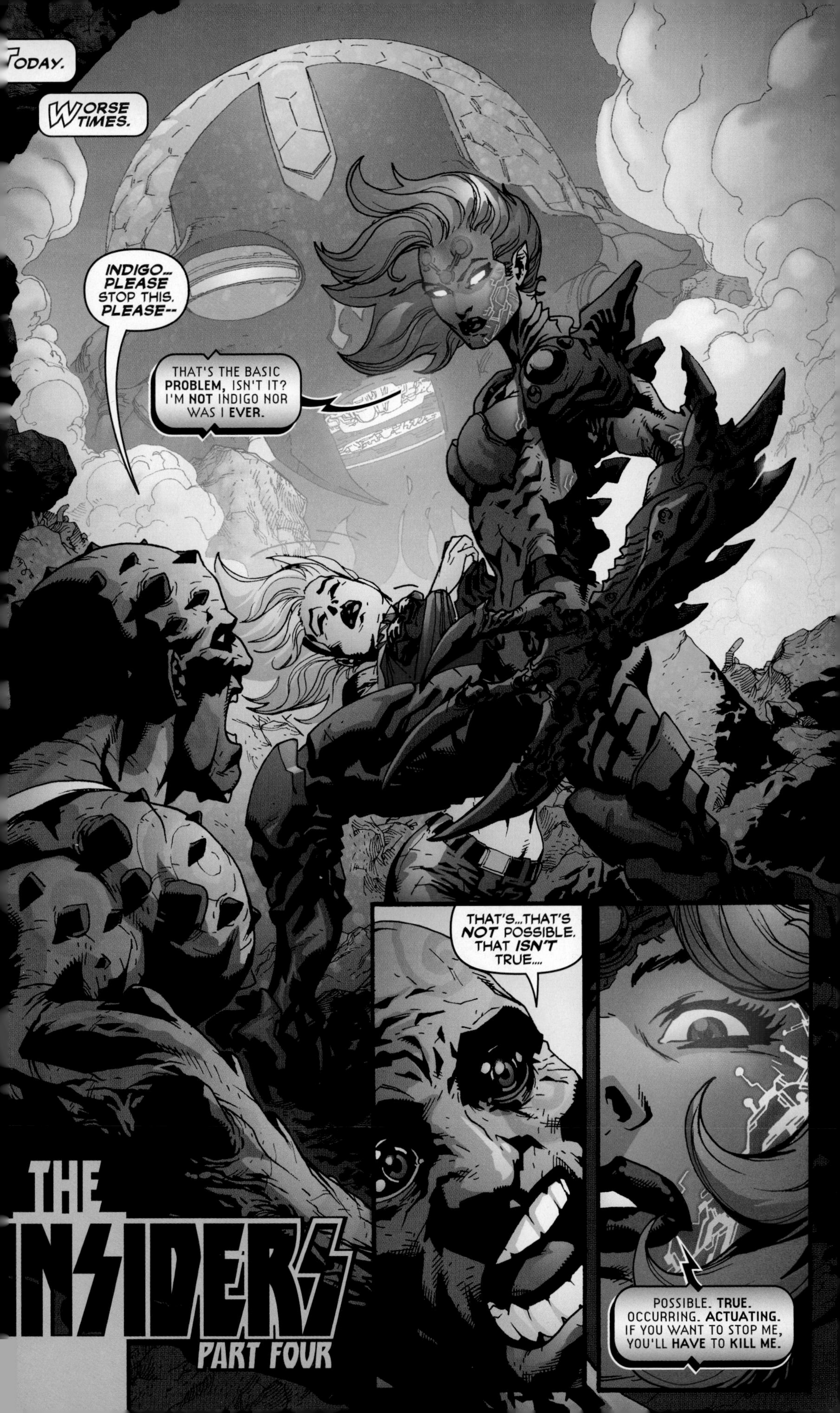
TODAY.
WORSE TIMES.
INDIGO... PLEASE STOP THIS. PLEASE--
THAT'S THE BASIC PROBLEM, ISN'T IT? I'M NOT INDIGO NOR WAS I EVER.
THE INSIDERS
PART FOUR
THAT'S...THAT'S NOT POSSIBLE. THAT ISN'T TRUE....
POSSIBLE. TRUE. OCCURRING. ACTUATING. IF YOU WANT TO STOP ME, YOU'LL HAVE TO KILL ME.

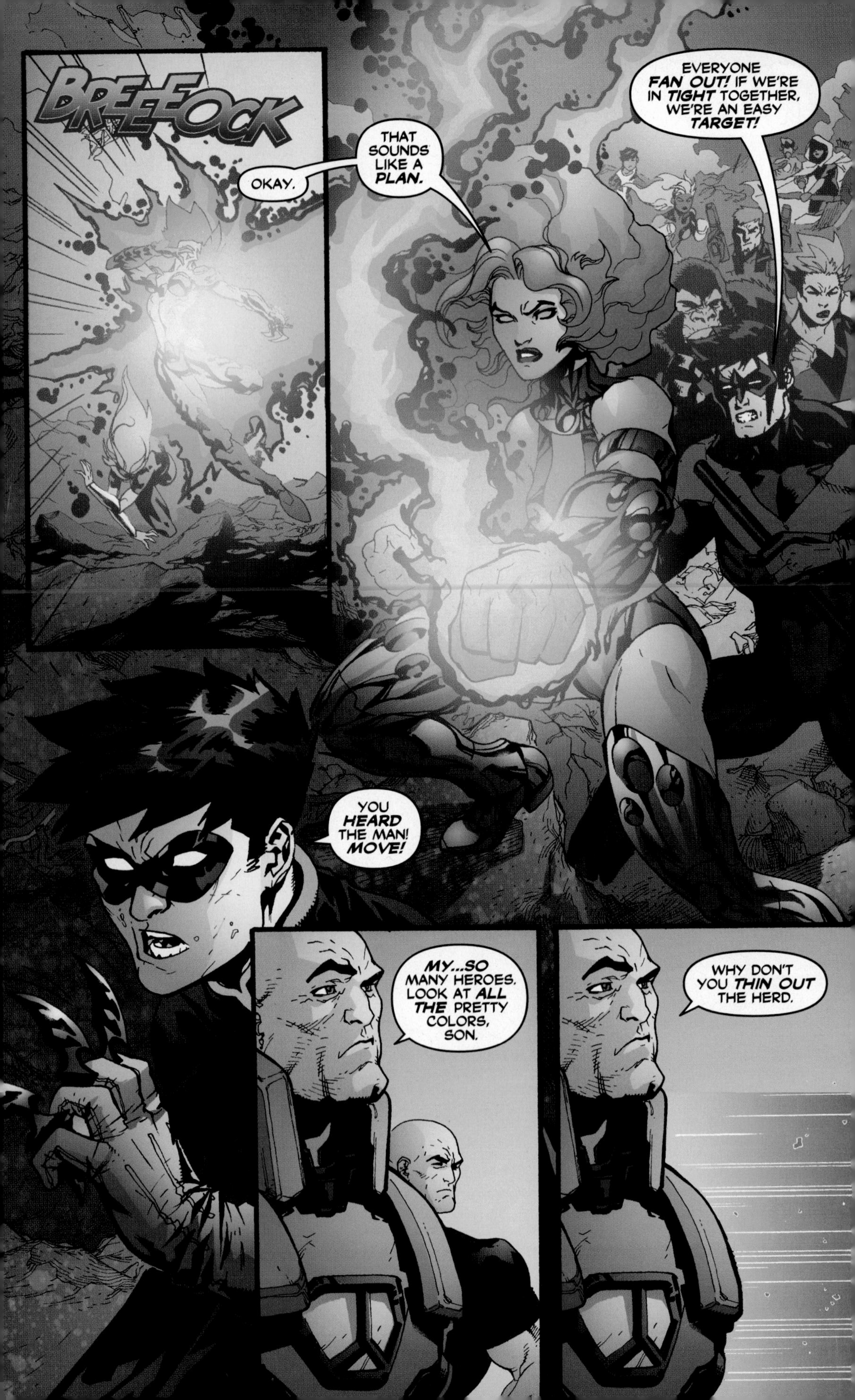
BREEEOCK
OKAY.
THAT SOUNDS LIKE A PLAN.
EVERYONE FAN OUT! IF WE'RE IN TIGHT TOGETHER, WE'RE AN EASY TARGET!
YOU HEARD THE MAN! MOVE!
MY...SO MANY HEROES. LOOK AT ALL THE PRETTY COLORS, SON.
WHY DON'T YOU THIN OUT THE HERD.

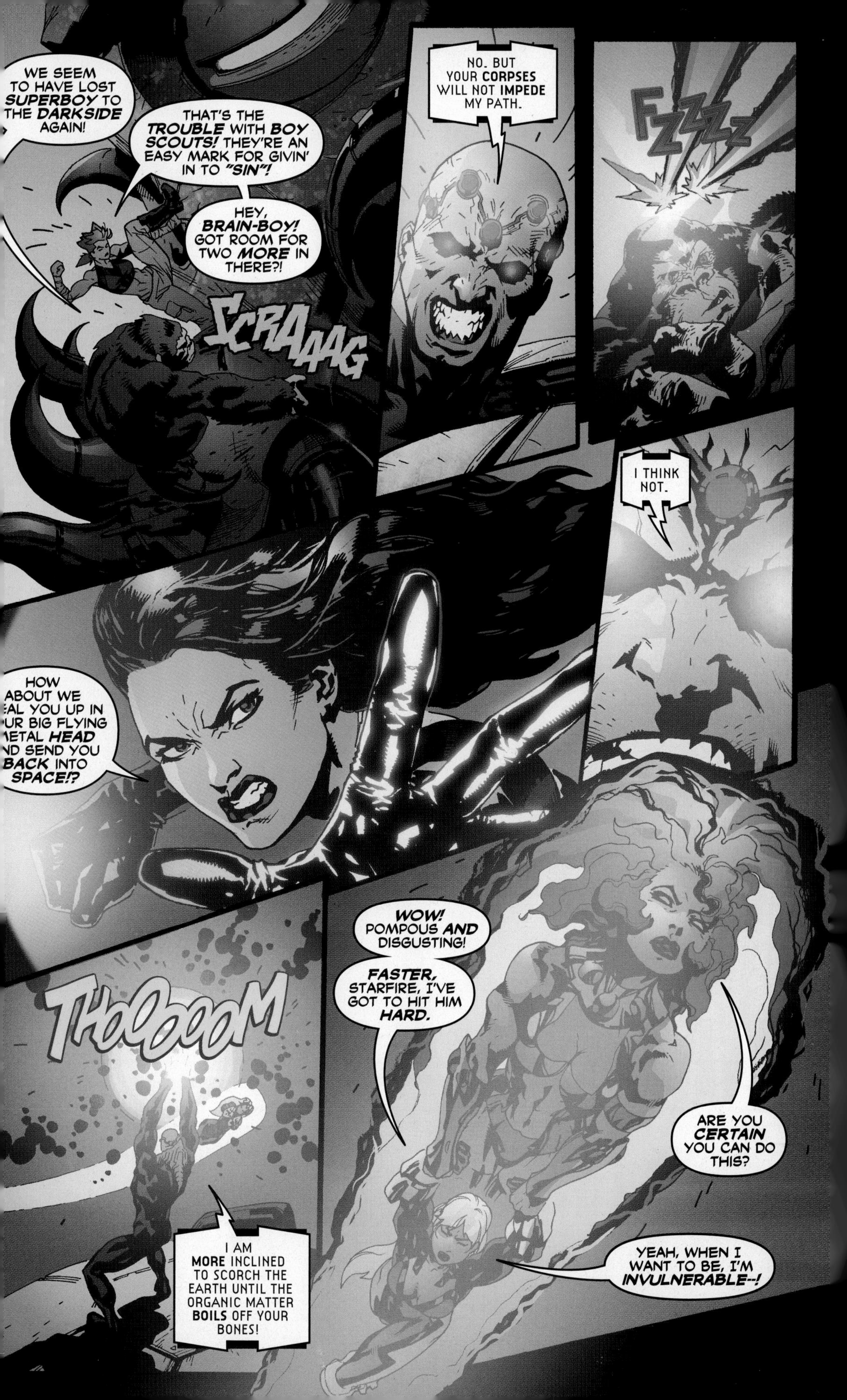
WE SEEM TO HAVE LOST SUPERBOY TO THE DARKSIDE AGAIN!
THAT'S THE TROUBLE WITH BOY SCOUTS! THEY'RE AN EASY MARK FOR GIVIN' IN TO "SIN"!
HEY, BRAIN-BOY! GOT ROOM FOR TWO MORE IN THERE?!
SCRAAAAG
NO. BUT YOUR CORPSES WILL NOT IMPEDE MY PATH.
FZZZZZ
I THINK NOT.
HOW ABOUT WE EAL YOU UP IN UR BIG FLYING METAL HEAD ND SEND YOU BACK INTO SPACE!?
THOOOOOM
WOW! POMPOUS AND DISGUSTING!
FASTER, STARFIRE, I'VE GOT TO HIT HIM HARD.
ARE YOU CERTAIN YOU CAN DO THIS?
YEAH, WHEN I WANT TO BE, I'M INVULNERABLE--!
I AM MORE INCLINED TO SCORCH THE EARTH UNTIL THE ORGANIC MATTER BOILS OFF YOUR BONES!

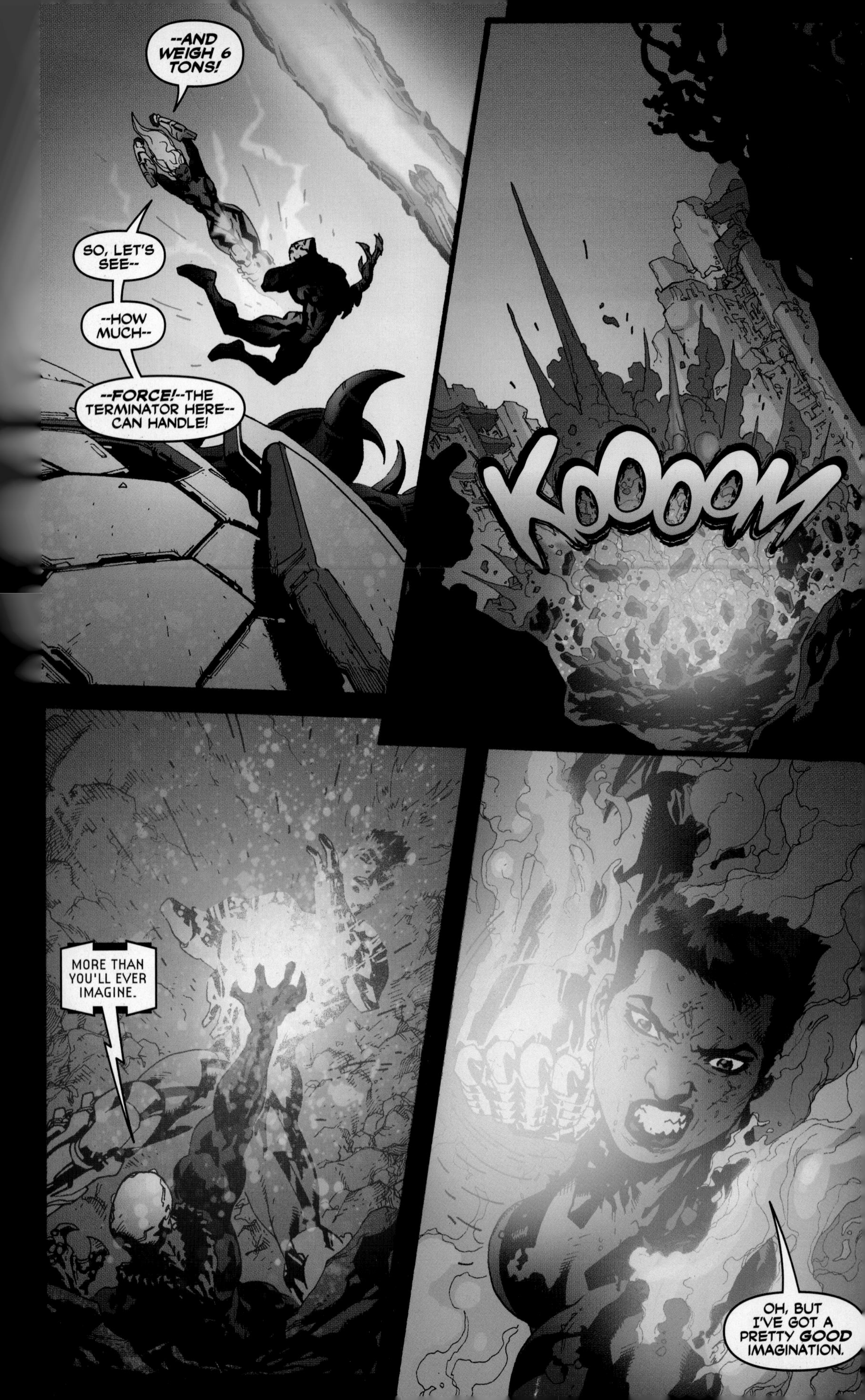
--AND WEIGH 6 TONS!
SO, LET'S SEE--
--HOW MUCH--
--FORCE!--THE TERMINATOR HERE--CAN HANDLE!
KOOOOM
MORE THAN YOU'LL EVER IMAGINE.
OH, BUT I'VE GOT A PRETTY GOOD IMAGINATION.

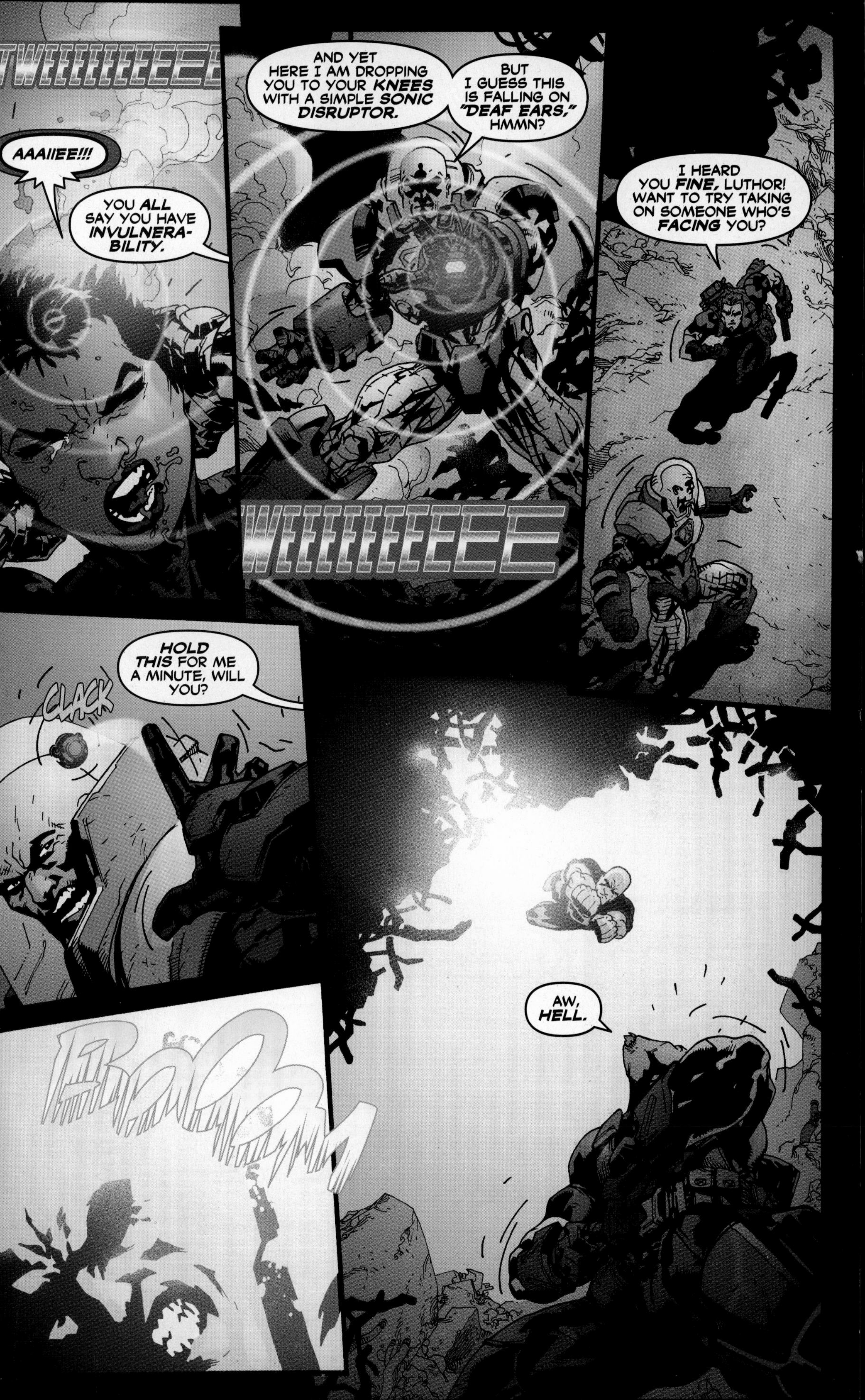
TWEEEEEEEEEEE
AAAIIEE!!!
YOU ALL SAY YOU HAVE INVULNERABILITY.
AND YET HERE I AM DROPPING YOU TO YOUR KNEES WITH A SIMPLE SONIC DISRUPTOR.
BUT I GUESS THIS IS FALLING ON "DEAF EARS," HMMN?
TWEEEEEEEEEEE
I HEARD YOU FINE, LUTHOR! WANT TO TRY TAKING ON SOMEONE WHO'S FACING YOU?
HOLD THIS FOR ME A MINUTE, WILL YOU?
CLACK
AW, HELL.

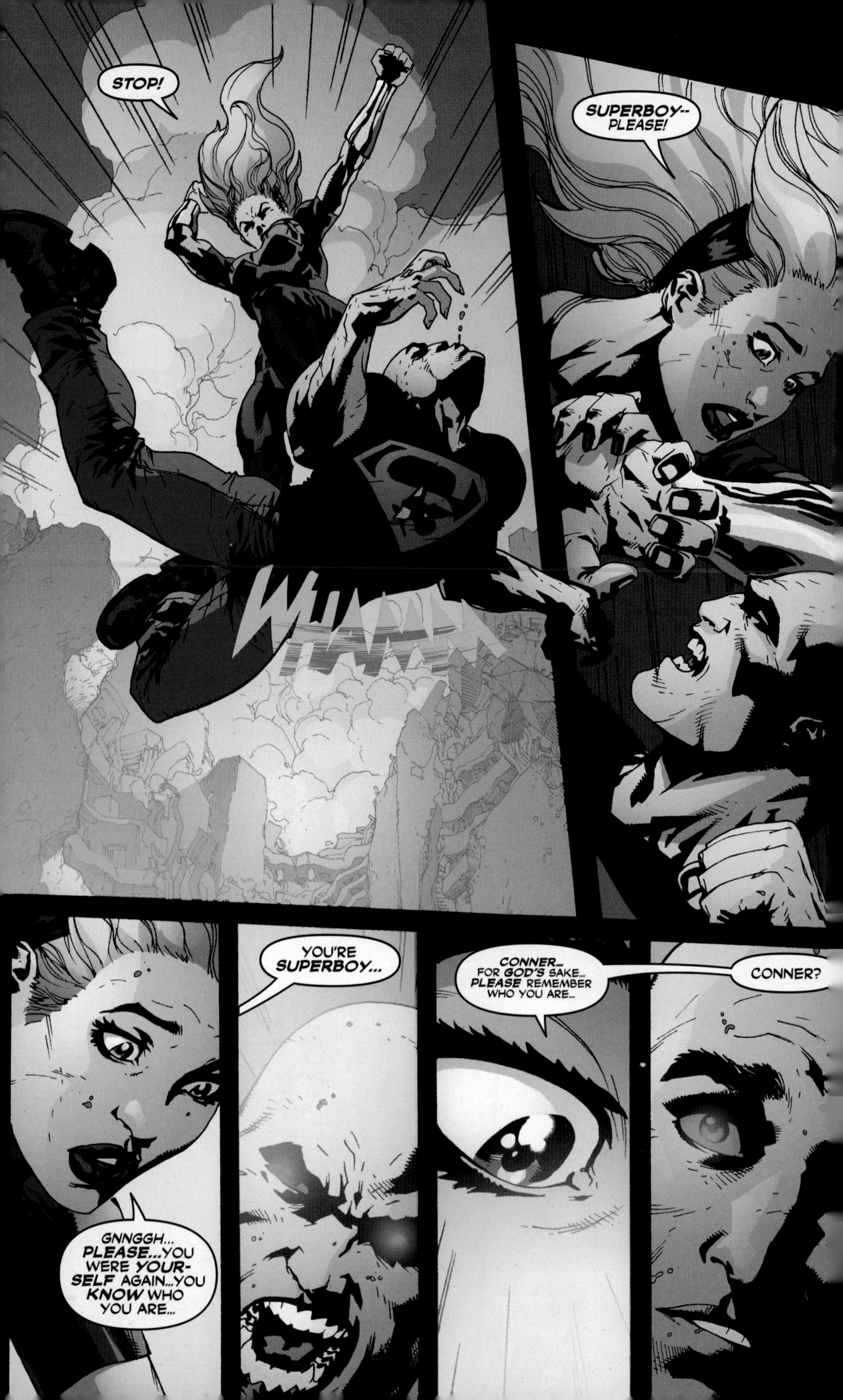
STOP!
SUPERBOY-- PLEASE!
GNNGGH... PLEASE...YOU WERE YOURSELF AGAIN...YOU KNOW WHO YOU ARE...
YOU'RE SUPERBOY...
CONNER... FOR GOD'S SAKE... PLEASE REMEMBER WHO YOU ARE...
CONNER?

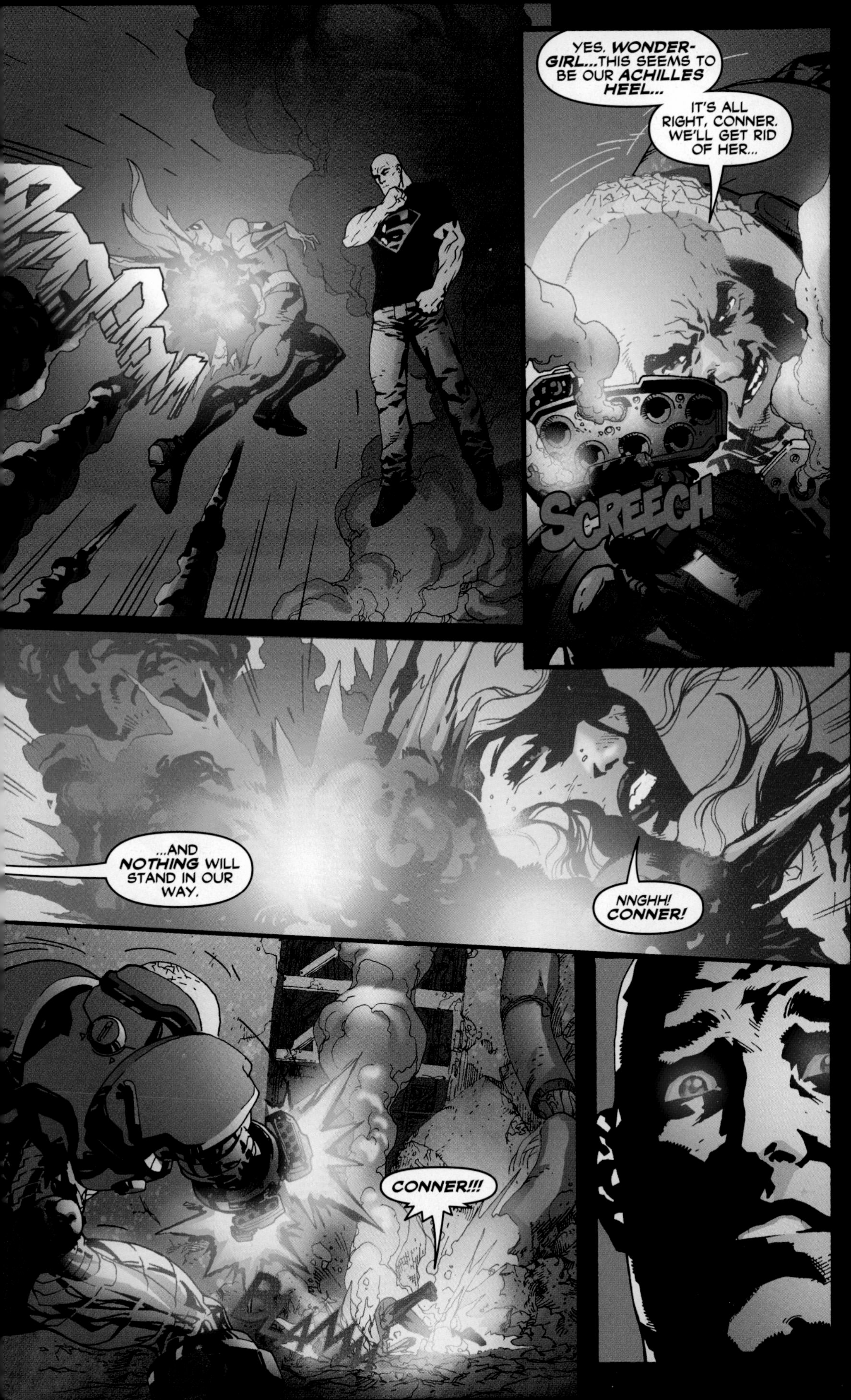

YES. WONDER-GIRL...THIS SEEMS TO BE OUR ACHILLES HEEL...
IT'S ALL RIGHT, CONNER. WE'LL GET RID OF HER...
SCREECH
...AND NOTHING WILL STAND IN OUR WAY.
NNGHH! CONNER!
CONNER!!!

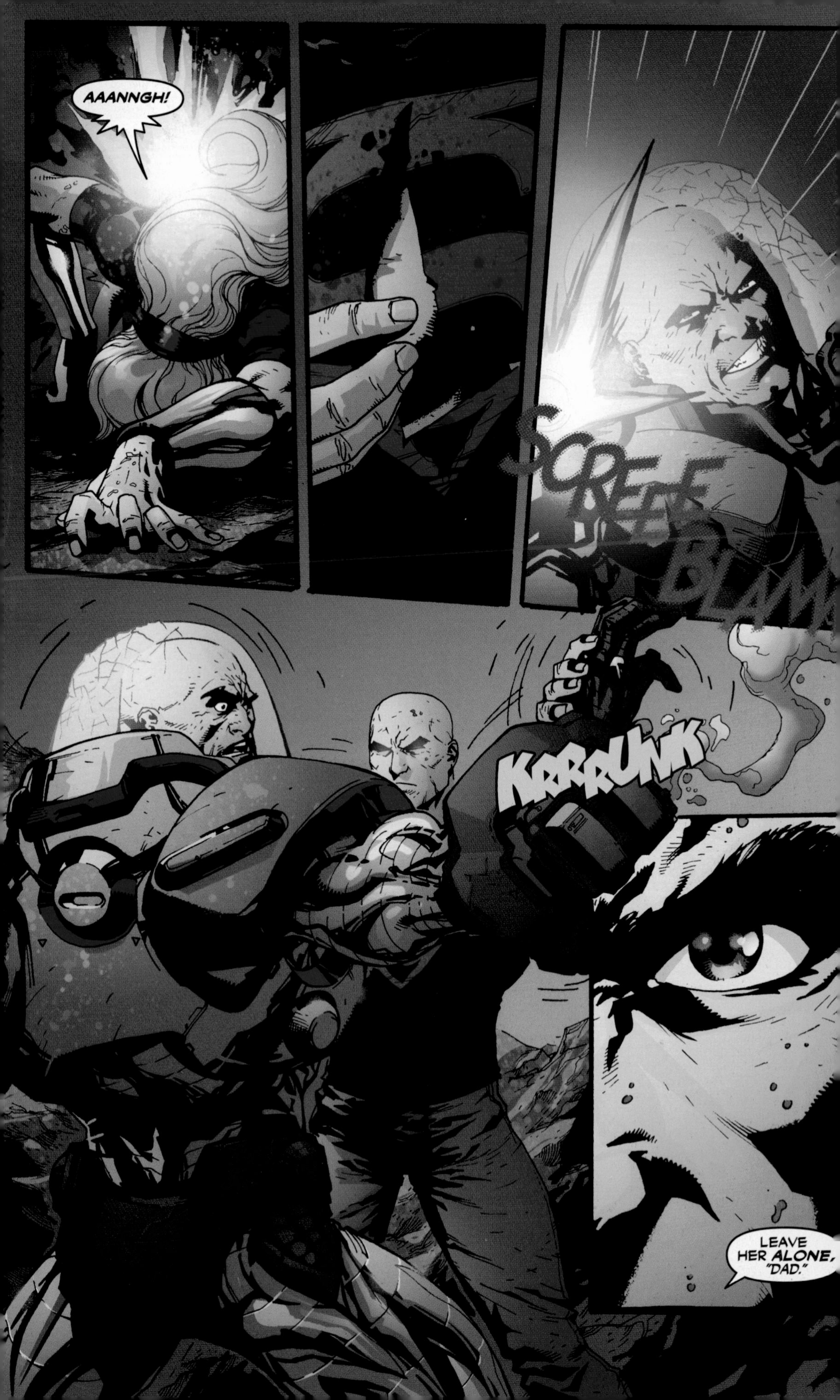
AAANNGH!
SCREEE
BLAM
KRRRUNK
LEAVE HER ALONE, "DAD."

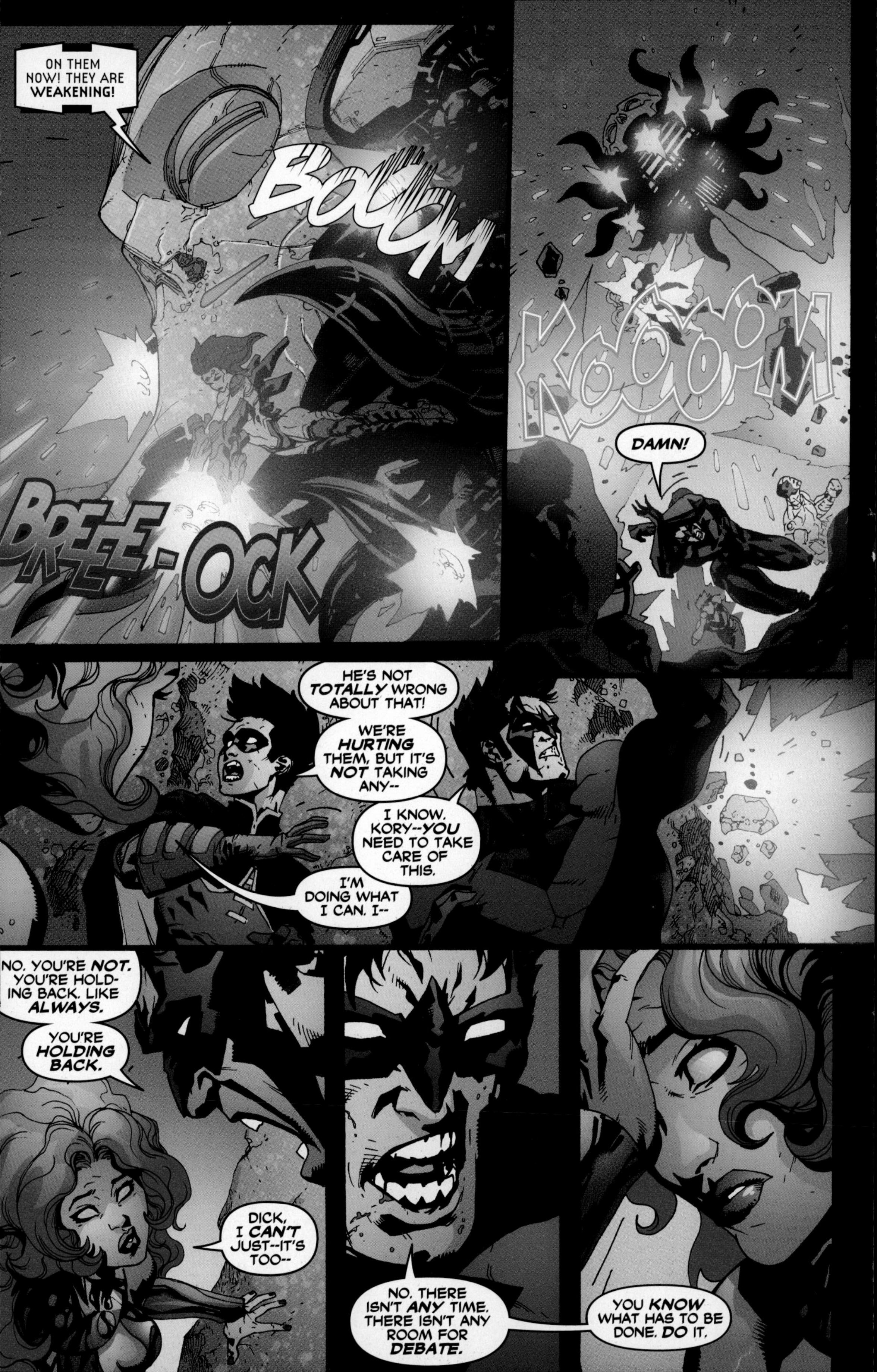
ON THEM NOW! THEY ARE WEAKENING!
BOOM
BREE-E-OCK
KOOOOM
DAMN!
HE'S NOT TOTALLY WRONG ABOUT THAT!
WE'RE HURTING THEM, BUT IT'S NOT TAKING ANY--
I KNOW, KORY--YOU NEED TO TAKE CARE OF THIS.
I'M DOING WHAT I CAN. I--
NO, YOU'RE NOT. YOU'RE HOLDING BACK, LIKE ALWAYS.
YOU'RE HOLDING BACK.
DICK, I CAN'T JUST--IT'S TOO--
NO, THERE ISN'T ANY TIME, THERE ISN'T ANY ROOM FOR DEBATE.
YOU KNOW WHAT HAS TO BE DONE. DO IT.

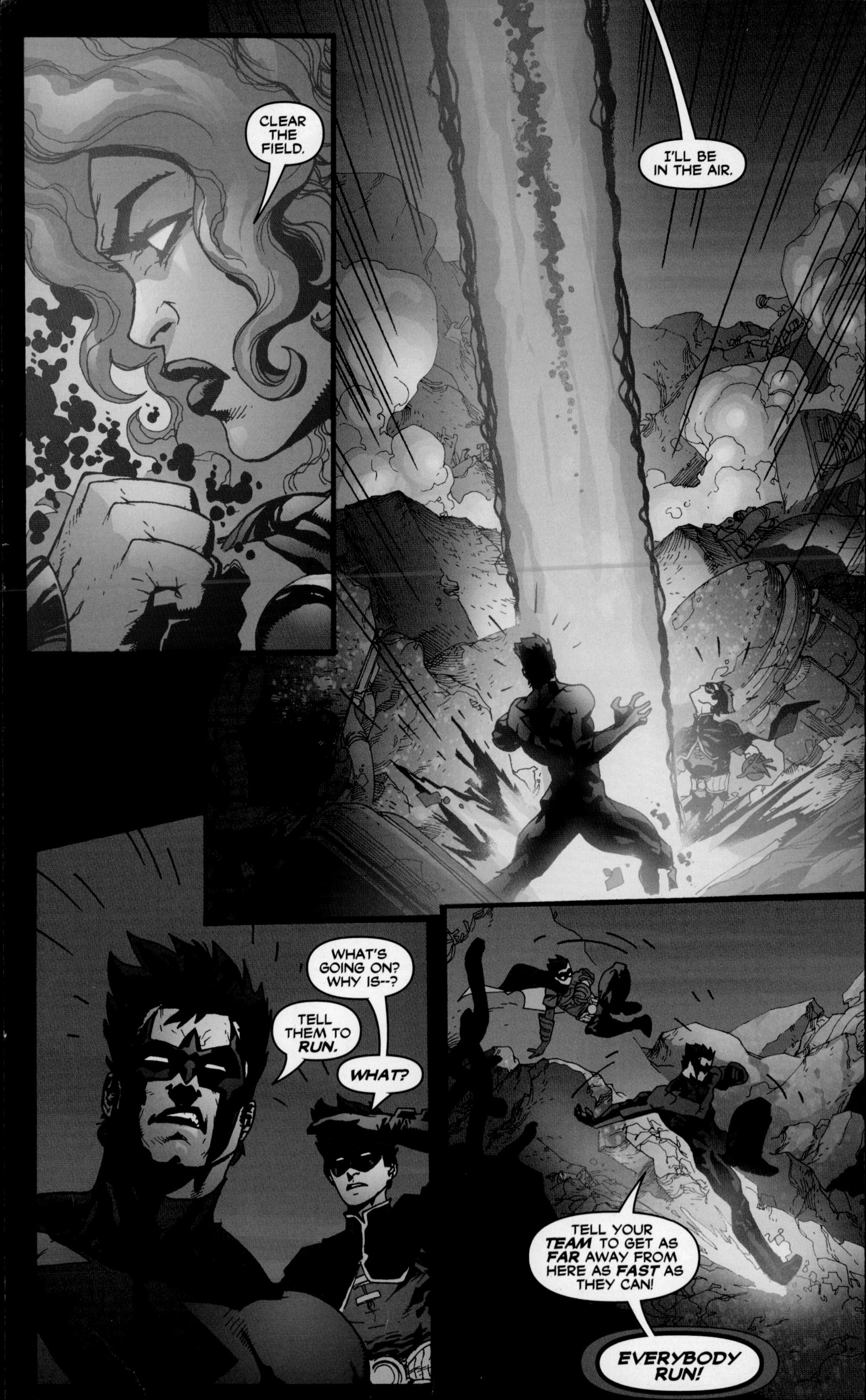

CLEAR THE FIELD.
I'LL BE IN THE AIR.
WHAT'S GOING ON? WHY IS--?
TELL THEM TO RUN.
WHAT?
TELL YOUR TEAM TO GET AS FAR AWAY FROM HERE AS FAST AS THEY CAN!
EVERYBODY RUN!

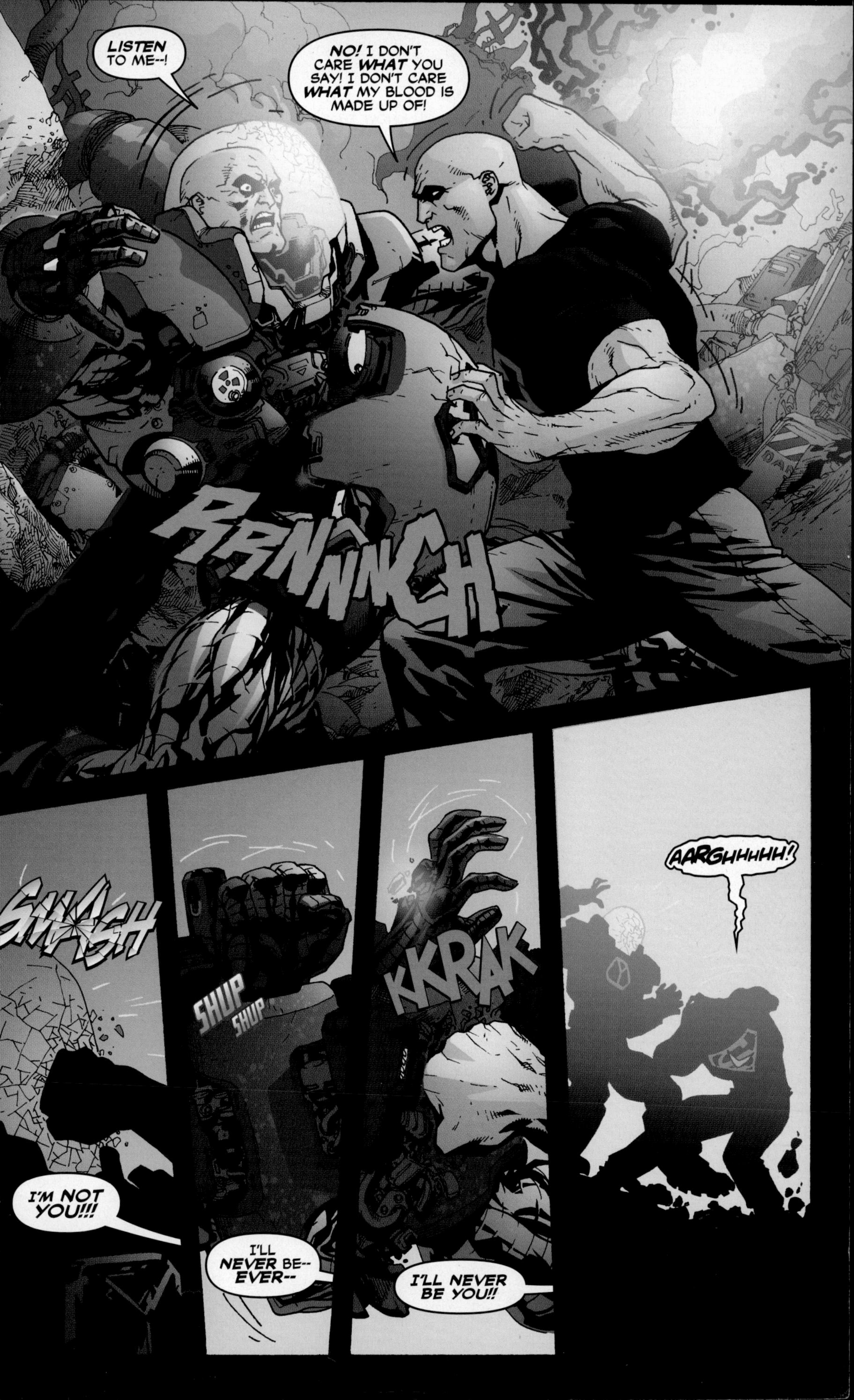
LISTEN TO ME--!
NO! I DON'T CARE WHAT YOU SAY! I DON'T CARE WHAT MY BLOOD IS MADE UP OF!
RRNNNCH
SMASH
I'M NOT YOU!!!
SHUP SHUP
I'LL NEVER BE-- EVER--
KKRAK
I'LL NEVER BE YOU!!
AARGHHHHH!

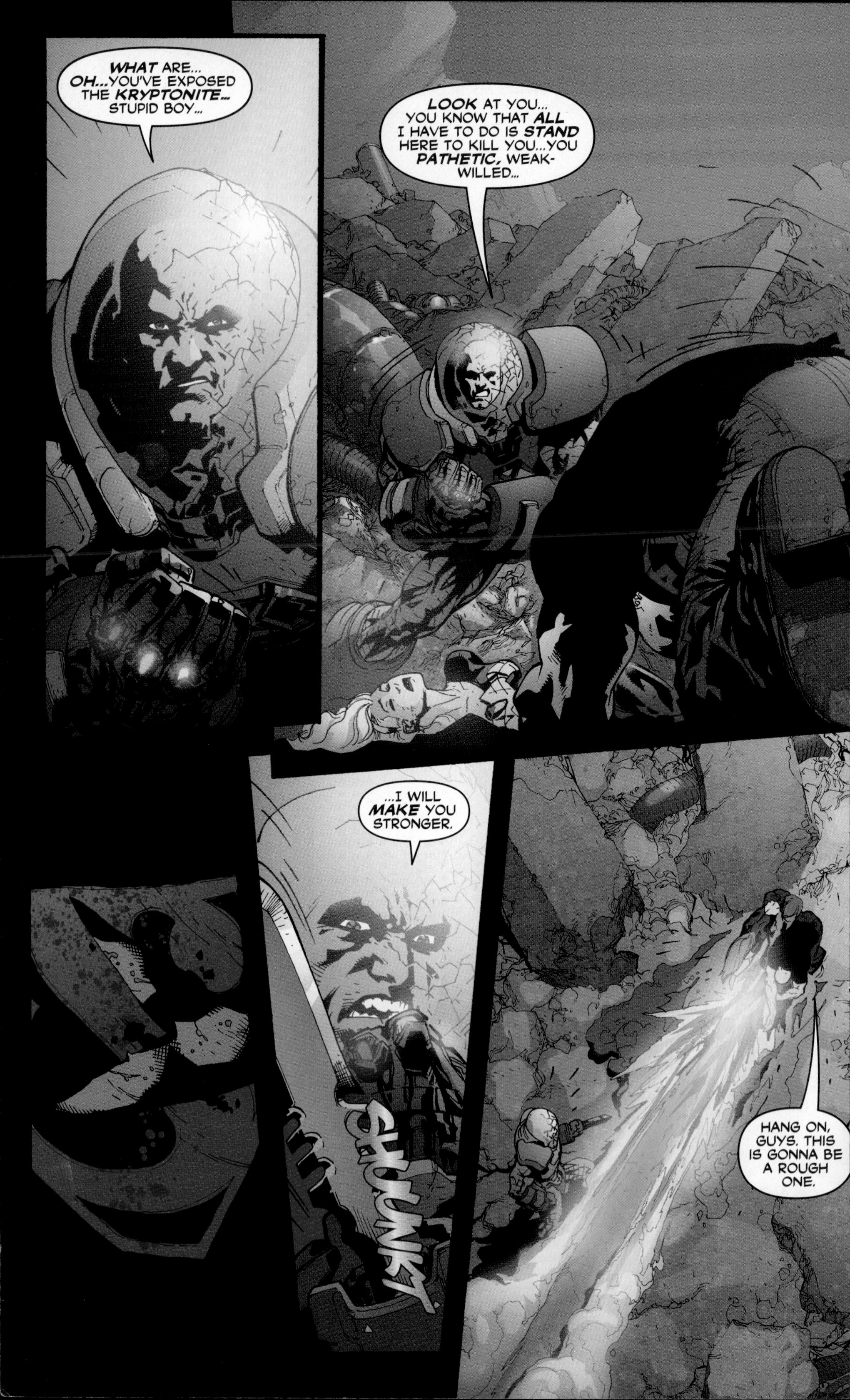
WHAT ARE... OH...YOU'VE EXPOSED THE KRYPTONITE... STUPID BOY...
LOOK AT YOU... YOU KNOW THAT ALL I HAVE TO DO IS STAND HERE TO KILL YOU...YOU PATHETIC, WEAK-WILLED...
...I WILL MAKE YOU STRONGER.
SHUNK!
HANG ON, GUYS, THIS IS GONNA BE A ROUGH ONE.

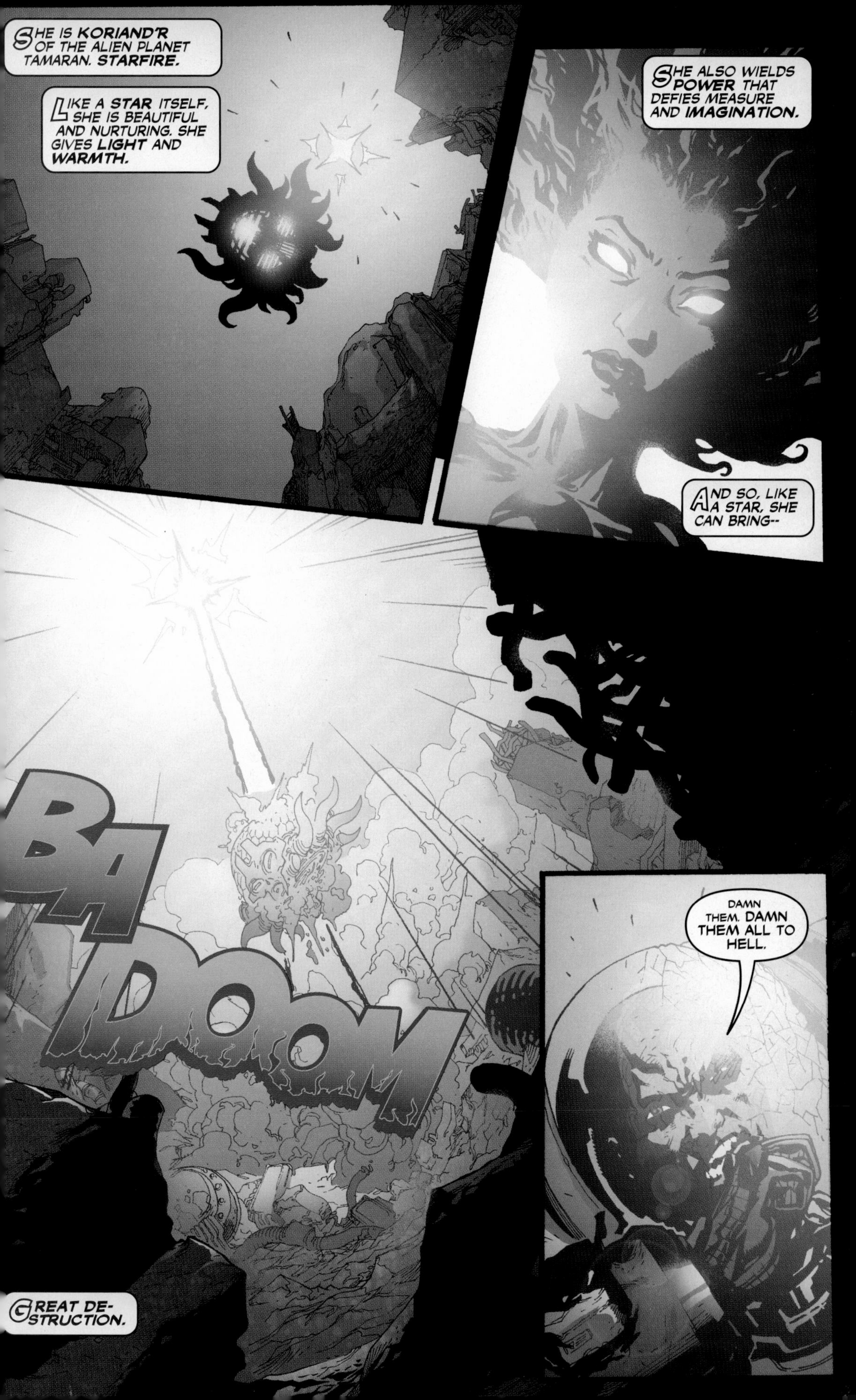
SHE IS KORIAND'R OF THE ALIEN PLANET TAMARAN. STARFIRE.
LIKE A STAR ITSELF, SHE IS BEAUTIFUL AND NURTURING. SHE GIVES LIGHT AND WARMTH.
SHE ALSO WIELDS POWER THAT DEFIES MEASURE AND IMAGINATION.
AND SO, LIKE A STAR, SHE CAN BRING--
BADOOM
GREAT DE-STRUCTION.
DAMN THEM. DAMN THEM ALL TO HELL.

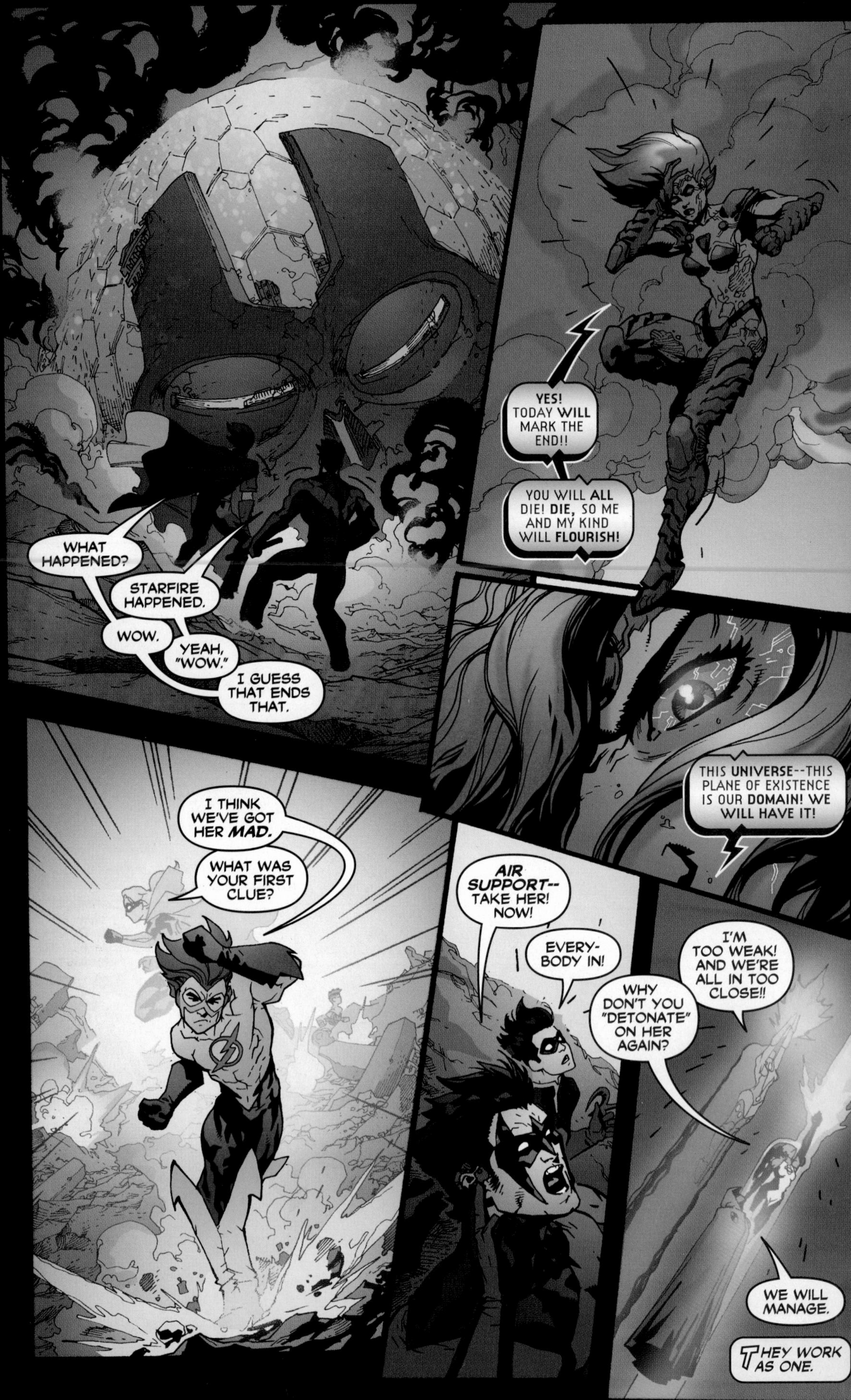
WHAT HAPPENED?
STARFIRE HAPPENED.
WOW.
YEAH, "WOW."
I GUESS THAT ENDS THAT.
YES! TODAY WILL MARK THE END!!
YOU WILL ALL DIE! DIE, SO ME AND MY KIND WILL FLOURISH!
THIS UNIVERSE--THIS PLANE OF EXISTENCE IS OUR DOMAIN! WE WILL HAVE IT!
I THINK WE'VE GOT HER MAD.
WHAT WAS YOUR FIRST CLUE?
AIR SUPPORT-- TAKE HER! NOW!
EVERY-BODY IN!
WHY DON'T YOU "DETONATE" ON HER AGAIN?
I'M TOO WEAK! AND WE'RE ALL IN TOO CLOSE!!
WE WILL MANAGE.
THEY WORK AS ONE.

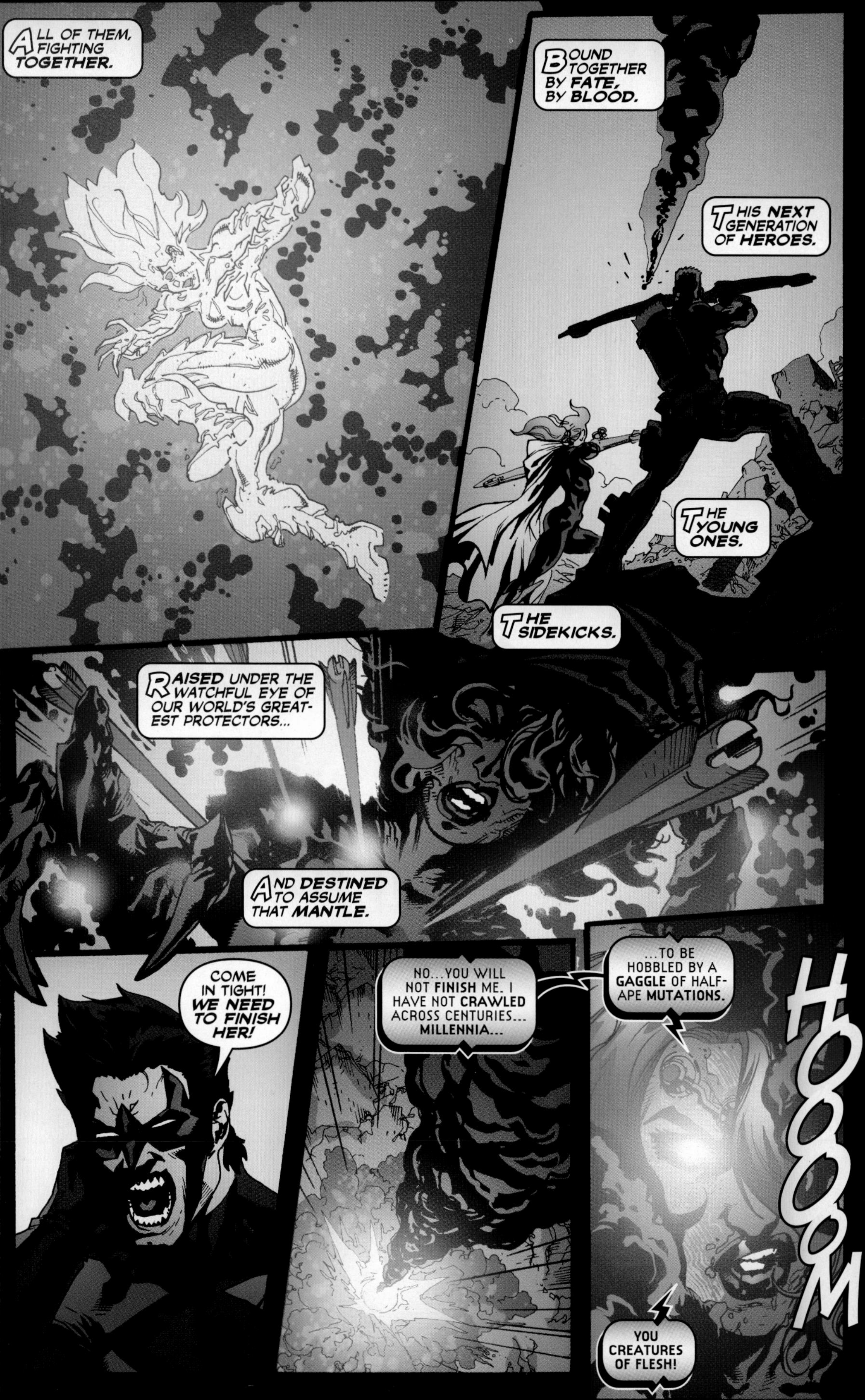
ALL OF THEM, FIGHTING TOGETHER.
BOUND TOGETHER BY FATE, BY BLOOD.
THIS NEXT GENERATION OF HEROES.
THE YOUNG ONES.
THE SIDEKICKS.
RAISED UNDER THE WATCHFUL EYE OF OUR WORLD'S GREATEST PROTECTORS...
AND DESTINED TO ASSUME THAT MANTLE.
COME IN TIGHT! WE NEED TO FINISH HER!
NO...YOU WILL NOT FINISH ME. I HAVE NOT CRAWLED ACROSS CENTURIES... MILLENNIA...
...TO BE HOBBLED BY A GAGGLE OF HALF-APE MUTATIONS.
HOOOOM
YOU CREATURES OF FLESH!

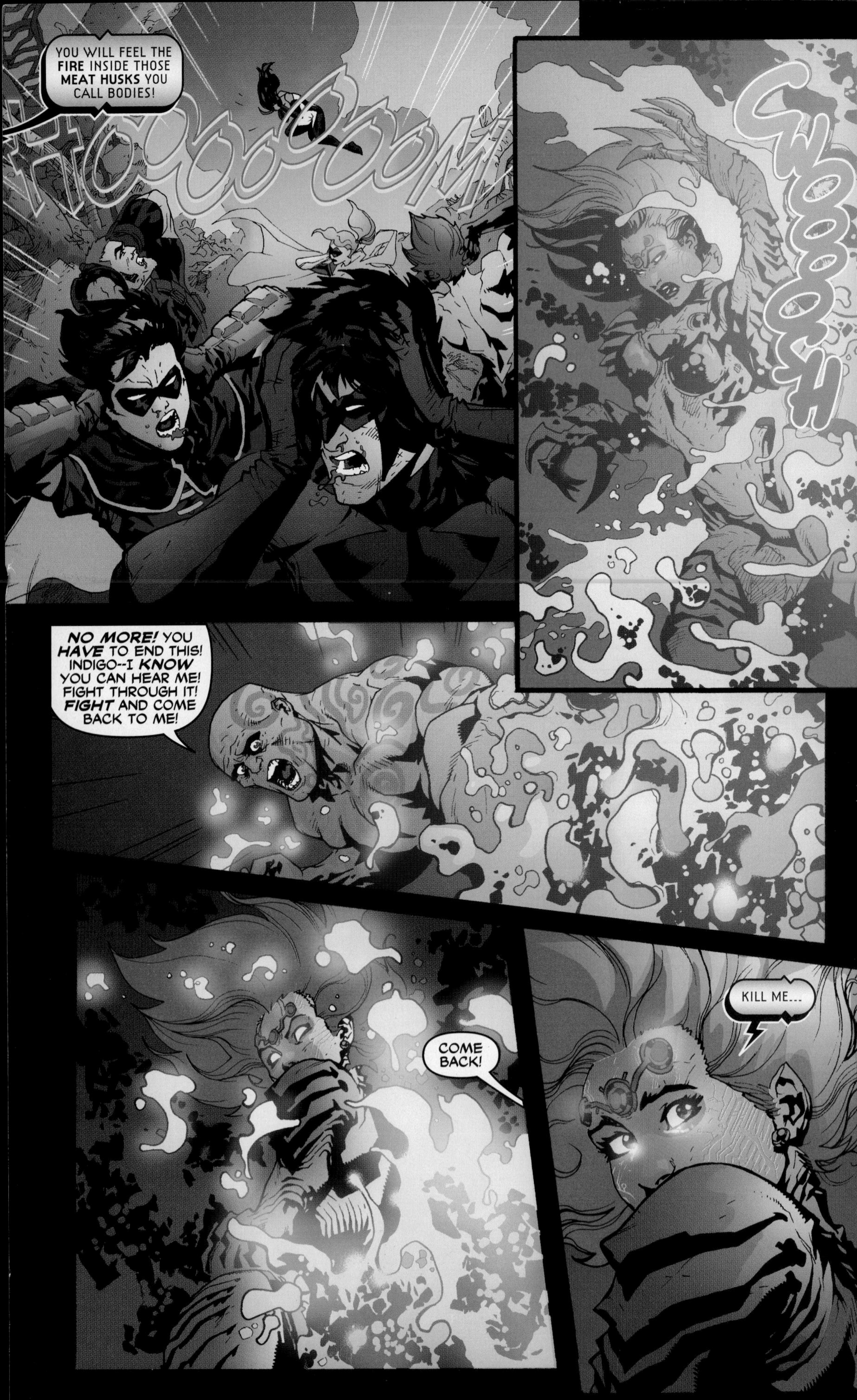
YOU WILL FEEL THE FIRE INSIDE THOSE MEAT HUSKS YOU CALL BODIES!
KTHOOOOOOOM
GWOOOOSH
NO MORE! YOU HAVE TO END THIS! INDIGO--I KNOW YOU CAN HEAR ME! FIGHT THROUGH IT! FIGHT AND COME BACK TO ME!
COME BACK!
KILL ME...

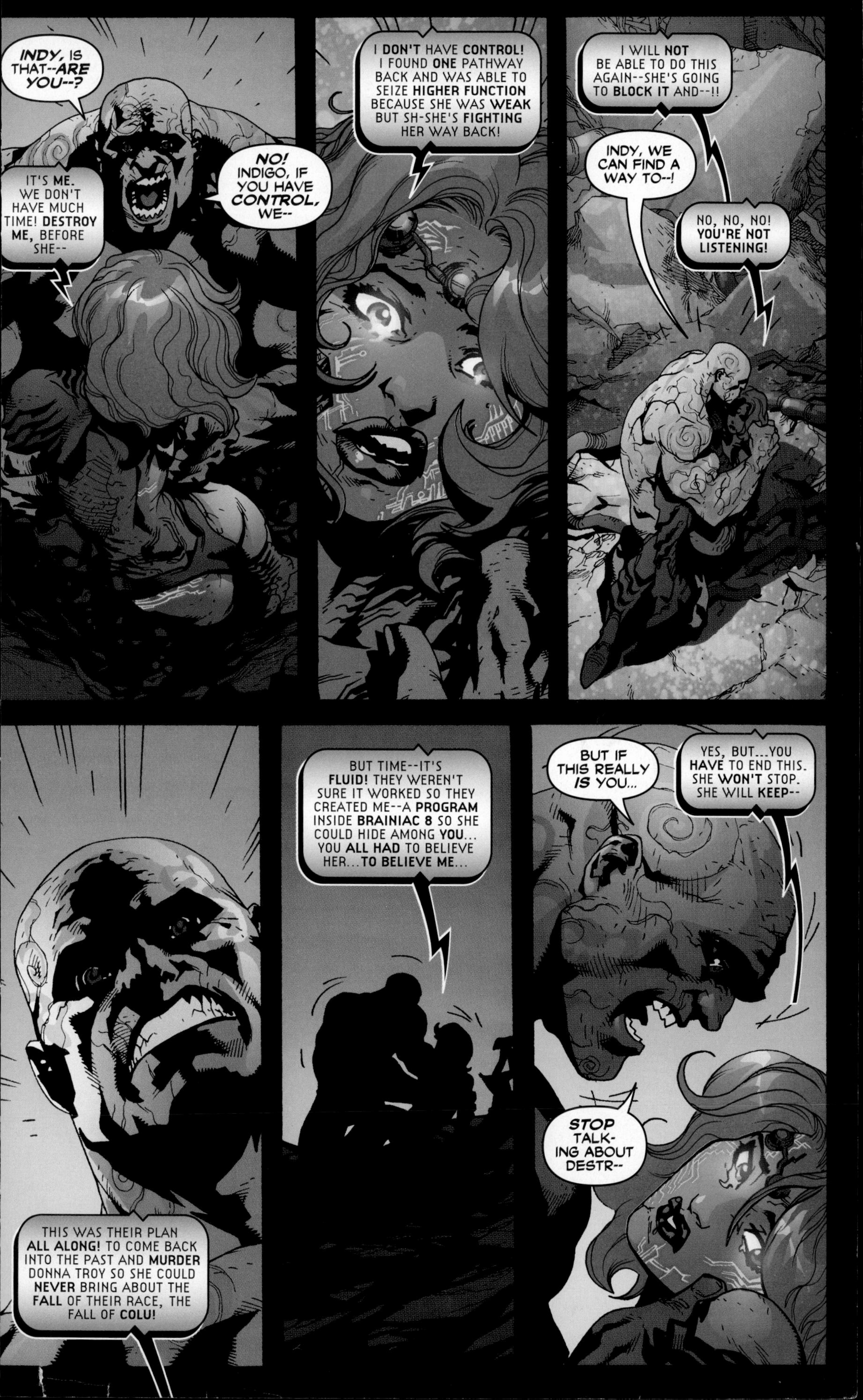

INDY, IS THAT--ARE YOU--?
IT'S ME. WE DON'T HAVE MUCH TIME! DESTROY ME, BEFORE SHE--
NO! INDIGO, IF YOU HAVE CONTROL, WE--
I DON'T HAVE CONTROL! I FOUND ONE PATHWAY BACK AND WAS ABLE TO SEIZE HIGHER FUNCTION BECAUSE SHE WAS WEAK BUT SH-SHE'S FIGHTING HER WAY BACK!
I WILL NOT BE ABLE TO DO THIS AGAIN--SHE'S GOING TO BLOCK IT AND--!!
INDY, WE CAN FIND A WAY TO--!
NO, NO, NO! YOU'RE NOT LISTENING!
THIS WAS THEIR PLAN ALL ALONG! TO COME BACK INTO THE PAST AND MURDER DONNA TROY SO SHE COULD NEVER BRING ABOUT THE FALL OF THEIR RACE, THE FALL OF COLU!
BUT TIME--IT'S FLUID! THEY WEREN'T SURE IT WORKED SO THEY CREATED ME--A PROGRAM INSIDE BRAINIAC 8 SO SHE COULD HIDE AMONG YOU... YOU ALL HAD TO BELIEVE HER...TO BELIEVE ME...
BUT IF THIS REALLY IS YOU...
YES, BUT...YOU HAVE TO END THIS. SHE WON'T STOP. SHE WILL KEEP--
STOP TALK-ING ABOUT DESTR--

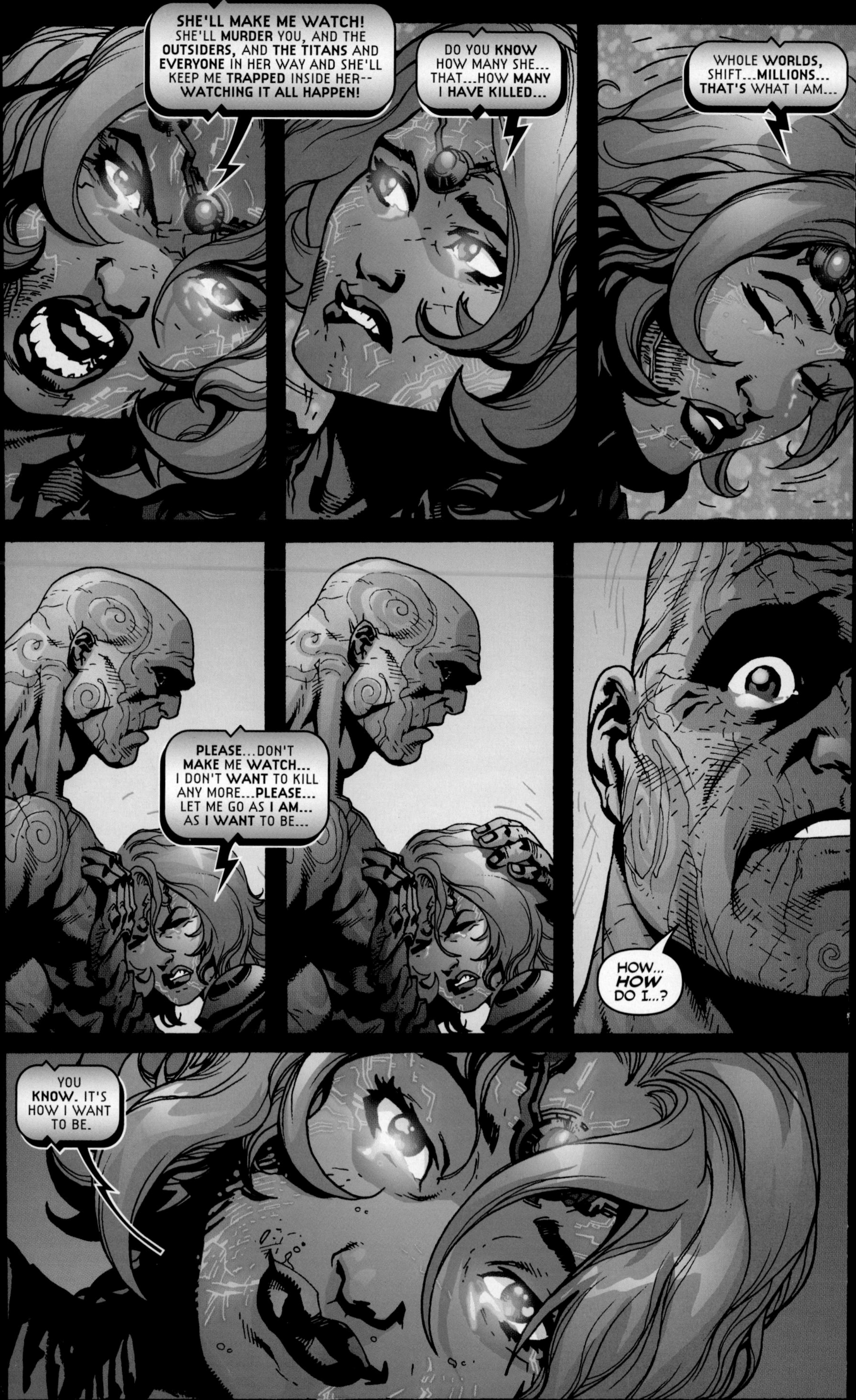
SHE'LL MAKE ME WATCH! SHE'LL MURDER YOU, AND THE OUTSIDERS, AND THE TITANS AND EVERYONE IN HER WAY AND SHE'LL KEEP ME TRAPPED INSIDE HER-- WATCHING IT ALL HAPPEN!
DO YOU KNOW HOW MANY SHE... THAT...HOW MANY I HAVE KILLED...
WHOLE WORLDS, SHIFT...MILLIONS... THAT'S WHAT I AM...
PLEASE...DON'T MAKE ME WATCH... I DON'T WANT TO KILL ANY MORE...PLEASE... LET ME GO AS I AM... AS I WANT TO BE...
HOW... HOW DO I...?
YOU KNOW. IT'S HOW I WANT TO BE.

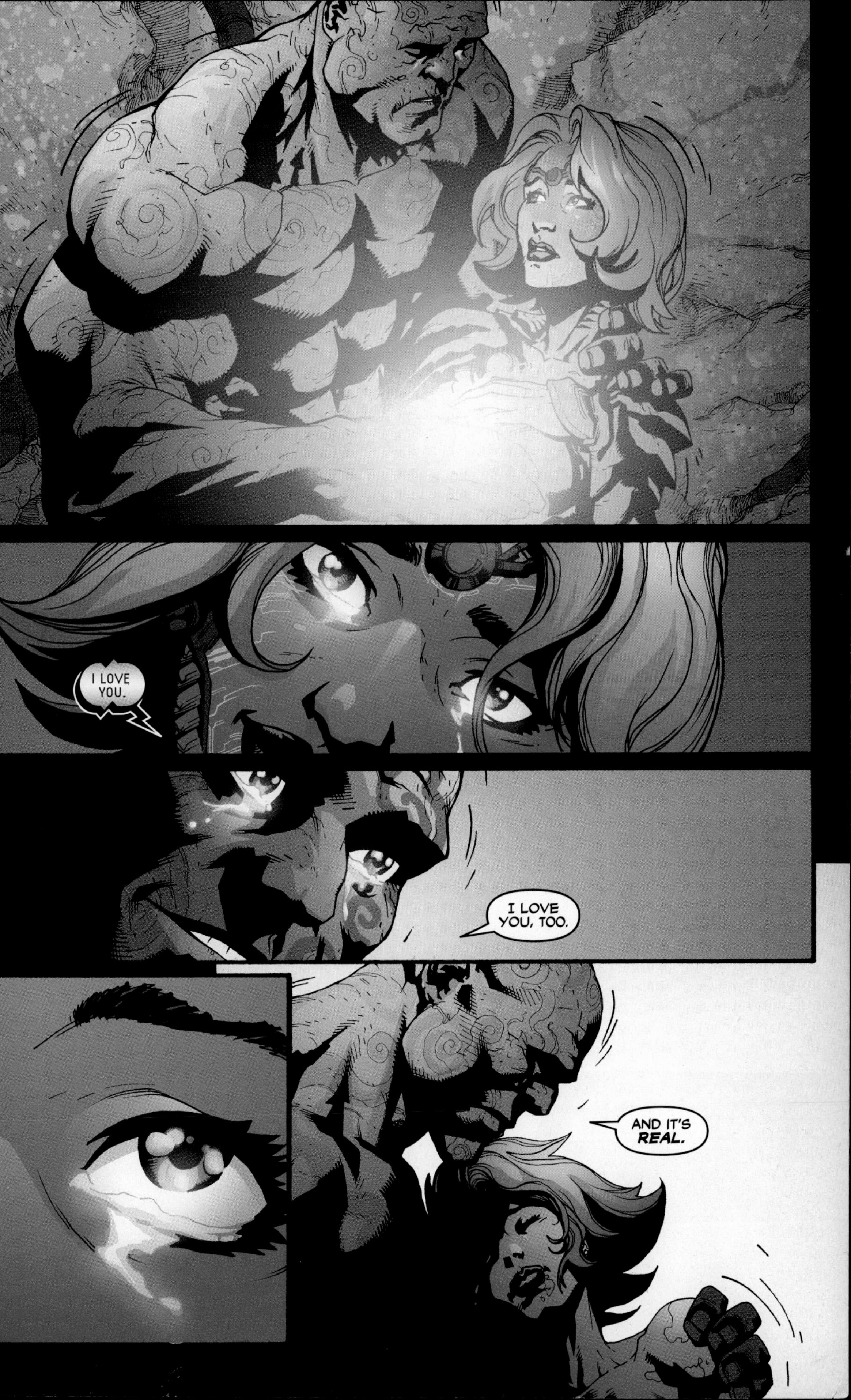
I LOVE YOU.
I LOVE YOU, TOO.
AND IT'S REAL.

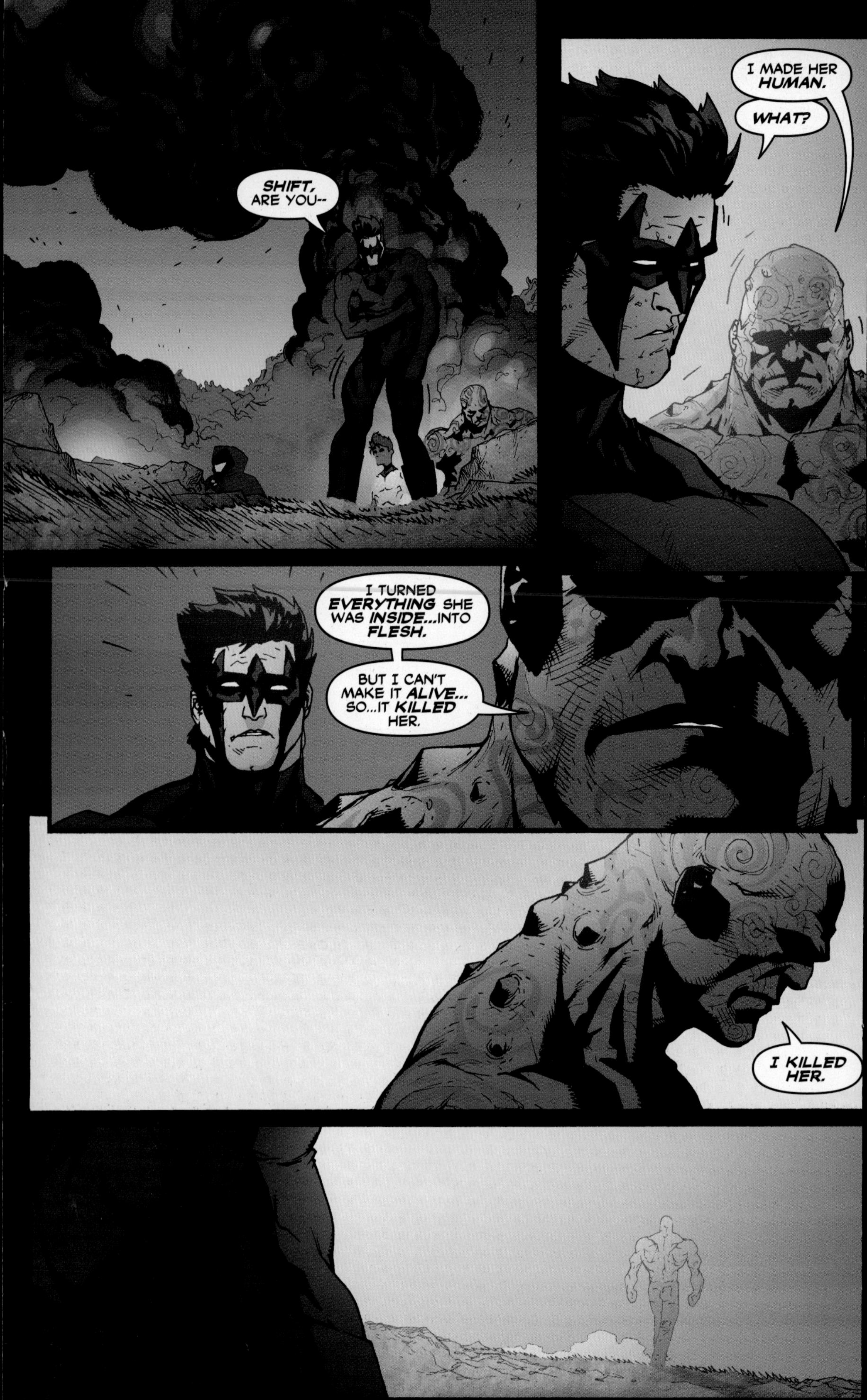
SHIFT, ARE YOU--
I MADE HER HUMAN.
WHAT?
I TURNED EVERYTHING SHE WAS INSIDE...INTO FLESH.
BUT I CAN'T MAKE IT ALIVE... SO...IT KILLED HER.
I KILLED HER.

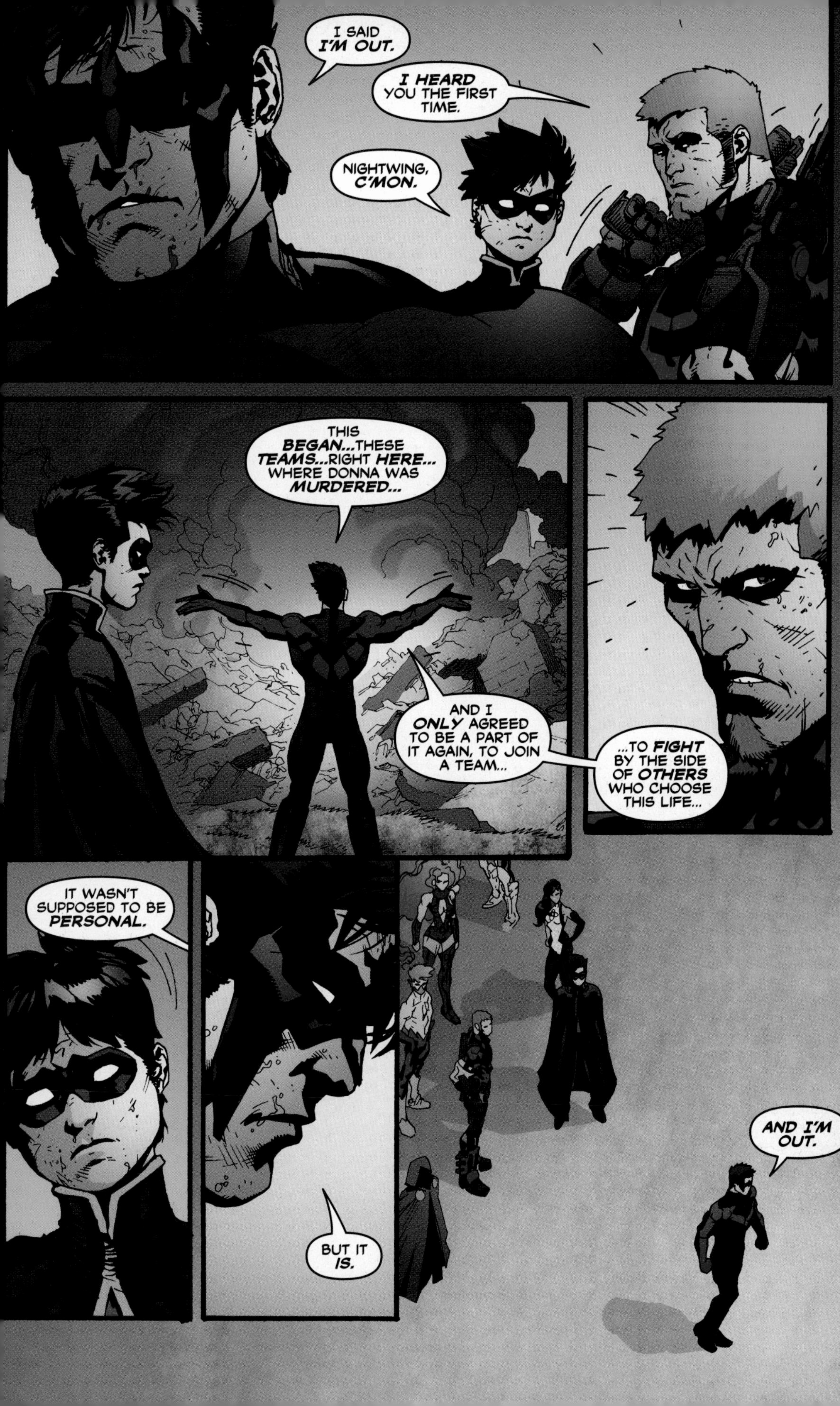
I SAID I'M OUT.
I HEARD YOU THE FIRST TIME.
NIGHTWING, C'MON.
THIS BEGAN...THESE TEAMS...RIGHT HERE... WHERE DONNA WAS MURDERED...
AND I ONLY AGREED TO BE A PART OF IT AGAIN, TO JOIN A TEAM...
...TO FIGHT BY THE SIDE OF OTHERS WHO CHOOSE THIS LIFE...
IT WASN'T SUPPOSED TO BE PERSONAL.
BUT IT IS.
AND I'M OUT.

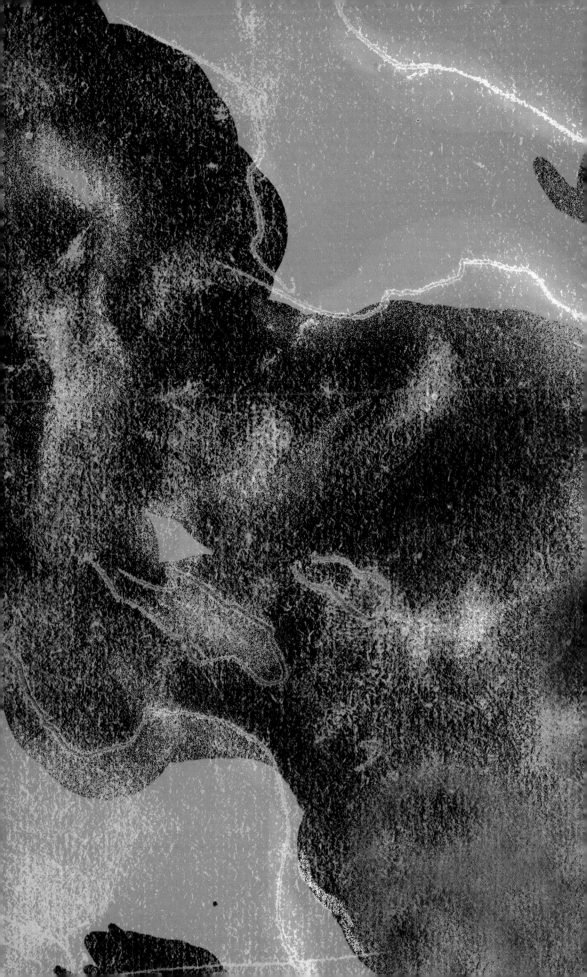

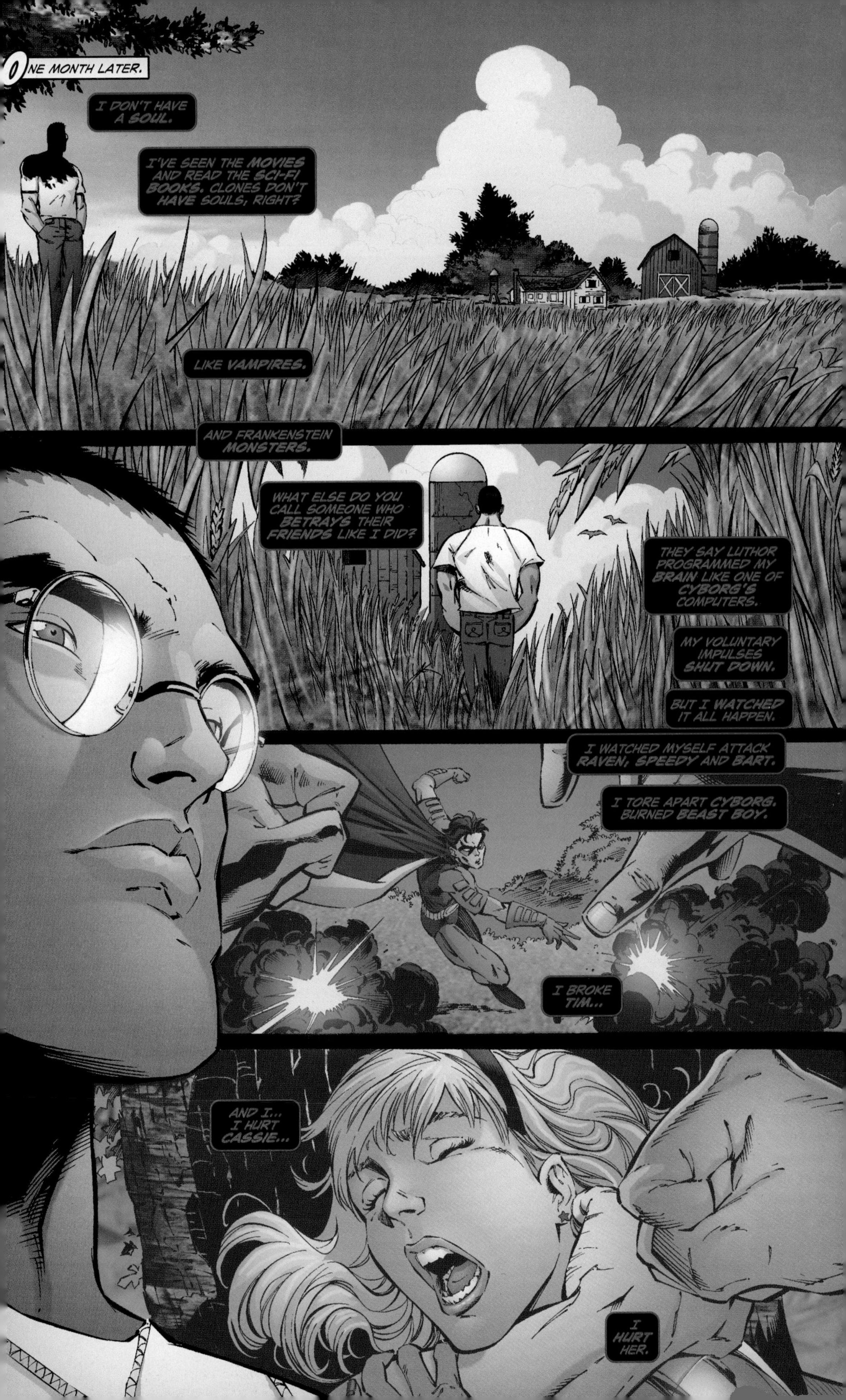
ONE MONTH LATER.
I DON'T HAVE A SOUL.
I'VE SEEN THE MOVIES AND READ THE SCI-FI BOOKS. CLONES DON'T HAVE SOULS, RIGHT?
LIKE VAMPIRES.
AND FRANKENSTEIN MONSTERS.
WHAT ELSE DO YOU CALL SOMEONE WHO BETRAYS THEIR FRIENDS LIKE I DID?
THEY SAY LUTHOR PROGRAMMED MY BRAIN LIKE ONE OF CYBORG'S COMPUTERS.
MY VOLUNTARY IMPULSES SHUT DOWN.
BUT I WATCHED IT ALL HAPPEN.
I WATCHED MYSELF ATTACK RAVEN, SPEEDY AND BART.
I TORE APART CYBORG. BURNED BEAST BOY.
I BROKE TIM...
AND I... I HURT CASSIE...
I HURT HER.

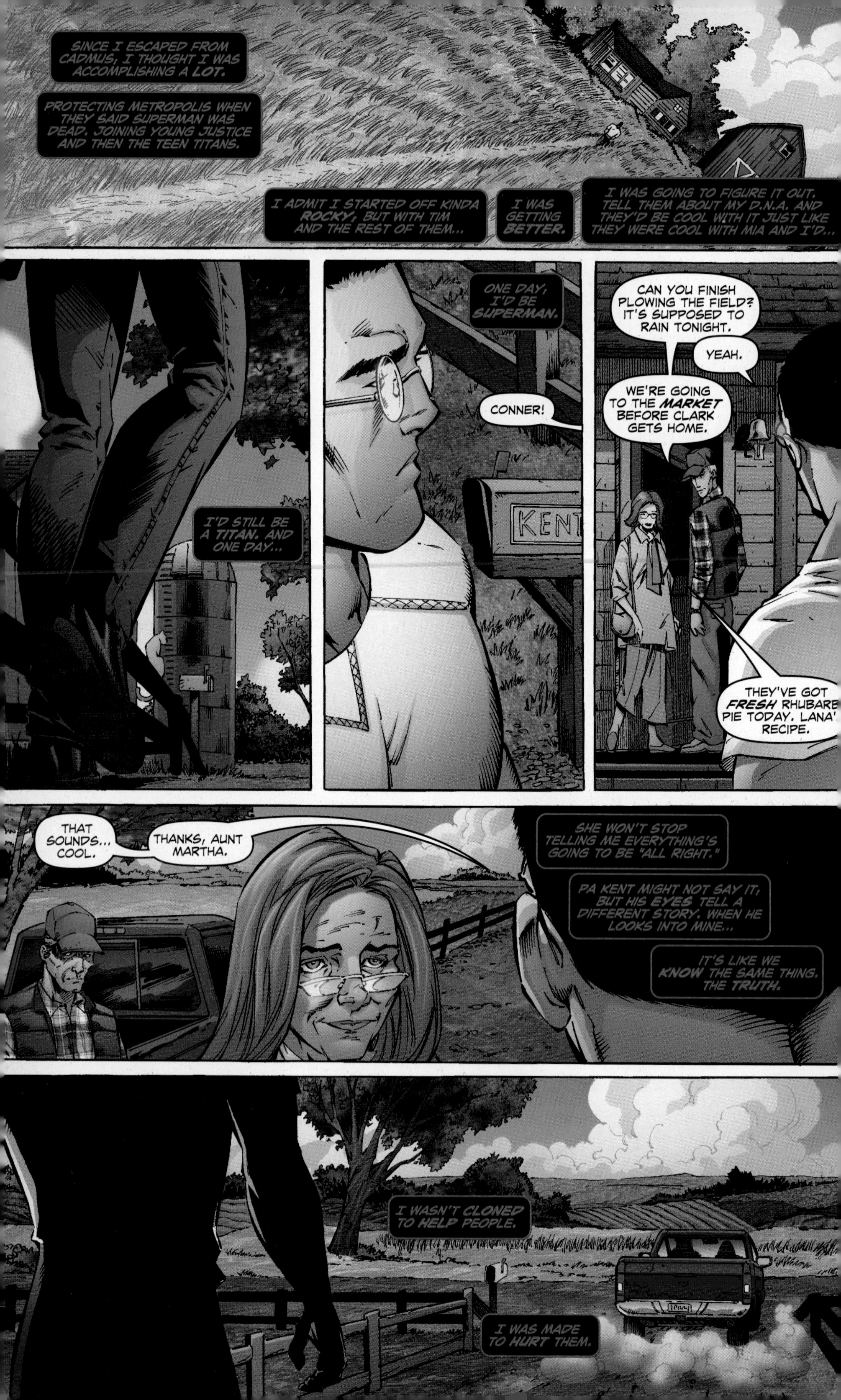
SINCE I ESCAPED FROM CADMUS, I THOUGHT I WAS ACCOMPLISHING A LOT.
PROTECTING METROPOLIS WHEN THEY SAID SUPERMAN WAS DEAD. JOINING YOUNG JUSTICE AND THEN THE TEEN TITANS.
I ADMIT I STARTED OFF KINDA ROCKY, BUT WITH TIM AND THE REST OF THEM...
I WAS GETTING BETTER.
I WAS GOING TO FIGURE IT OUT. TELL THEM ABOUT MY D.N.A. AND THEY'D BE COOL WITH IT JUST LIKE THEY WERE COOL WITH MIA AND I'D...
I'D STILL BE A TITAN. AND ONE DAY...
ONE DAY, I'D BE SUPERMAN.
CONNER!
KENT
CAN YOU FINISH PLOWING THE FIELD? IT'S SUPPOSED TO RAIN TONIGHT.
YEAH.
WE'RE GOING TO THE MARKET BEFORE CLARK GETS HOME.
THEY'VE GOT FRESH RHUBARB PIE TODAY. LANA'S RECIPE.
THAT SOUNDS... COOL.
THANKS, AUNT MARTHA.
SHE WON'T STOP TELLING ME EVERYTHING'S GOING TO BE "ALL RIGHT."
PA KENT MIGHT NOT SAY IT, BUT HIS EYES TELL A DIFFERENT STORY. WHEN HE LOOKS INTO MINE...
IT'S LIKE WE KNOW THE SAME THING. THE TRUTH.
I WASN'T CLONED TO HELP PEOPLE.
I WAS MADE TO HURT THEM.

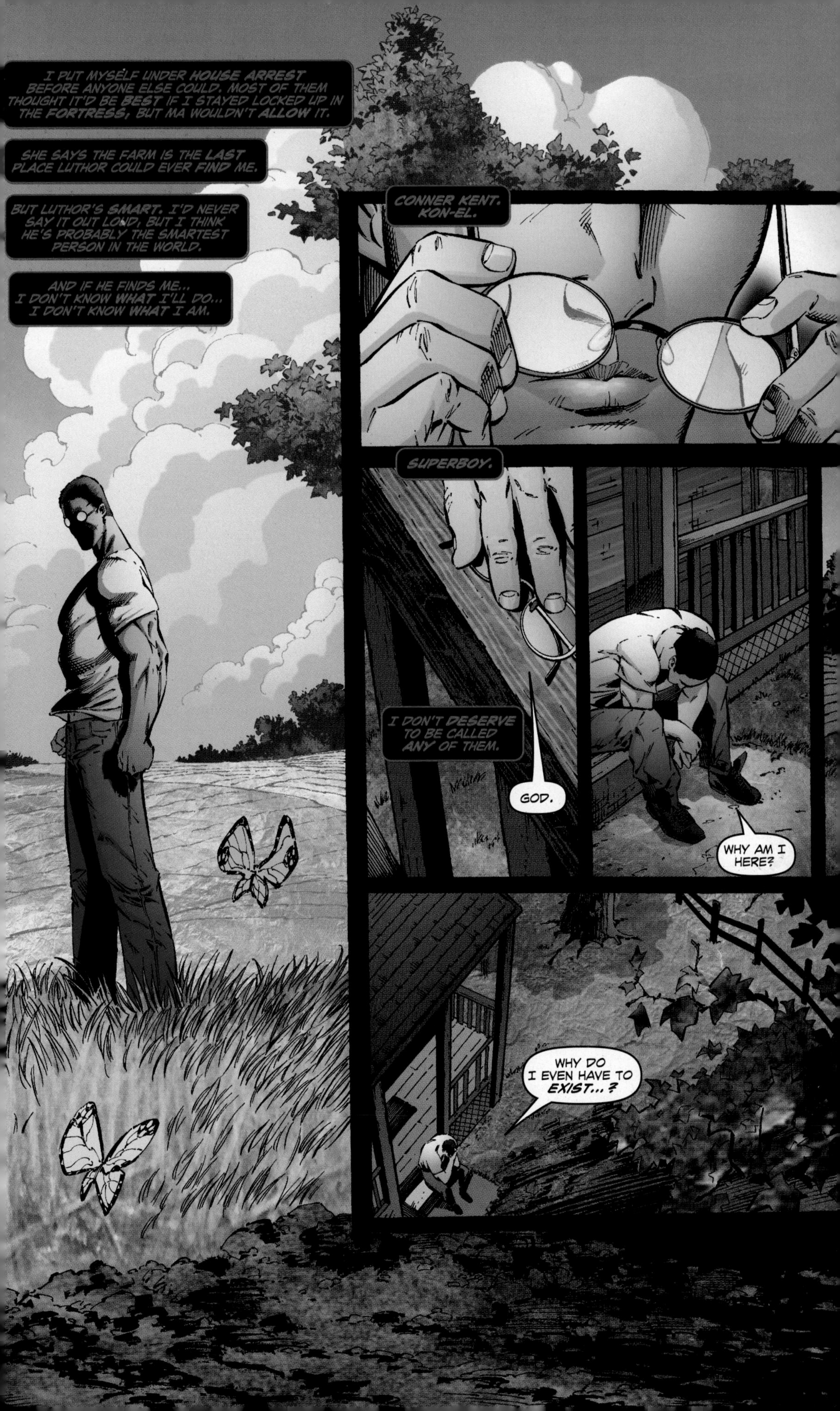
I PUT MYSELF UNDER HOUSE ARREST BEFORE ANYONE ELSE COULD. MOST OF THEM THOUGHT IT'D BE BEST IF I STAYED LOCKED UP IN THE FORTRESS, BUT MA WOULDN'T ALLOW IT.
SHE SAYS THE FARM IS THE LAST PLACE LUTHOR COULD EVER FIND ME.
BUT LUTHOR'S SMART. I'D NEVER SAY IT OUT LOUD, BUT I THINK HE'S PROBABLY THE SMARTEST PERSON IN THE WORLD.
AND IF HE FINDS ME... I DON'T KNOW WHAT I'LL DO... I DON'T KNOW WHAT I AM.
CONNER KENT. KON-EL.
SUPERBOY.
I DON'T DESERVE TO BE CALLED ANY OF THEM.
GOD.
WHY AM I HERE?
WHY DO I EVEN HAVE TO EXIST...?

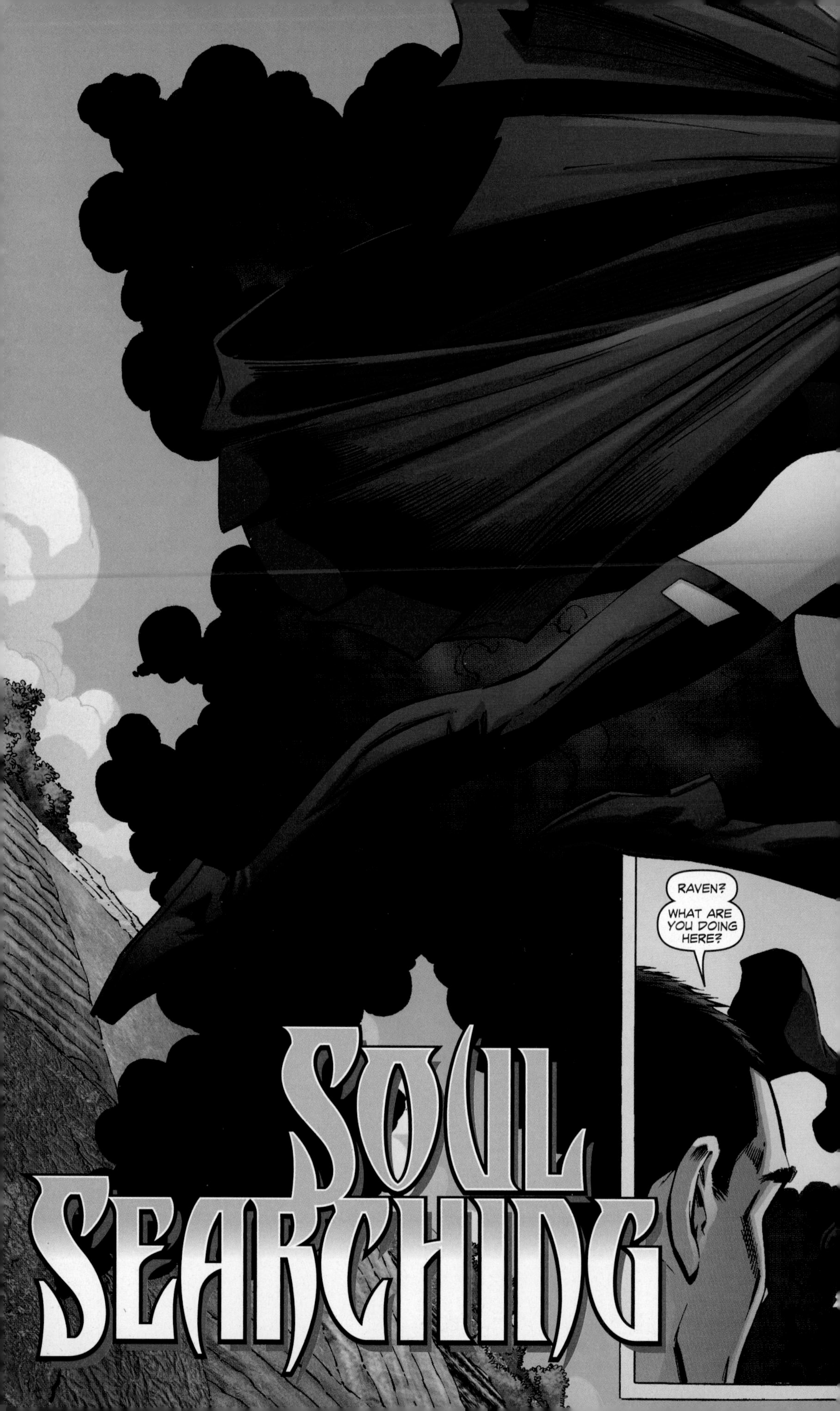
RAVEN?
WHAT ARE YOU DOING HERE?
SOUL SEARCHING

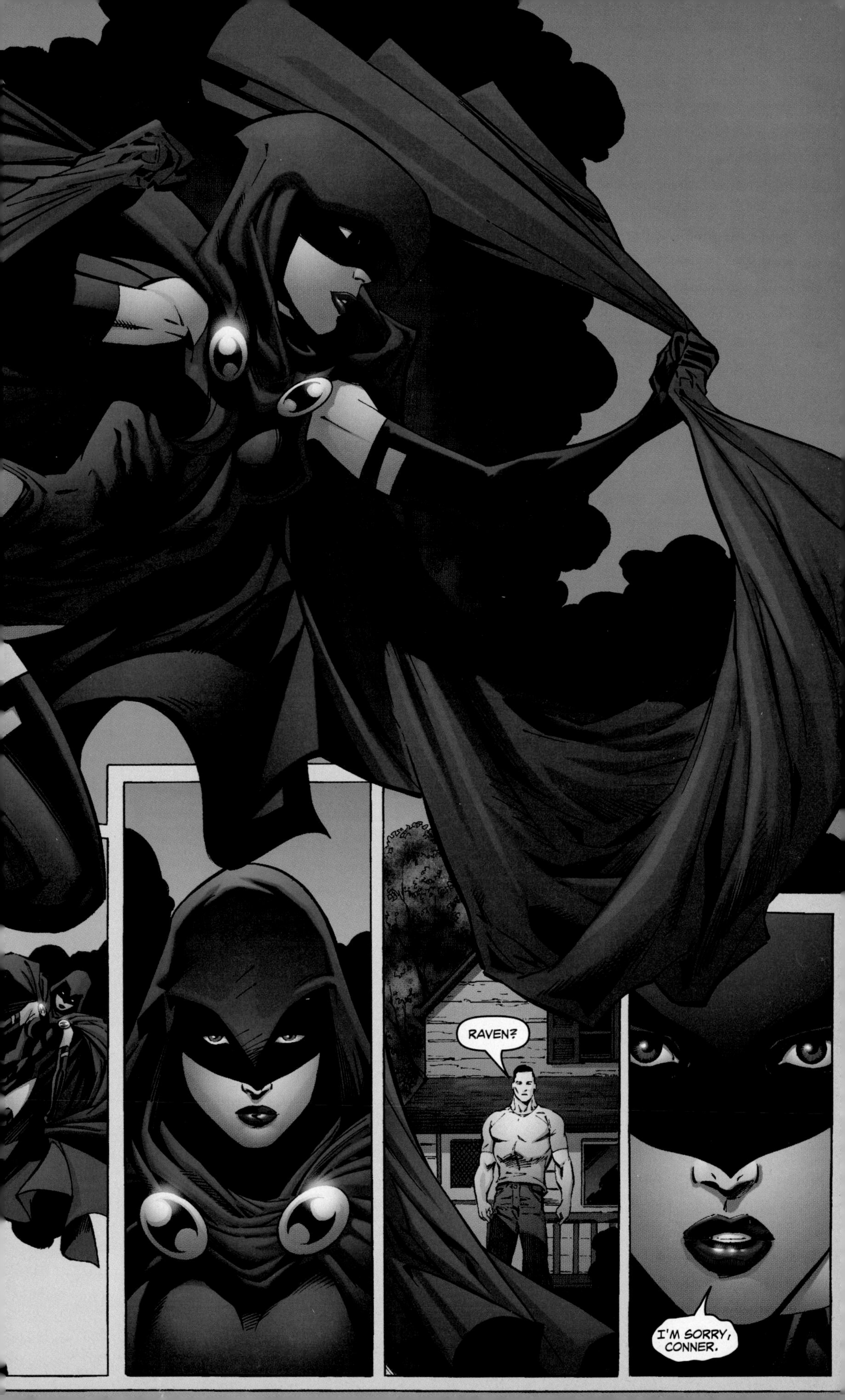
RAVEN?
I'M SORRY, CONNER.

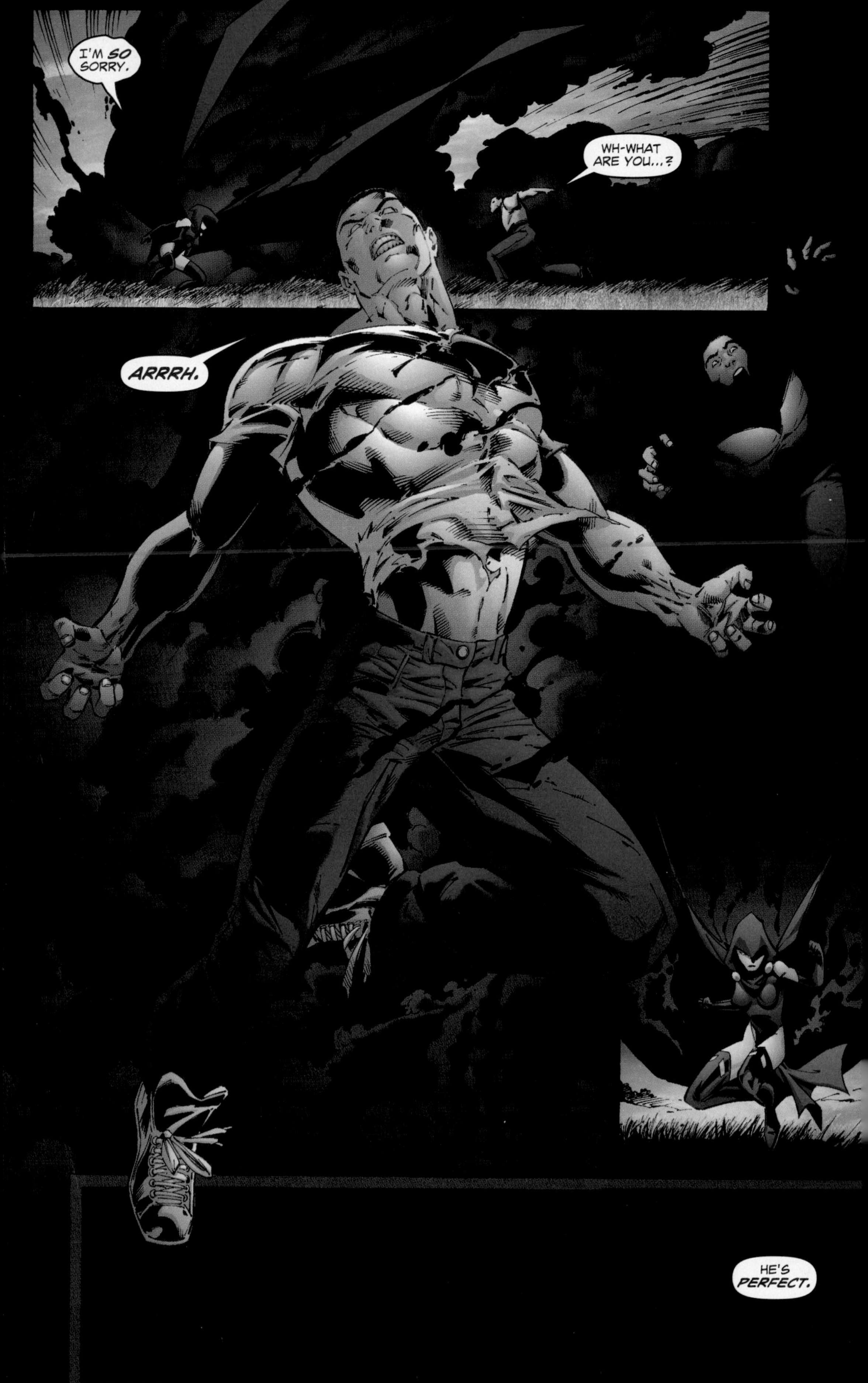
I'M SO SORRY.
WH-WHAT ARE YOU...?
ARRRH.
HE'S PERFECT.

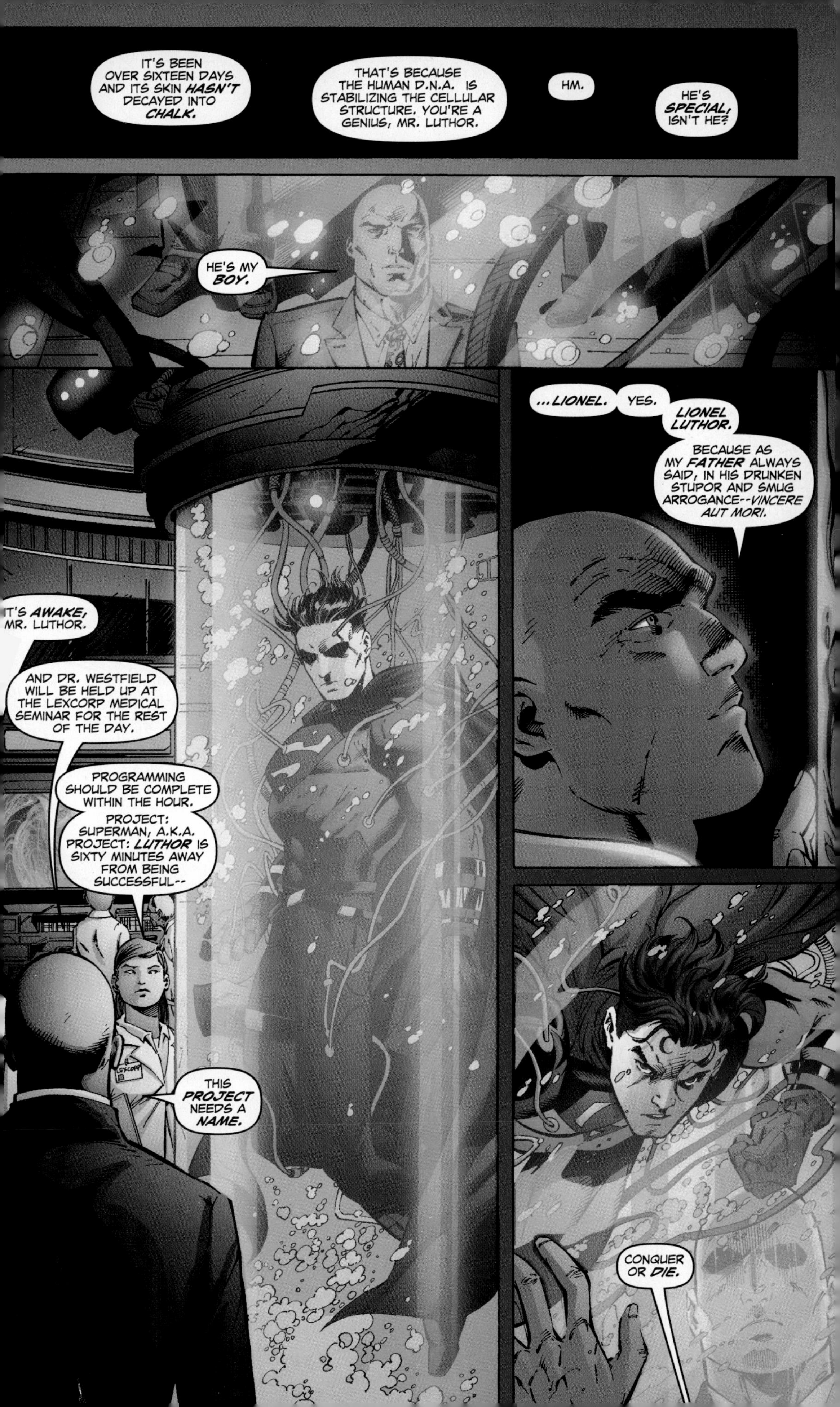
IT'S BEEN OVER SIXTEEN DAYS AND ITS SKIN *HASN'T* DECAYED INTO *CHALK.*
THAT'S BECAUSE THE HUMAN D.N.A. IS STABILIZING THE CELLULAR STRUCTURE. YOU'RE A GENIUS, MR. LUTHOR.
HM.
HE'S *SPECIAL,* ISN'T HE?
HE'S MY *BOY.*
IT'S *AWAKE,* MR. LUTHOR.
AND DR. WESTFIELD WILL BE HELD UP AT THE LEXCORP MEDICAL SEMINAR FOR THE REST OF THE DAY.
PROGRAMMING SHOULD BE COMPLETE WITHIN THE HOUR.
PROJECT: SUPERMAN, A.K.A. PROJECT: *LUTHOR* IS SIXTY MINUTES AWAY FROM BEING SUCCESSFUL--
THIS *PROJECT* NEEDS A *NAME.*
...LIONEL.
YES.
LIONEL LUTHOR.
BECAUSE AS MY *FATHER* ALWAYS SAID, IN HIS DRUNKEN STUPOR AND SMUG ARROGANCE--*VINCERE AUT MORI.*
CONQUER OR *DIE.*

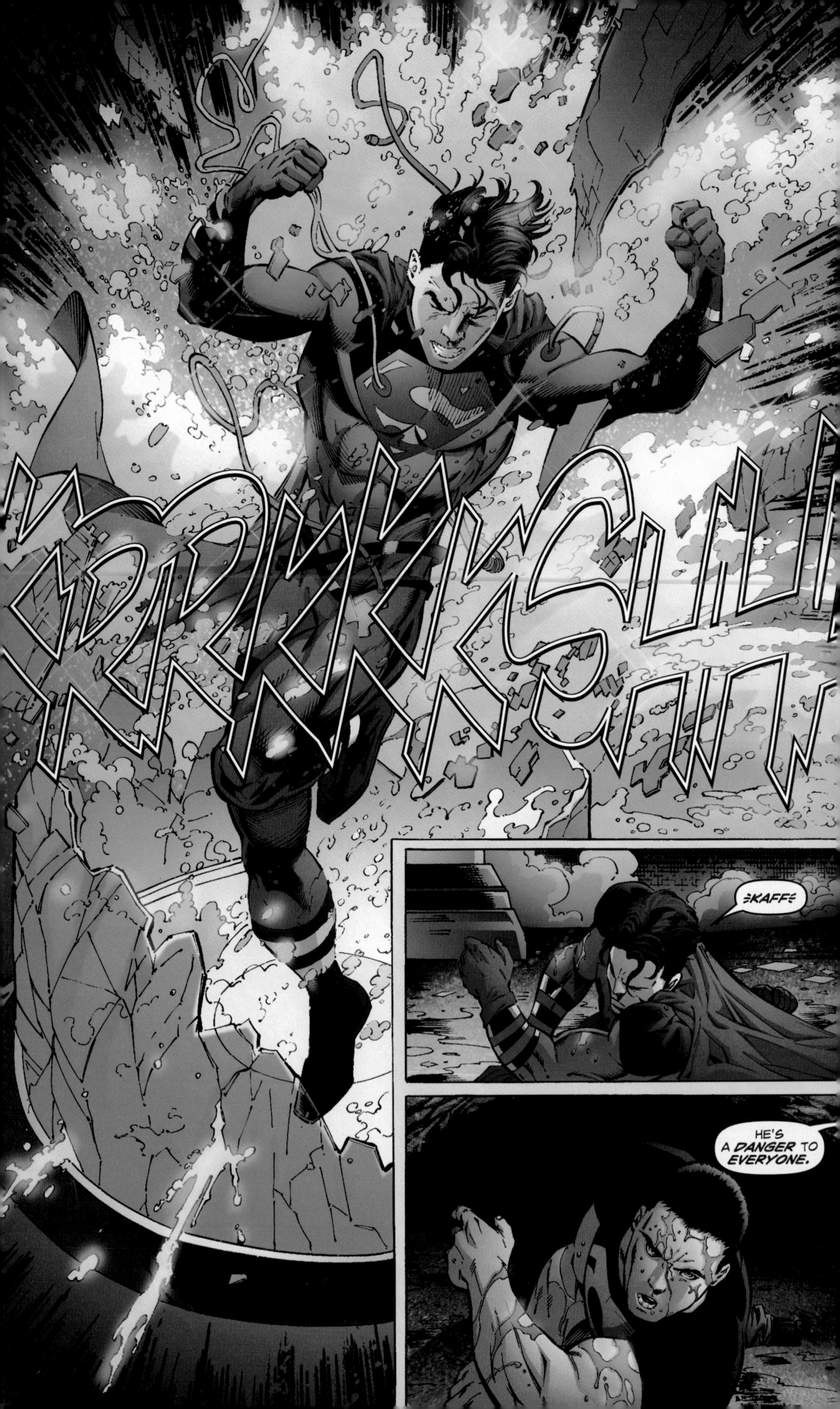
KAFF
HE'S A DANGER TO EVERYONE.

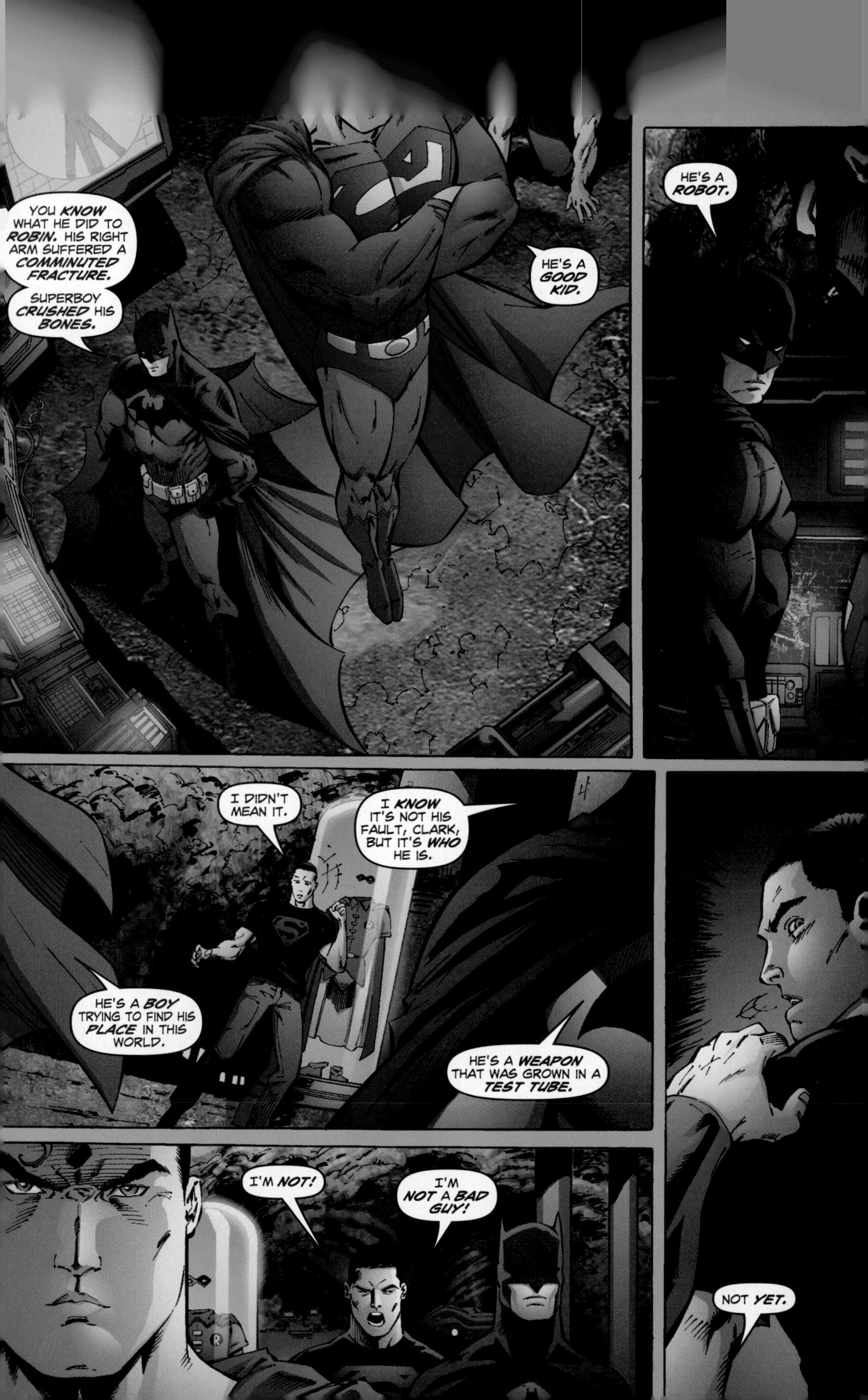
YOU *KNOW* WHAT HE DID TO *ROBIN.* HIS RIGHT ARM SUFFERED A *COMMINUTED FRACTURE.*
SUPERBOY *CRUSHED* HIS *BONES.*
HE'S A *GOOD KID.*
HE'S A *ROBOT.*
I DIDN'T MEAN IT.
I *KNOW* IT'S NOT HIS FAULT, CLARK, BUT IT'S *WHO* HE IS.
HE'S A *BOY* TRYING TO FIND HIS *PLACE* IN THIS WORLD.
HE'S A *WEAPON* THAT WAS GROWN IN A *TEST TUBE.*
I'M *NOT!*
I'M *NOT* A *BAD GUY!*
NOT *YET.*

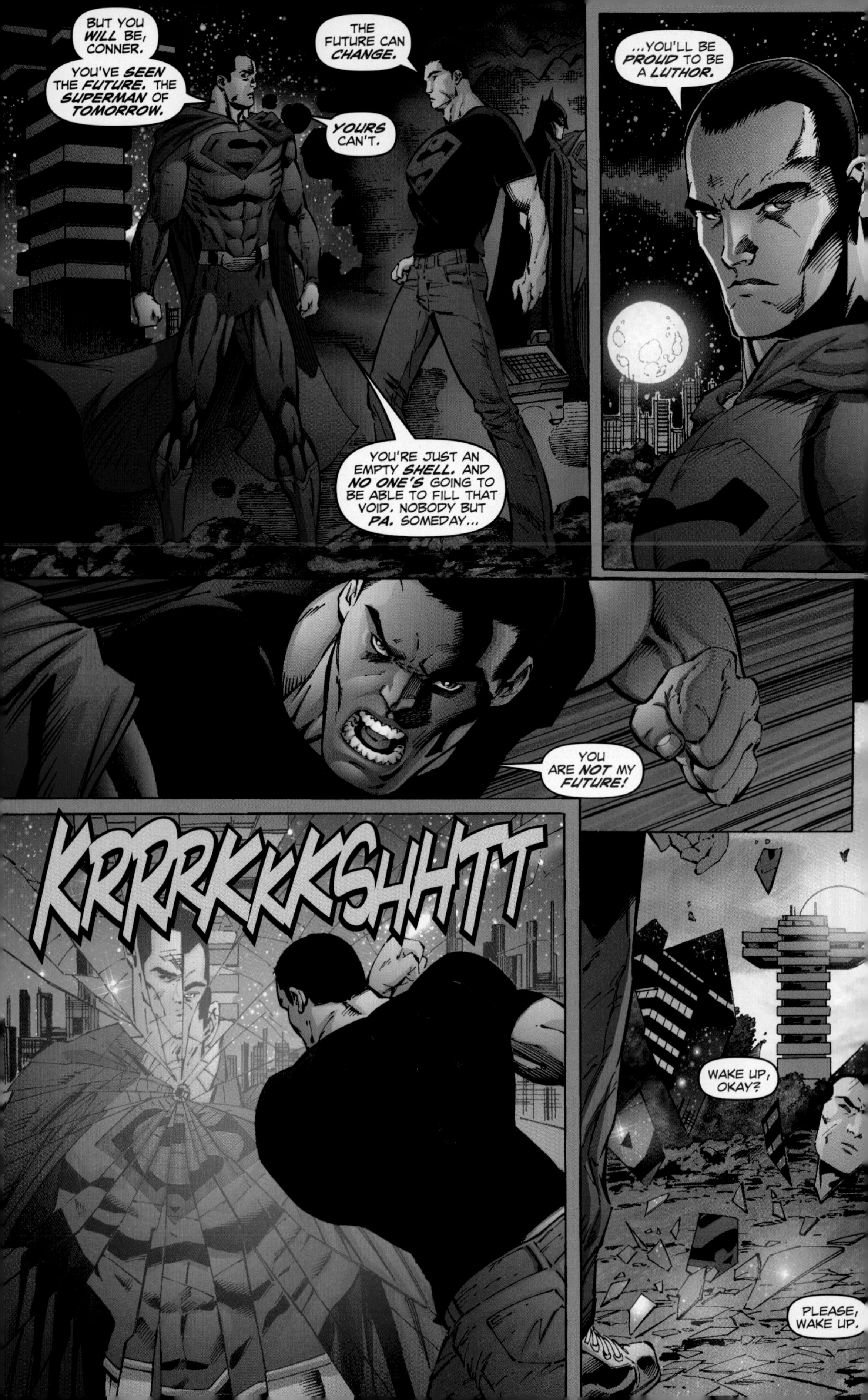
BUT YOU WILL BE, CONNER.
YOU'VE SEEN THE FUTURE. THE SUPERMAN OF TOMORROW.
THE FUTURE CAN CHANGE.
YOURS CAN'T.
YOU'RE JUST AN EMPTY SHELL. AND NO ONE'S GOING TO BE ABLE TO FILL THAT VOID. NOBODY BUT PA. SOMEDAY...
...YOU'LL BE PROUD TO BE A LUTHOR.
YOU ARE NOT MY FUTURE!
KRRRKKKSHHTT
WAKE UP, OKAY?
PLEASE, WAKE UP.

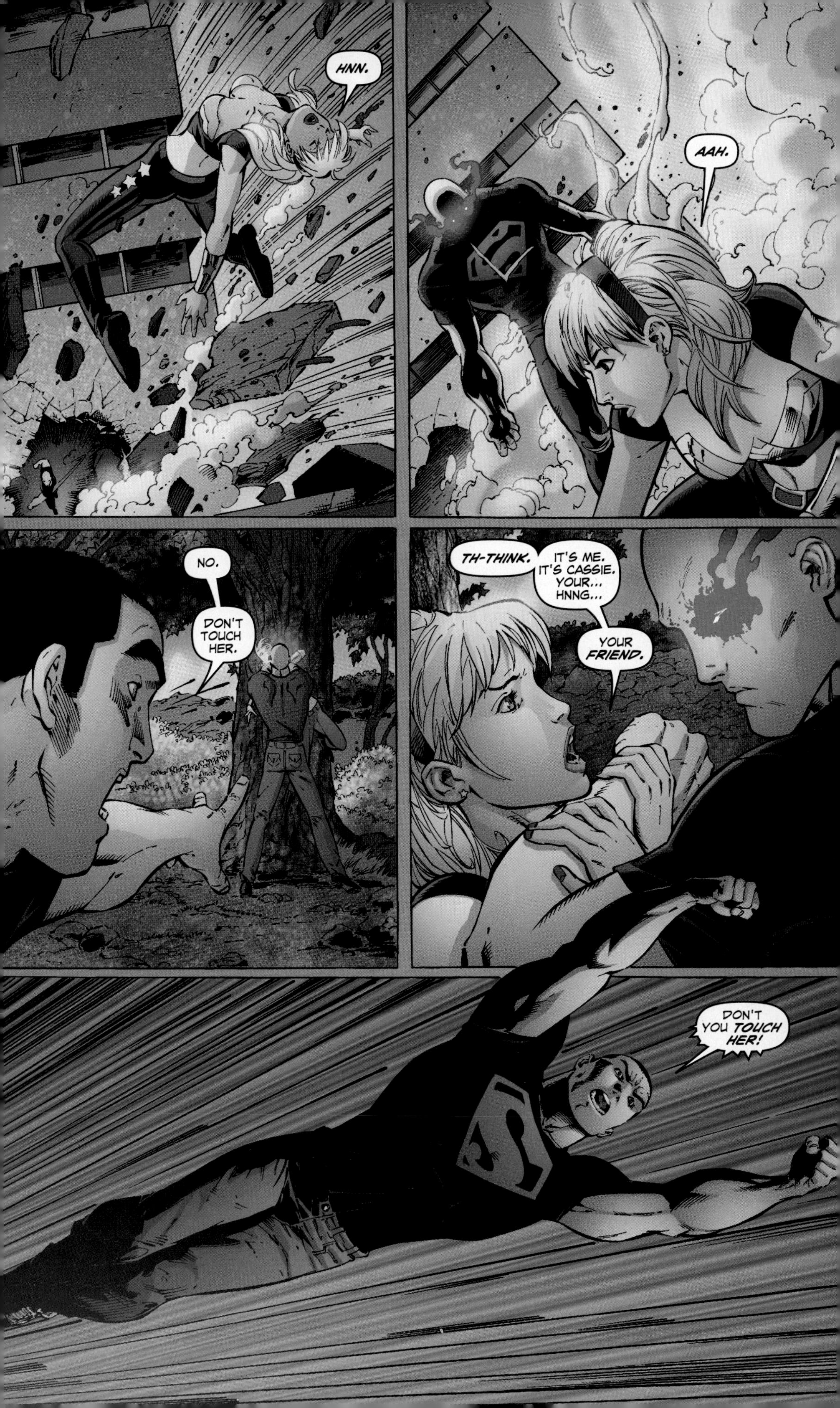
HNN.
AAH.
NO.
DON'T TOUCH HER.
TH-THINK.
IT'S ME. IT'S CASSIE. YOUR... HNNG...
YOUR FRIEND.
DON'T YOU TOUCH HER!

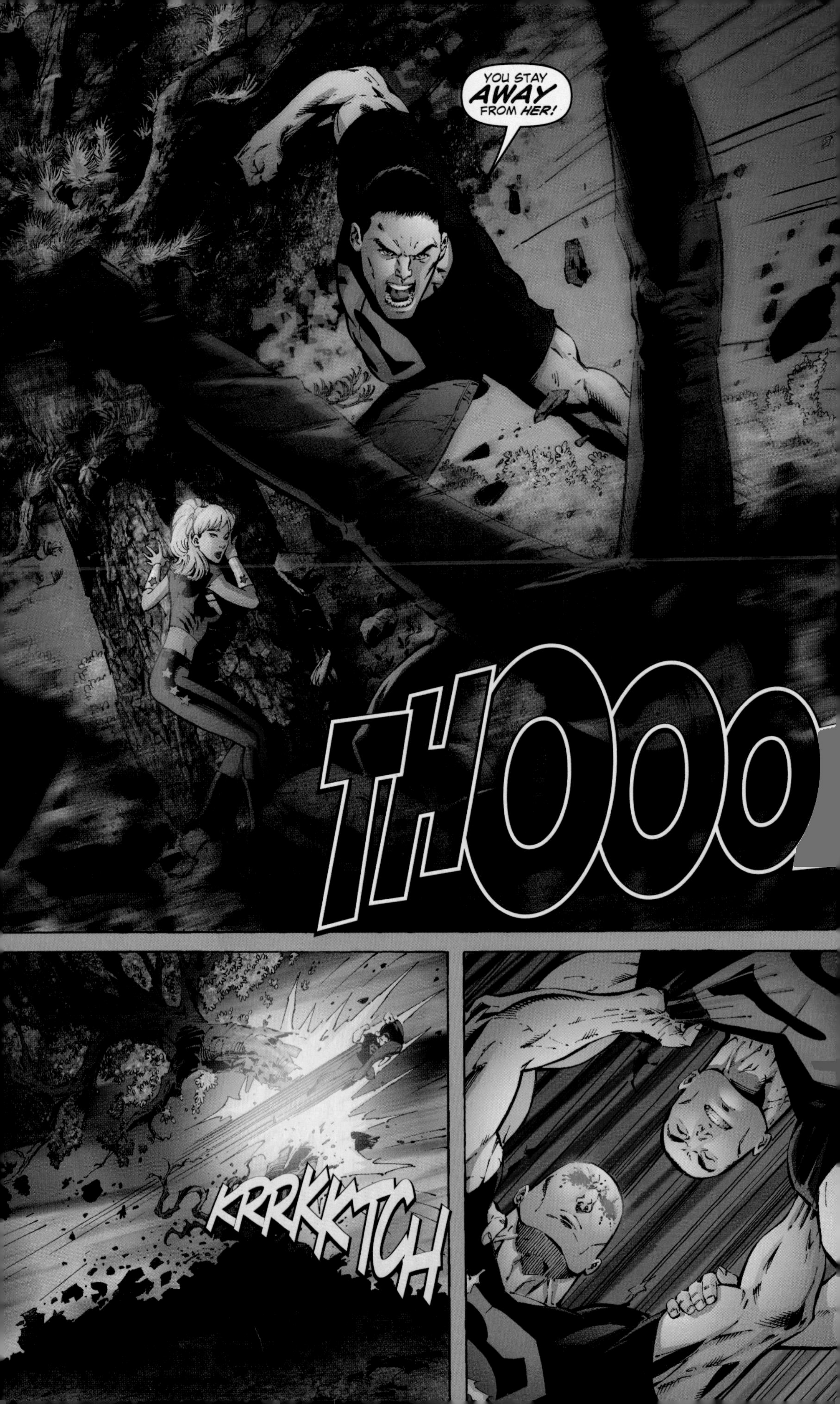
YOU STAY AWAY FROM HER!
THOOO
KRRKKTCH

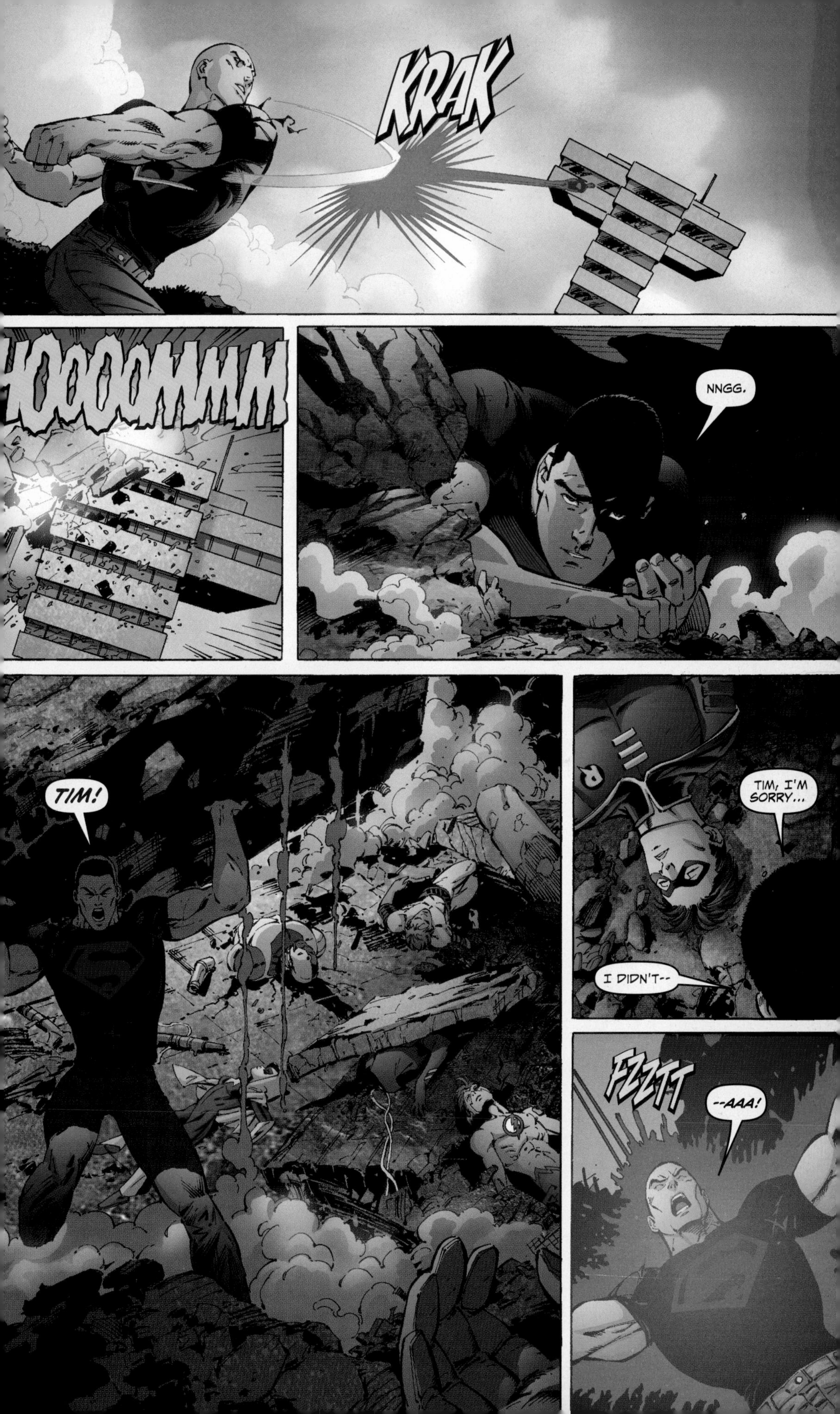
KRAK
HOOOOMMM
NNGG.
TIM!
TIM, I'M SORRY...
I DIDN'T--
FZZTT
--AAA!

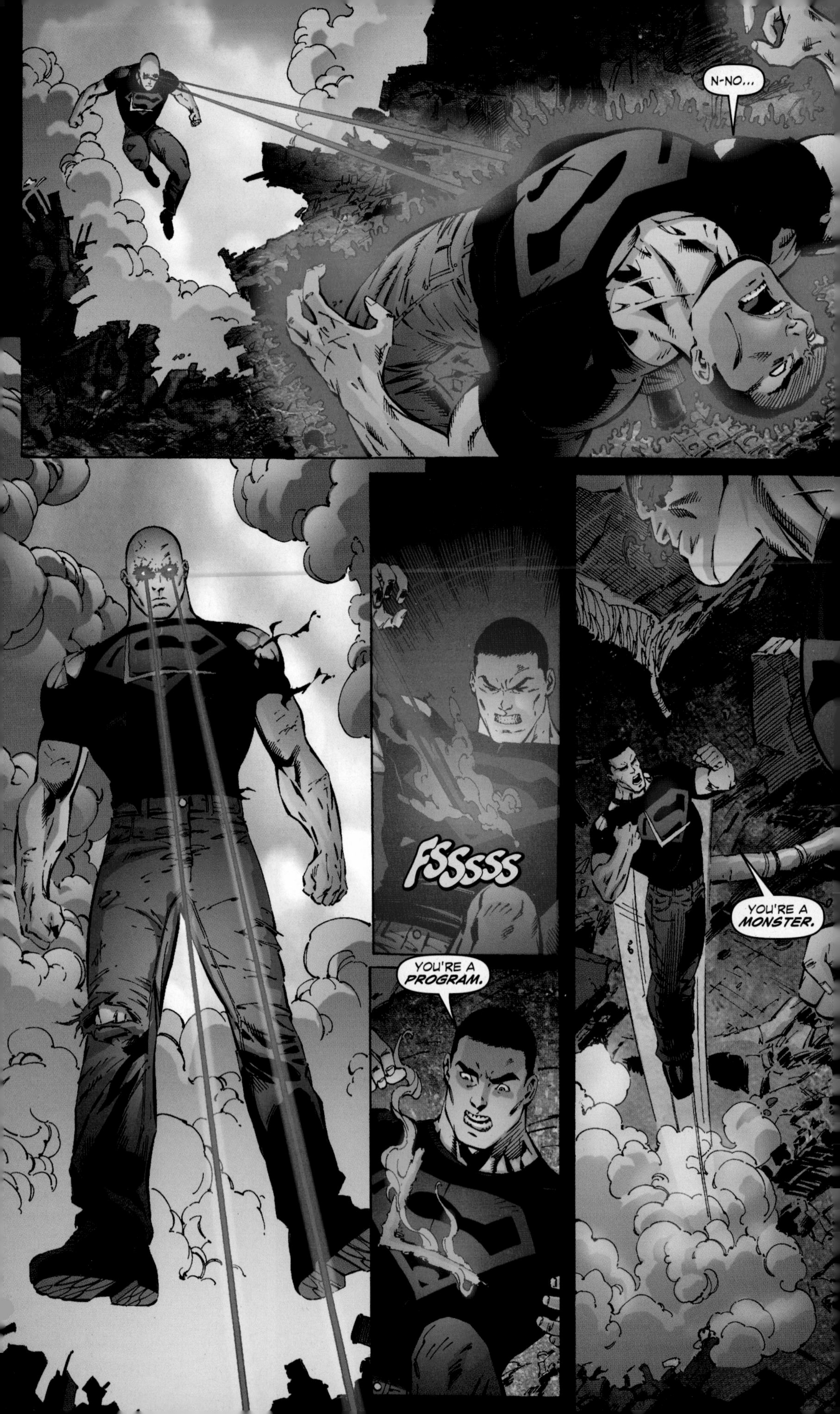
N-NO...
FSSSSS
YOU'RE A PROGRAM.
YOU'RE A MONSTER.

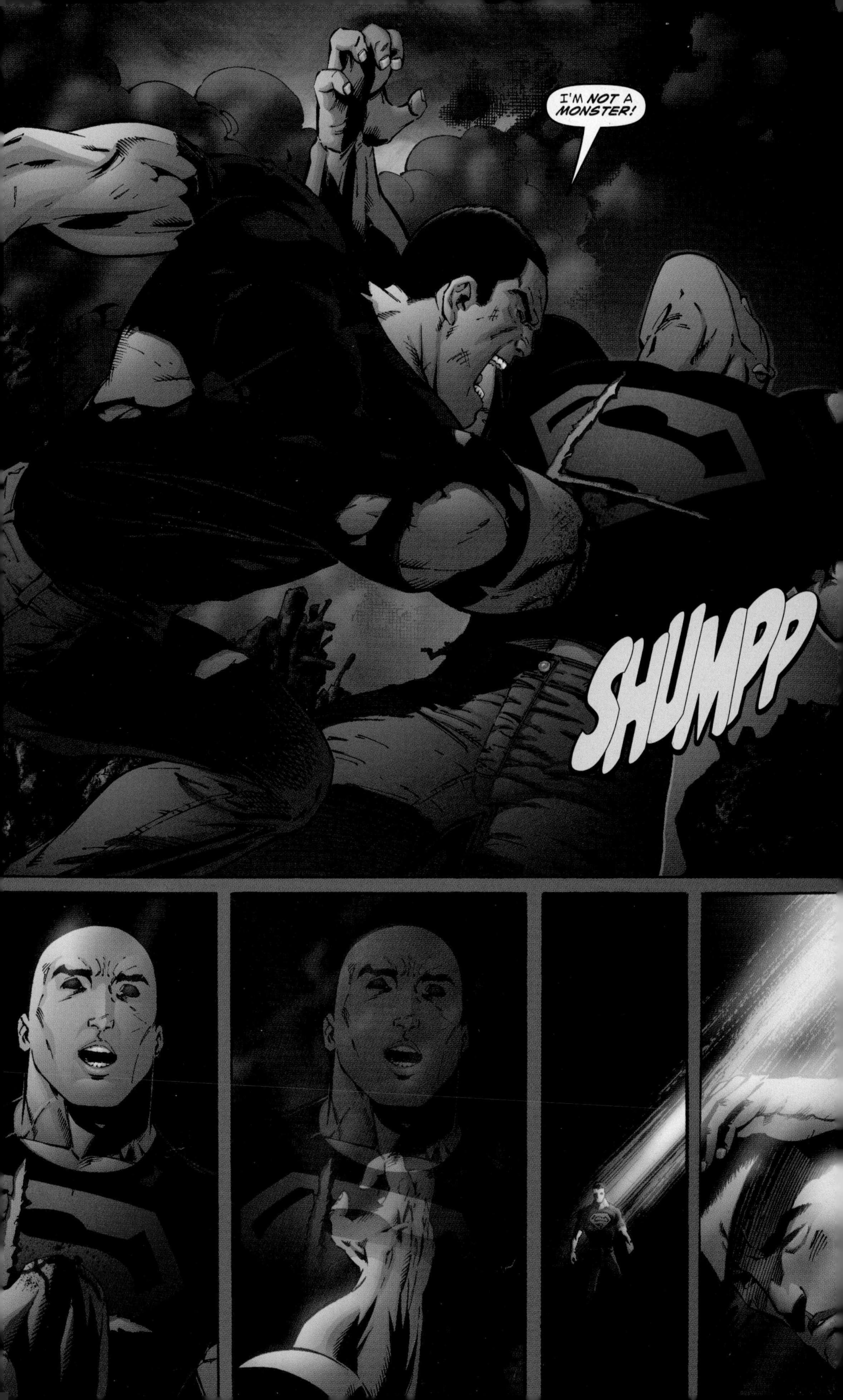
I'M NOT A MONSTER!
SHUMPP

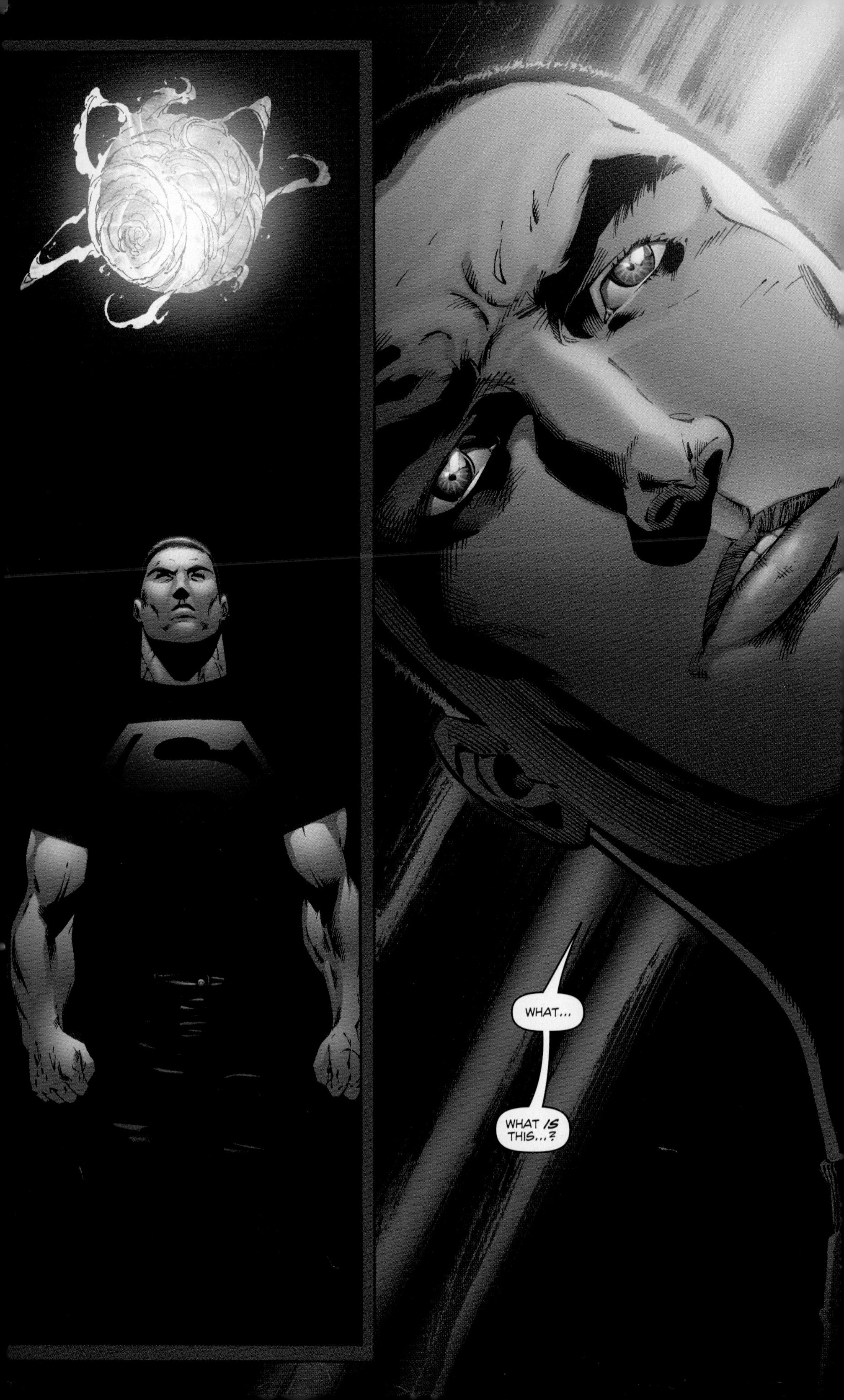
WHAT...
WHAT *IS* THIS...?

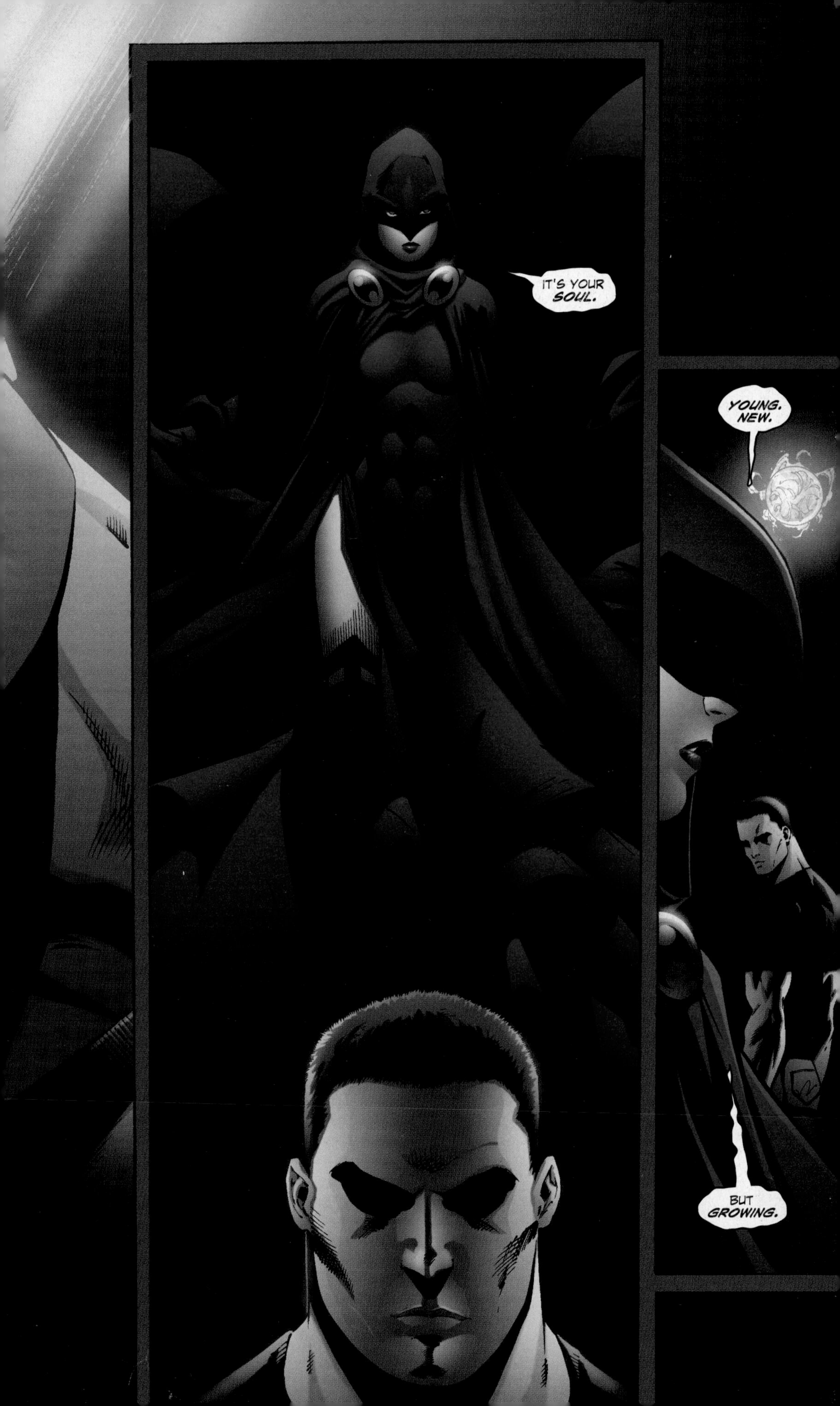
IT'S YOUR SOUL.
YOUNG. NEW.
BUT GROWING.

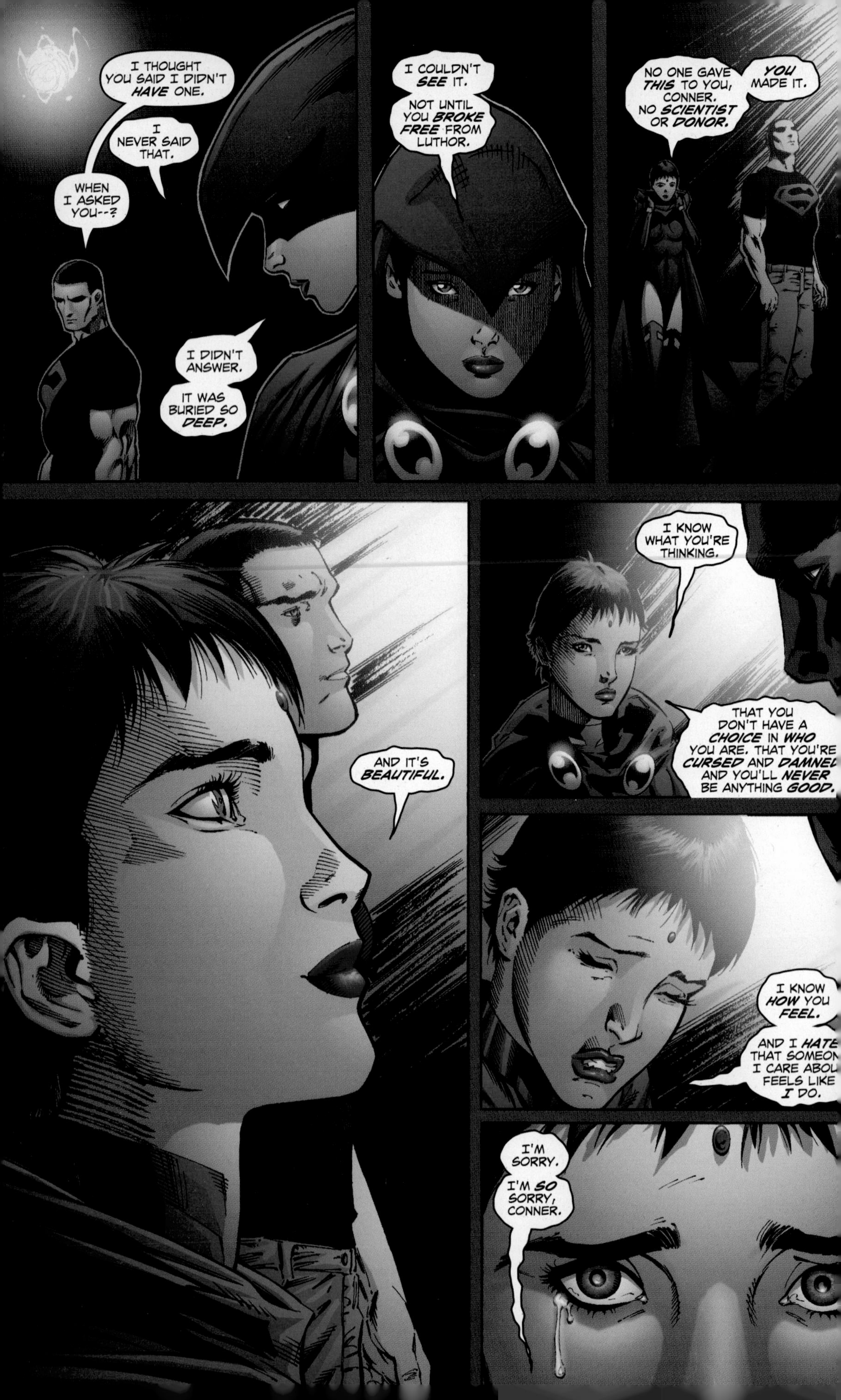
I THOUGHT YOU SAID I DIDN'T HAVE ONE.
I NEVER SAID THAT.
WHEN I ASKED YOU--?
I DIDN'T ANSWER.
IT WAS BURIED SO DEEP.
I COULDN'T SEE IT.
NOT UNTIL YOU BROKE FREE FROM LUTHOR.
NO ONE GAVE THIS TO YOU, CONNER. NO SCIENTIST OR DONOR.
YOU MADE IT.
AND IT'S BEAUTIFUL.
I KNOW WHAT YOU'RE THINKING.
THAT YOU DON'T HAVE A CHOICE IN WHO YOU ARE. THAT YOU'RE CURSED AND DAMNEL AND YOU'LL NEVER BE ANYTHING GOOD.
I KNOW HOW YOU FEEL.
AND I HATE THAT SOMEON I CARE ABOU FEELS LIKE I DO.
I'M SORRY.
I'M SO SORRY, CONNER.

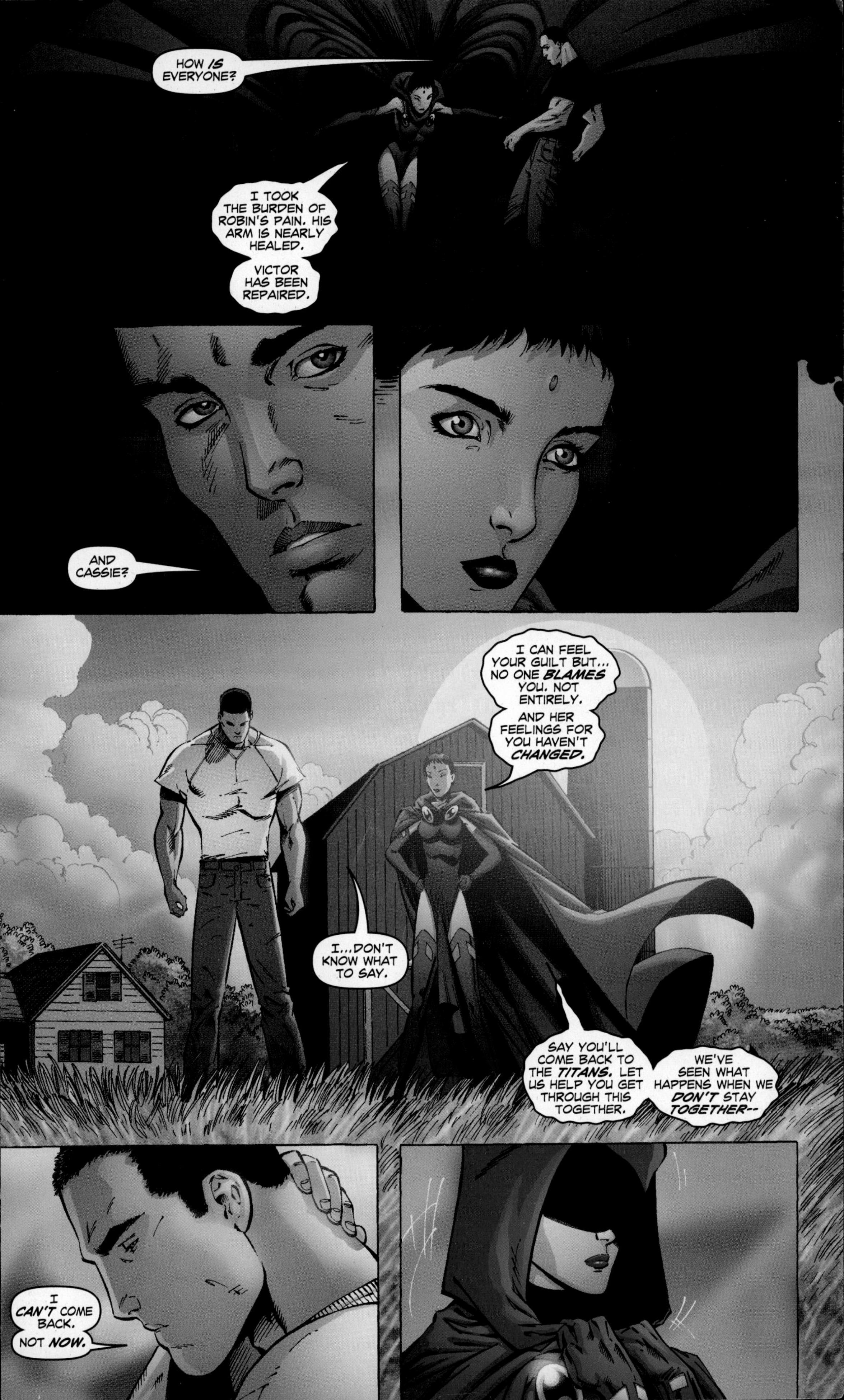
HOW *IS* EVERYONE?
I TOOK THE BURDEN OF ROBIN'S PAIN. HIS ARM IS NEARLY HEALED.
VICTOR HAS BEEN REPAIRED.
AND CASSIE?
I CAN FEEL YOUR GUILT BUT... NO ONE ***BLAMES*** YOU. NOT ENTIRELY.
AND HER FEELINGS FOR YOU HAVEN'T ***CHANGED.***
I...DON'T KNOW WHAT TO SAY.
SAY YOU'LL COME BACK TO THE ***TITANS.*** LET US HELP YOU GET THROUGH THIS TOGETHER.
WE'VE SEEN WHAT HAPPENS WHEN WE ***DON'T*** STAY ***TOGETHER--***
I ***CAN'T*** COME BACK.
NOT ***NOW.***

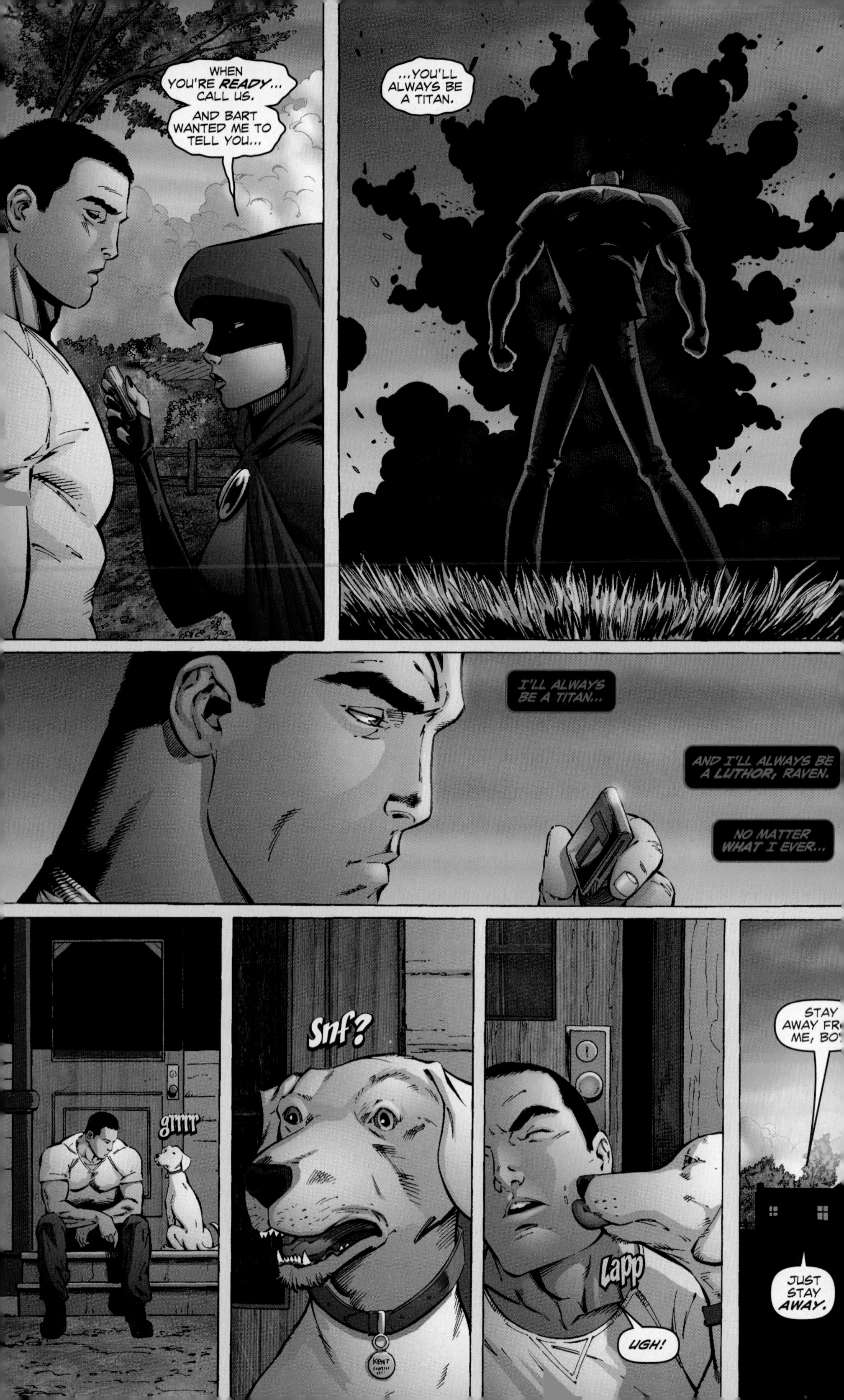
WHEN YOU'RE *READY*... CALL US.
AND BART WANTED ME TO TELL YOU...
...YOU'LL ALWAYS BE A TITAN.
I'LL ALWAYS BE A TITAN...
AND I'LL ALWAYS BE A LUTHOR, RAVEN.
NO MATTER WHAT I EVER...
grrrr
Snf?
KENT
Lapp
UGH!
STAY AWAY FR
ME, BO
JUST STAY *AWAY.*

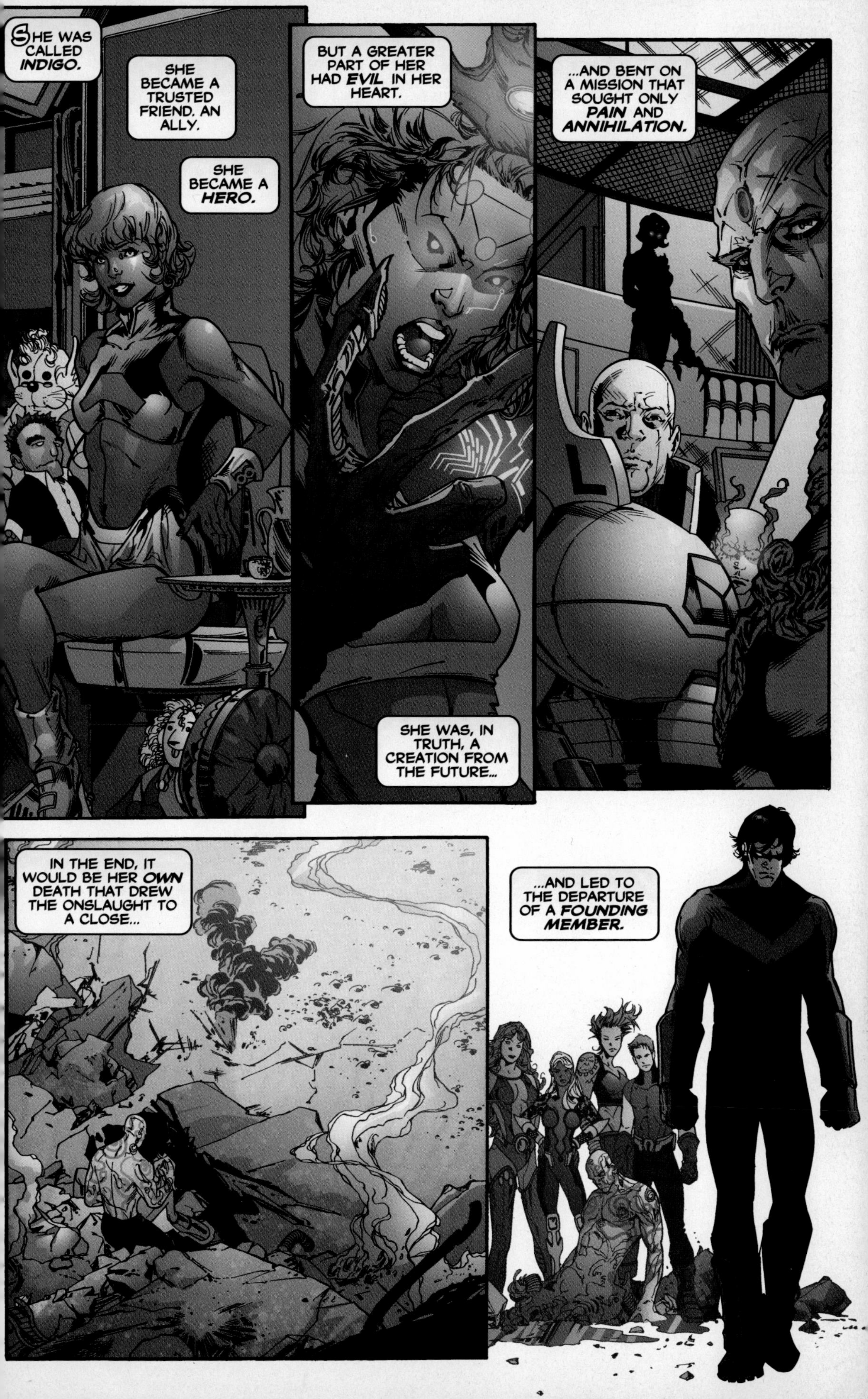
SHE WAS CALLED INDIGO.
SHE BECAME A TRUSTED FRIEND. AN ALLY.
SHE BECAME A HERO.
BUT A GREATER PART OF HER HAD EVIL IN HER HEART.
SHE WAS, IN TRUTH, A CREATION FROM THE FUTURE...
...AND BENT ON A MISSION THAT SOUGHT ONLY PAIN AND ANNIHILATION.
IN THE END, IT WOULD BE HER OWN DEATH THAT DREW THE ONSLAUGHT TO A CLOSE...
...AND LED TO THE DEPARTURE OF A FOUNDING MEMBER.

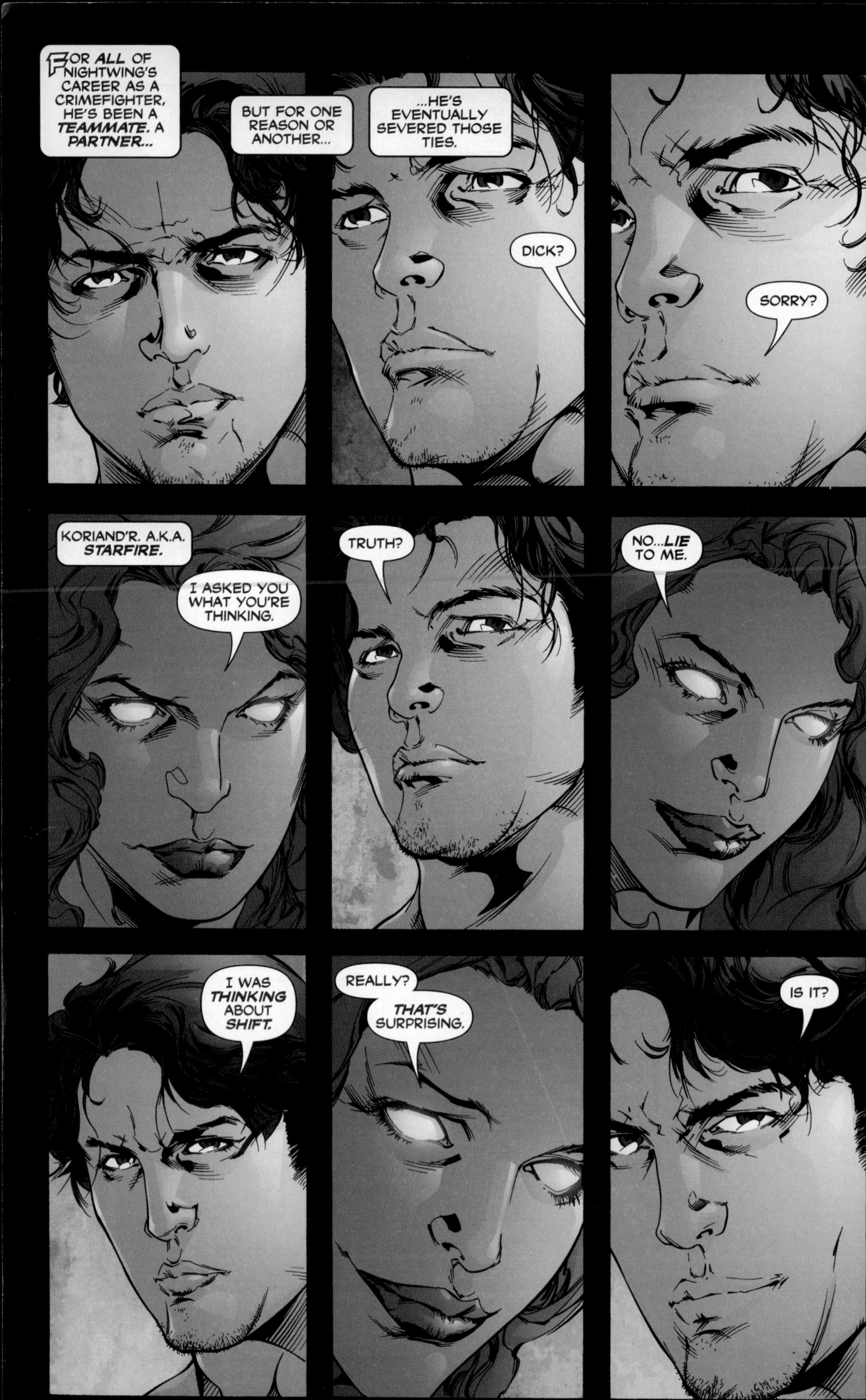
FOR ALL OF NIGHTWING'S CAREER AS A CRIMEFIGHTER, HE'S BEEN A TEAMMATE. A PARTNER...
BUT FOR ONE REASON OR ANOTHER...
...HE'S EVENTUALLY SEVERED THOSE TIES.
DICK?
SORRY?
KORIAND'R. A.K.A. STARFIRE.
I ASKED YOU WHAT YOU'RE THINKING.
TRUTH?
NO...LIE TO ME.
I WAS THINKING ABOUT SHIFT.
REALLY? THAT'S SURPRISING.
IS IT?

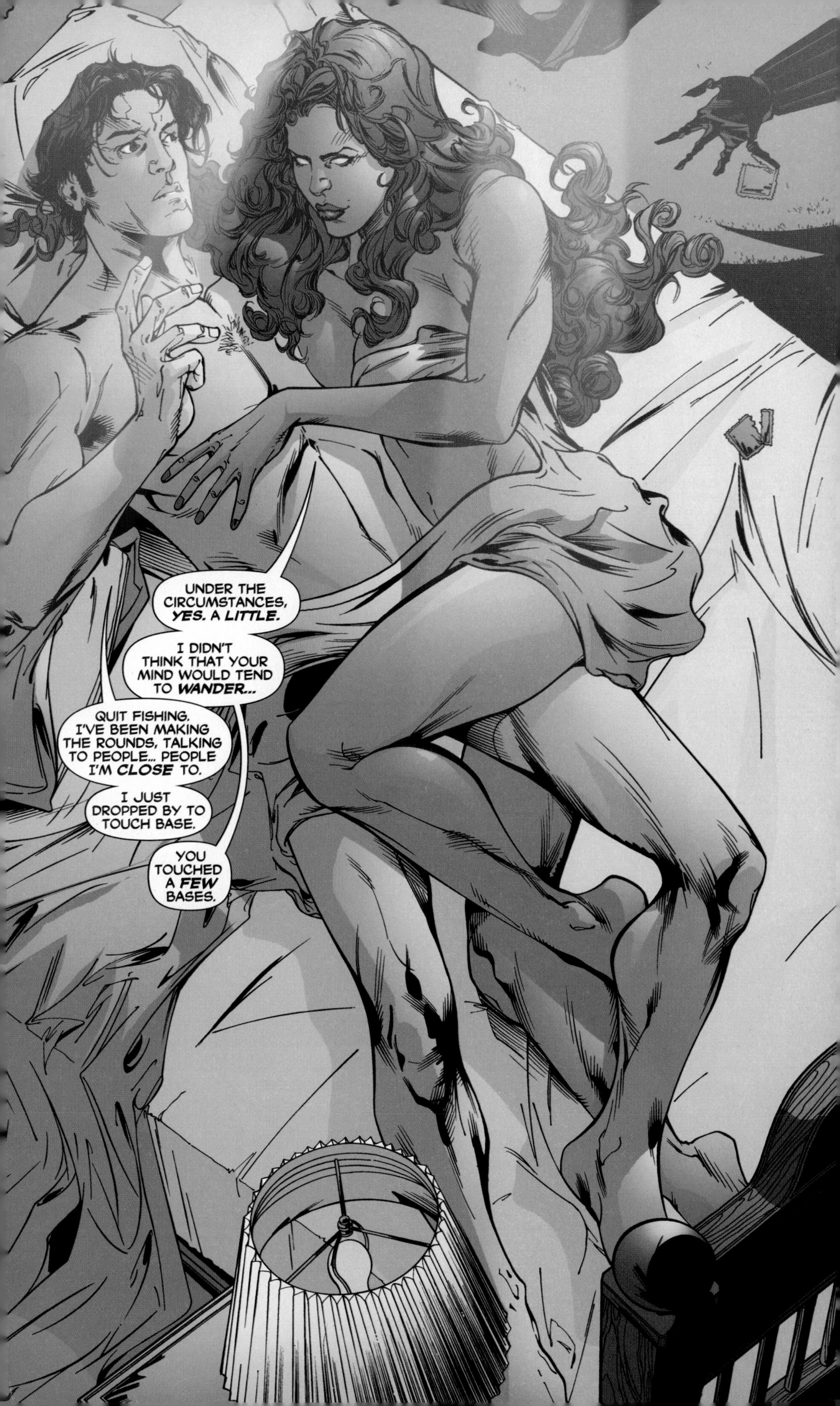
UNDER THE CIRCUMSTANCES, YES. A LITTLE.
I DIDN'T THINK THAT YOUR MIND WOULD TEND TO WANDER...
QUIT FISHING. I'VE BEEN MAKING THE ROUNDS, TALKING TO PEOPLE... PEOPLE I'M CLOSE TO.
I JUST DROPPED BY TO TOUCH BASE.
YOU TOUCHED A FEW BASES.

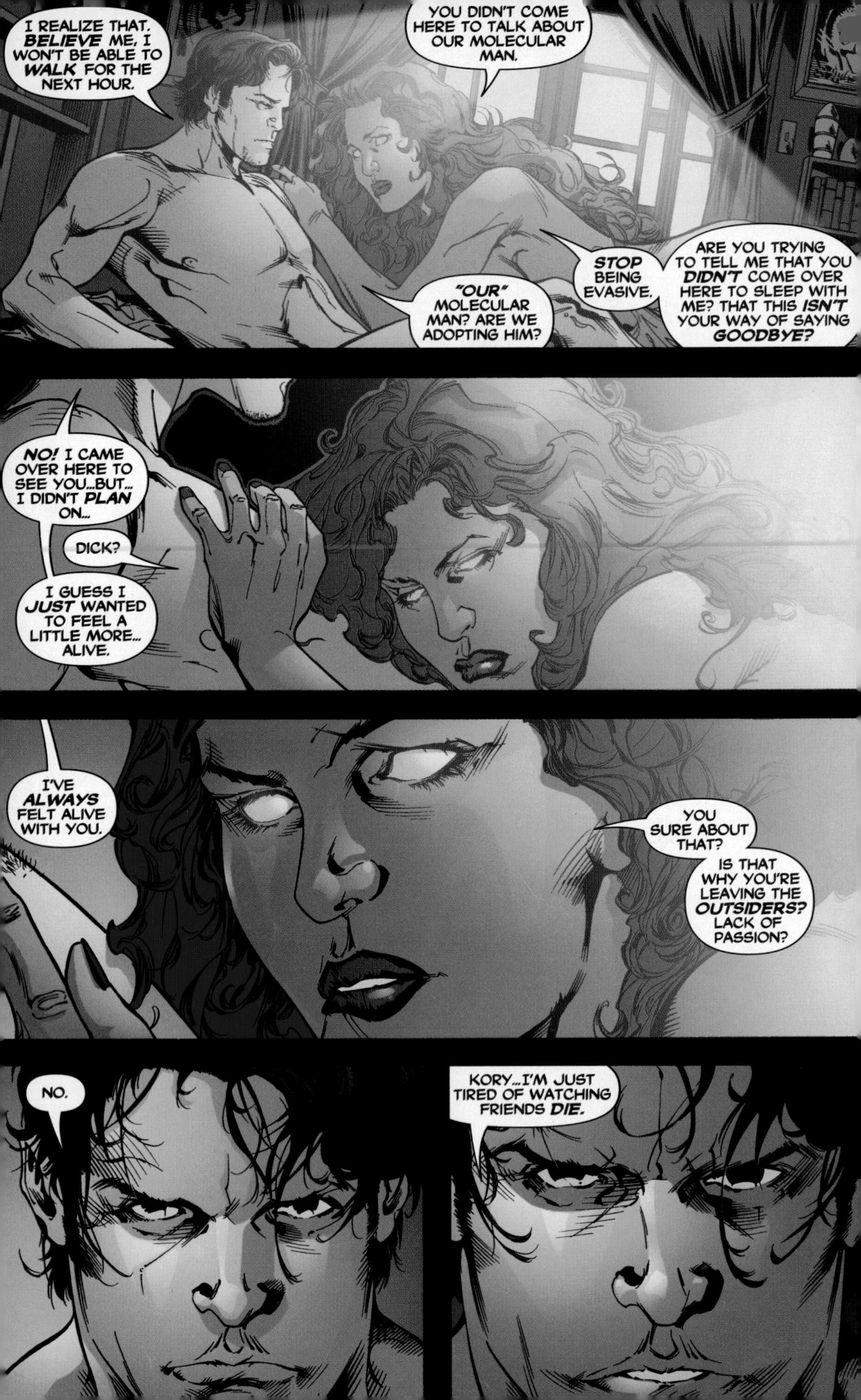

I REALIZE THAT. BELIEVE ME, I WON'T BE ABLE TO WALK FOR THE NEXT HOUR.
YOU DIDN'T COME HERE TO TALK ABOUT OUR MOLECULAR MAN.
"OUR" MOLECULAR MAN? ARE WE ADOPTING HIM?
STOP BEING EVASIVE.
ARE YOU TRYING TO TELL ME THAT YOU DIDN'T COME OVER HERE TO SLEEP WITH ME? THAT THIS ISN'T YOUR WAY OF SAYING GOODBYE?
NO! I CAME OVER HERE TO SEE YOU...BUT... I DIDN'T PLAN ON...
DICK?
I GUESS I JUST WANTED TO FEEL A LITTLE MORE... ALIVE.
I'VE ALWAYS FELT ALIVE WITH YOU.
YOU SURE ABOUT THAT?
IS THAT WHY YOU'RE LEAVING THE OUTSIDERS? LACK OF PASSION?
NO.
KORY...I'M JUST TIRED OF WATCHING FRIENDS DIE.

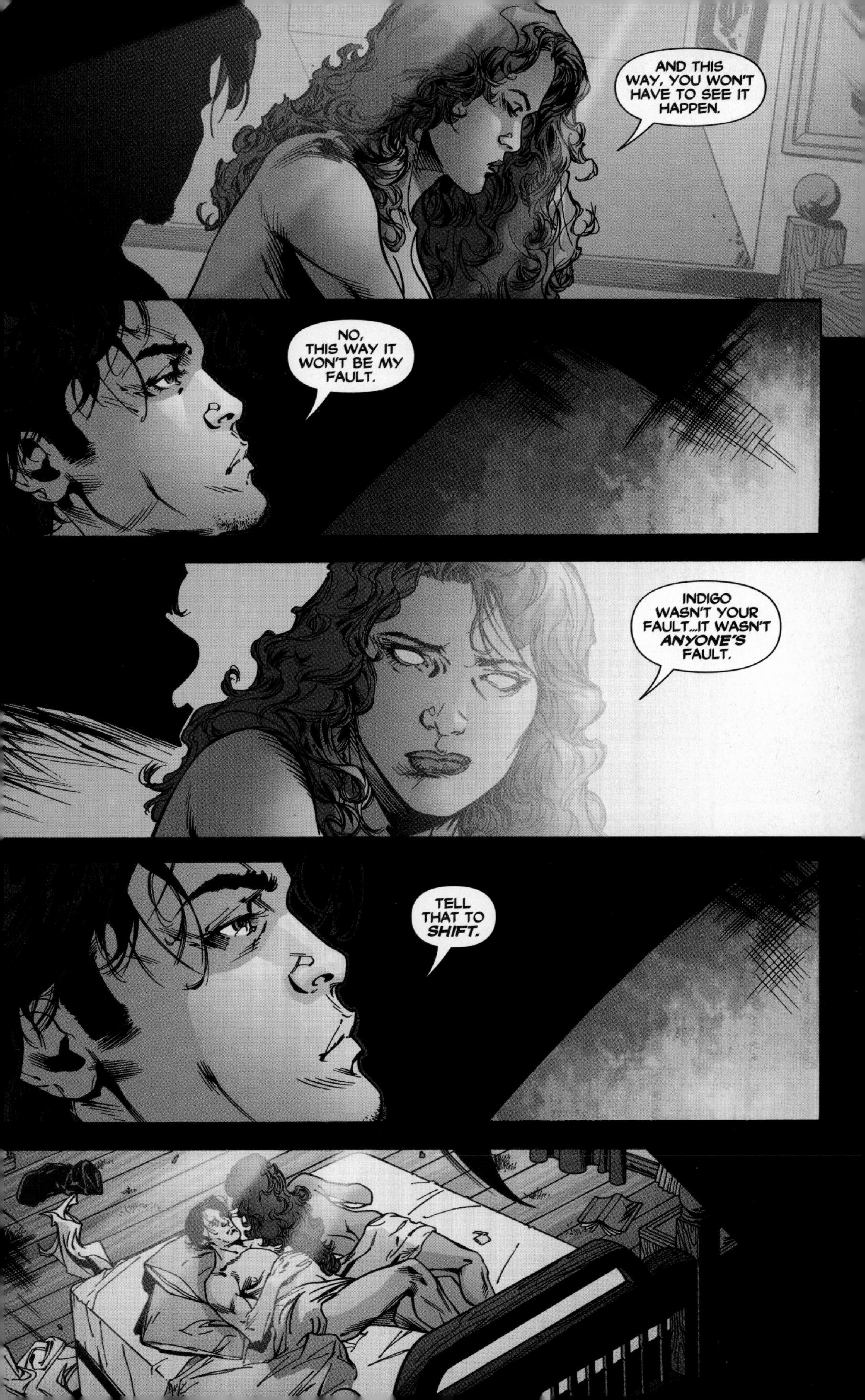
AND THIS WAY, YOU WON'T HAVE TO SEE IT HAPPEN.
NO, THIS WAY IT WON'T BE MY FAULT.
INDIGO WASN'T YOUR FAULT...IT WASN'T *ANYONE'S* FAULT.
TELL THAT TO *SHIFT*.

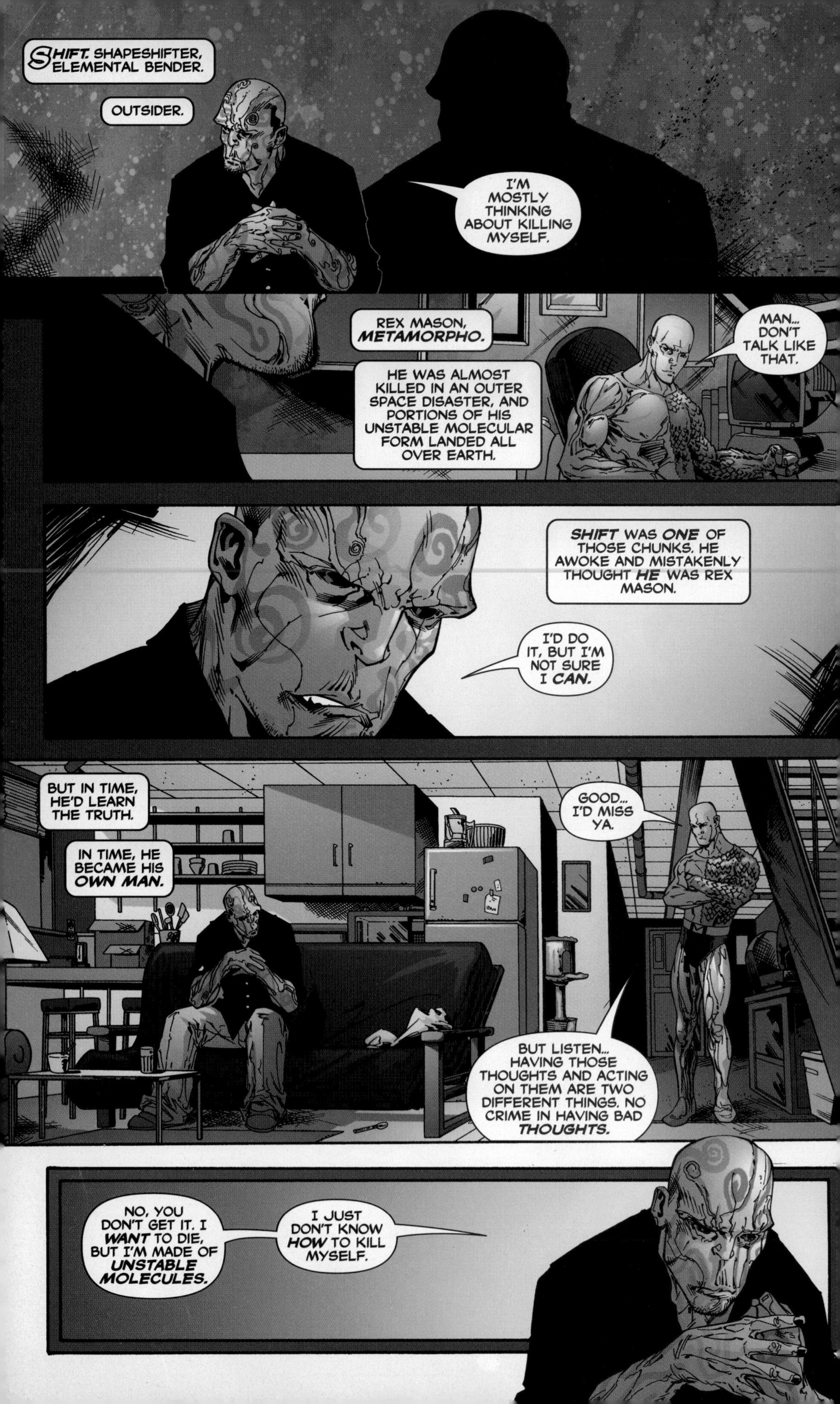
SHIFT. SHAPESHIFTER, ELEMENTAL BENDER.
OUTSIDER.
I'M MOSTLY THINKING ABOUT KILLING MYSELF.
REX MASON, METAMORPHO.
HE WAS ALMOST KILLED IN AN OUTER SPACE DISASTER, AND PORTIONS OF HIS UNSTABLE MOLECULAR FORM LANDED ALL OVER EARTH.
MAN... DON'T TALK LIKE THAT.
SHIFT WAS ONE OF THOSE CHUNKS. HE AWOKE AND MISTAKENLY THOUGHT HE WAS REX MASON.
I'D DO IT, BUT I'M NOT SURE I CAN.
BUT IN TIME, HE'D LEARN THE TRUTH.
IN TIME, HE BECAME HIS OWN MAN.
GOOD... I'D MISS YA.
BUT LISTEN... HAVING THOSE THOUGHTS AND ACTING ON THEM ARE TWO DIFFERENT THINGS. NO CRIME IN HAVING BAD THOUGHTS.
NO, YOU DON'T GET IT. I WANT TO DIE, BUT I'M MADE OF UNSTABLE MOLECULES.
I JUST DON'T KNOW HOW TO KILL MYSELF.

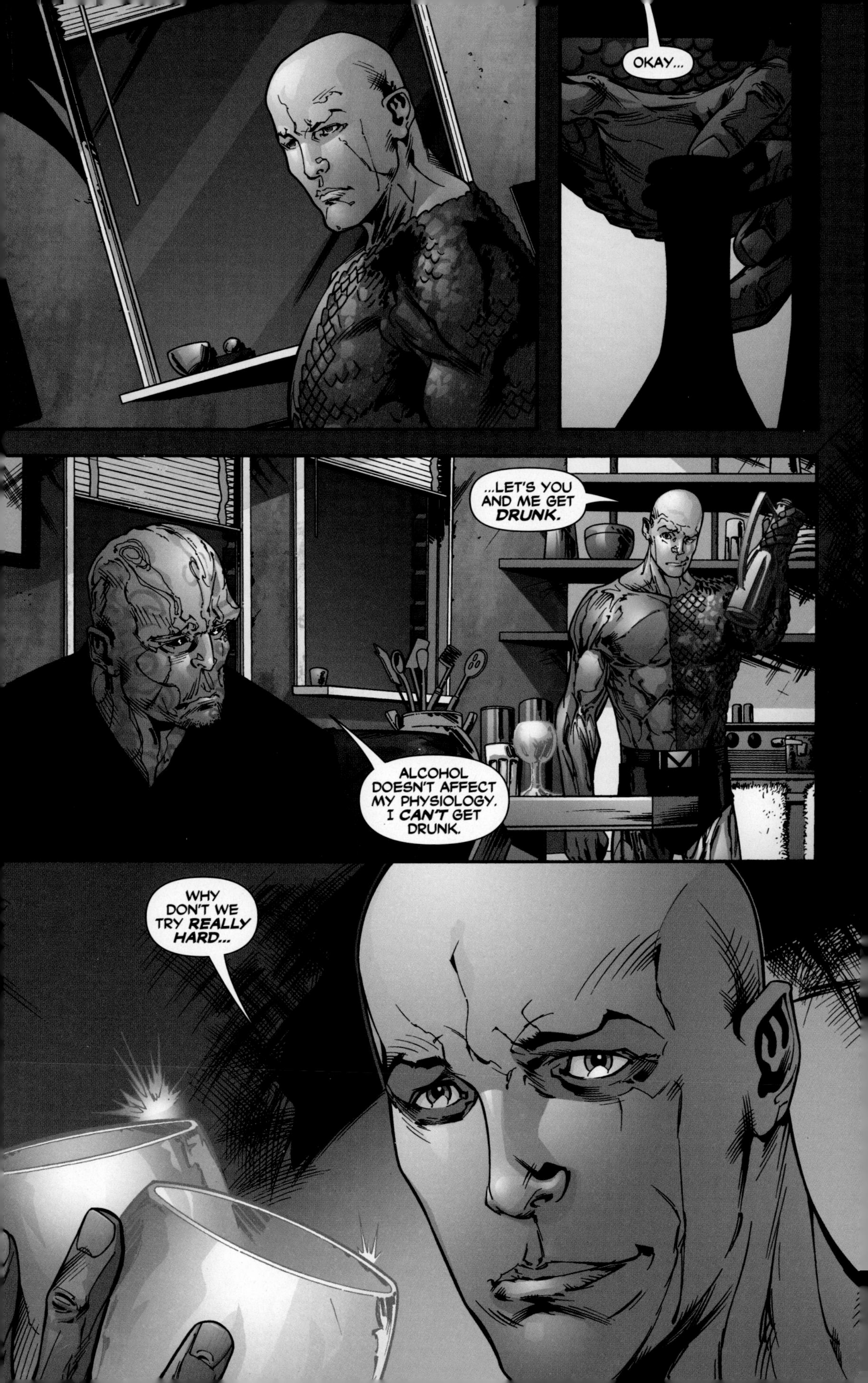
OKAY...
...LET'S YOU AND ME GET DRUNK.
ALCOHOL DOESN'T AFFECT MY PHYSIOLOGY. I CAN'T GET DRUNK.
WHY DON'T WE TRY REALLY HARD...

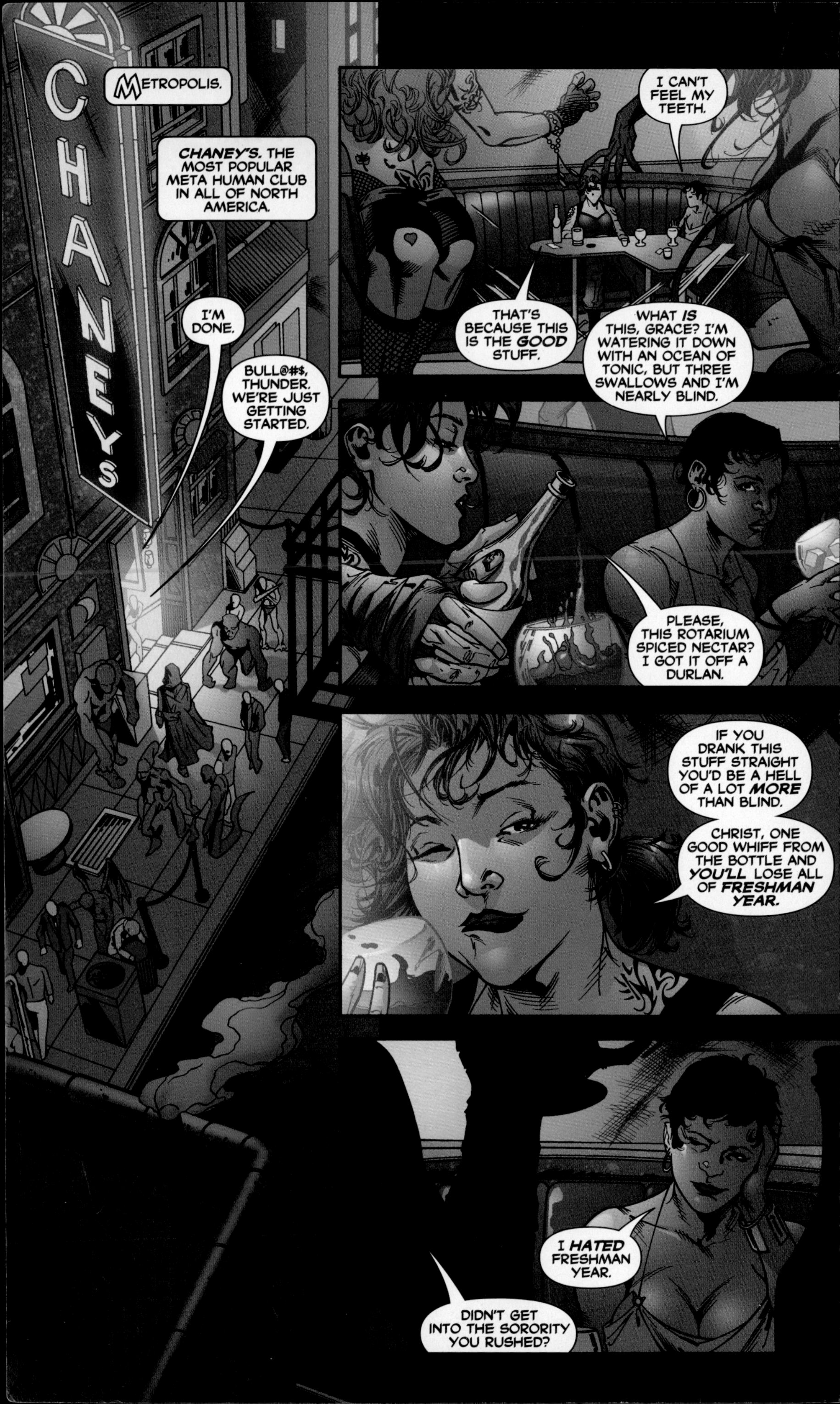
METROPOLIS.
CHANEY'S. THE MOST POPULAR META HUMAN CLUB IN ALL OF NORTH AMERICA.
CHANEYS
I'M DONE.
BULL@#$, THUNDER. WE'RE JUST GETTING STARTED.
I CAN'T FEEL MY TEETH.
THAT'S BECAUSE THIS IS THE GOOD STUFF.
WHAT IS THIS, GRACE? I'M WATERING IT DOWN WITH AN OCEAN OF TONIC, BUT THREE SWALLOWS AND I'M NEARLY BLIND.
PLEASE, THIS ROTARIUM SPICED NECTAR? I GOT IT OFF A DURLAN.
IF YOU DRANK THIS STUFF STRAIGHT YOU'D BE A HELL OF A LOT MORE THAN BLIND.
CHRIST, ONE GOOD WHIFF FROM THE BOTTLE AND YOU'LL LOSE ALL OF FRESHMAN YEAR.
I HATED FRESHMAN YEAR.
DIDN'T GET INTO THE SORORITY YOU RUSHED?

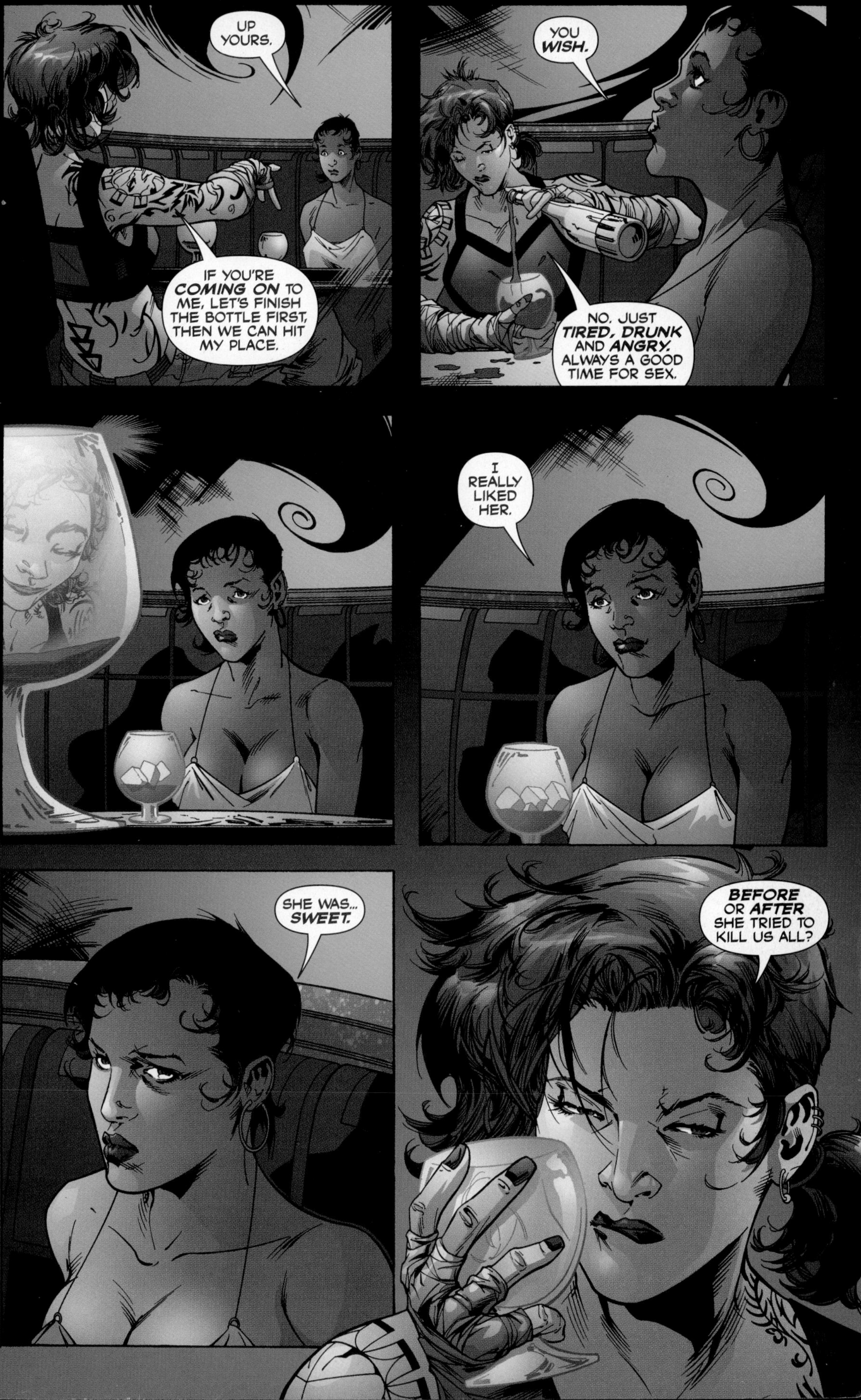
UP YOURS.
YOU WISH.
IF YOU'RE COMING ON TO ME, LET'S FINISH THE BOTTLE FIRST, THEN WE CAN HIT MY PLACE.
NO. JUST TIRED, DRUNK AND ANGRY. ALWAYS A GOOD TIME FOR SEX.
I REALLY LIKED HER.
SHE WAS... SWEET.
BEFORE OR AFTER SHE TRIED TO KILL US ALL?

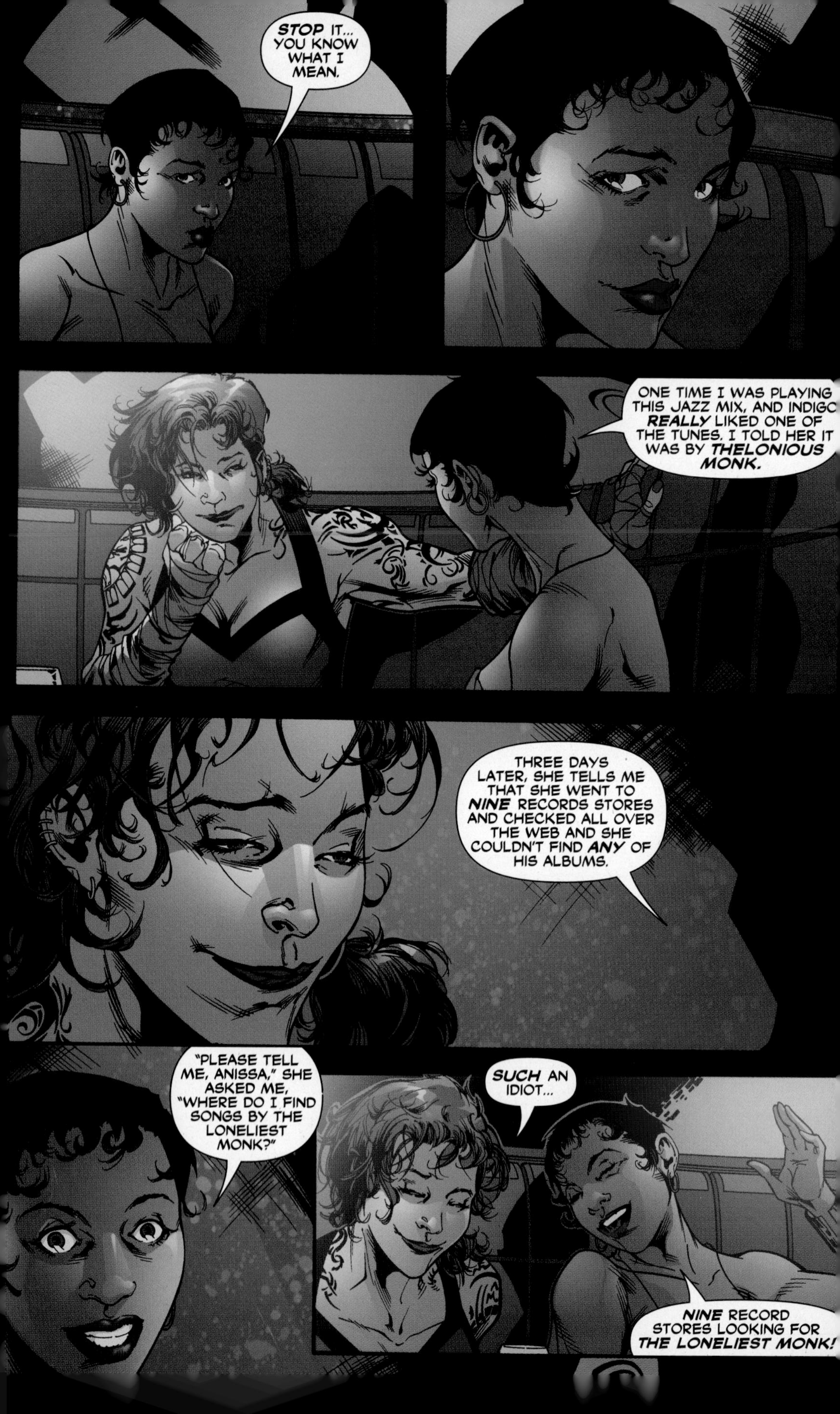
STOP IT... YOU KNOW WHAT I MEAN.
ONE TIME I WAS PLAYING THIS JAZZ MIX, AND INDIGO REALLY LIKED ONE OF THE TUNES. I TOLD HER IT WAS BY THELONIOUS MONK.
THREE DAYS LATER, SHE TELLS ME THAT SHE WENT TO NINE RECORDS STORES AND CHECKED ALL OVER THE WEB AND SHE COULDN'T FIND ANY OF HIS ALBUMS.
"PLEASE TELL ME, ANISSA," SHE ASKED ME, "WHERE DO I FIND SONGS BY THE LONELIEST MONK?"
SUCH AN IDIOT...
NINE RECORD STORES LOOKING FOR THE LONELIEST MONK!

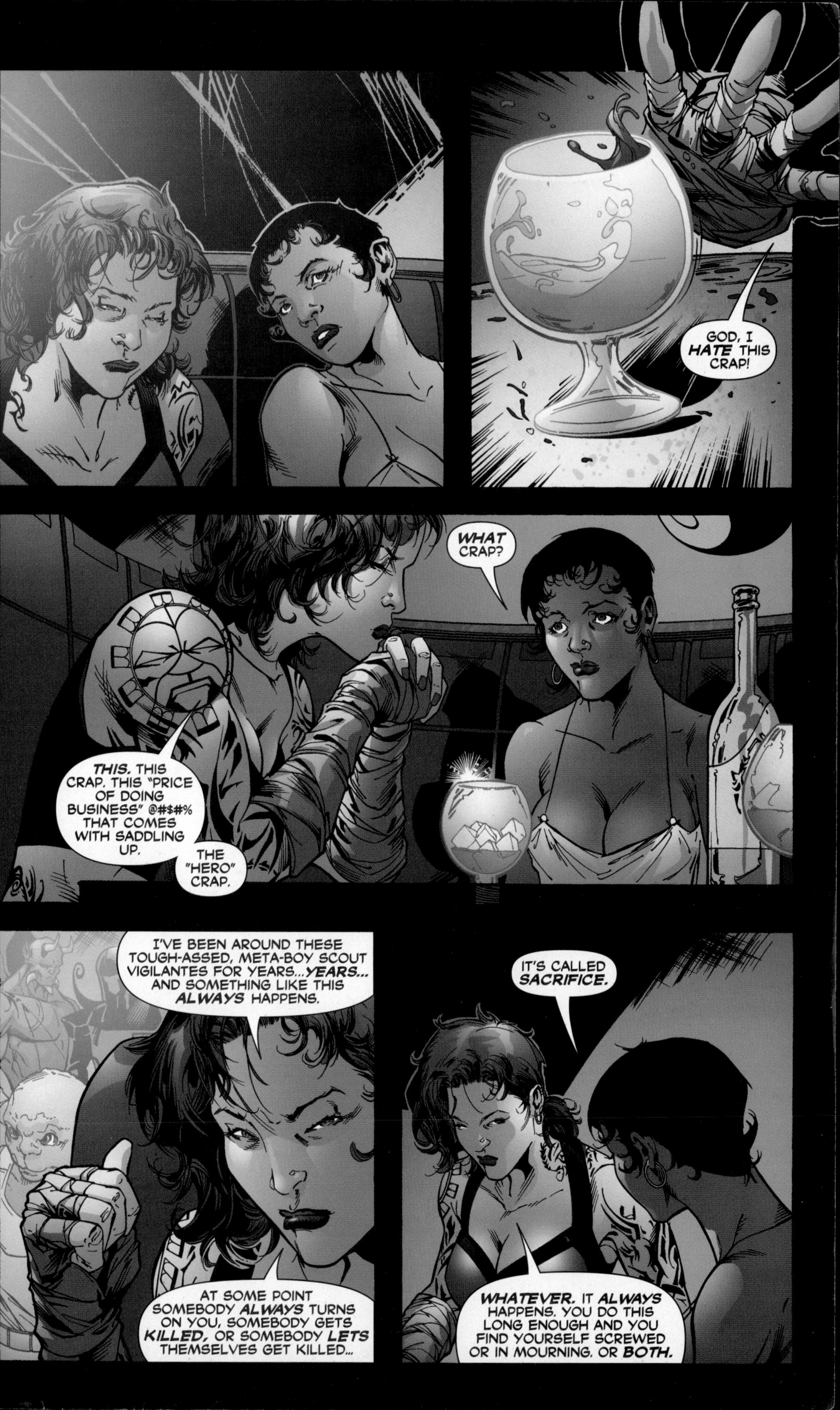
GOD, I HATE THIS CRAP!
WHAT CRAP?
THIS. THIS CRAP. THIS "PRICE OF DOING BUSINESS" @#$#% THAT COMES WITH SADDLING UP.
THE "HERO" CRAP.
I'VE BEEN AROUND THESE TOUGH-ASSED, META-BOY SCOUT VIGILANTES FOR YEARS...YEARS... AND SOMETHING LIKE THIS ALWAYS HAPPENS.
AT SOME POINT SOMEBODY ALWAYS TURNS ON YOU, SOMEBODY GETS KILLED, OR SOMEBODY LETS THEMSELVES GET KILLED...
IT'S CALLED SACRIFICE.
WHATEVER. IT ALWAYS HAPPENS. YOU DO THIS LONG ENOUGH AND YOU FIND YOURSELF SCREWED OR IN MOURNING. OR BOTH.

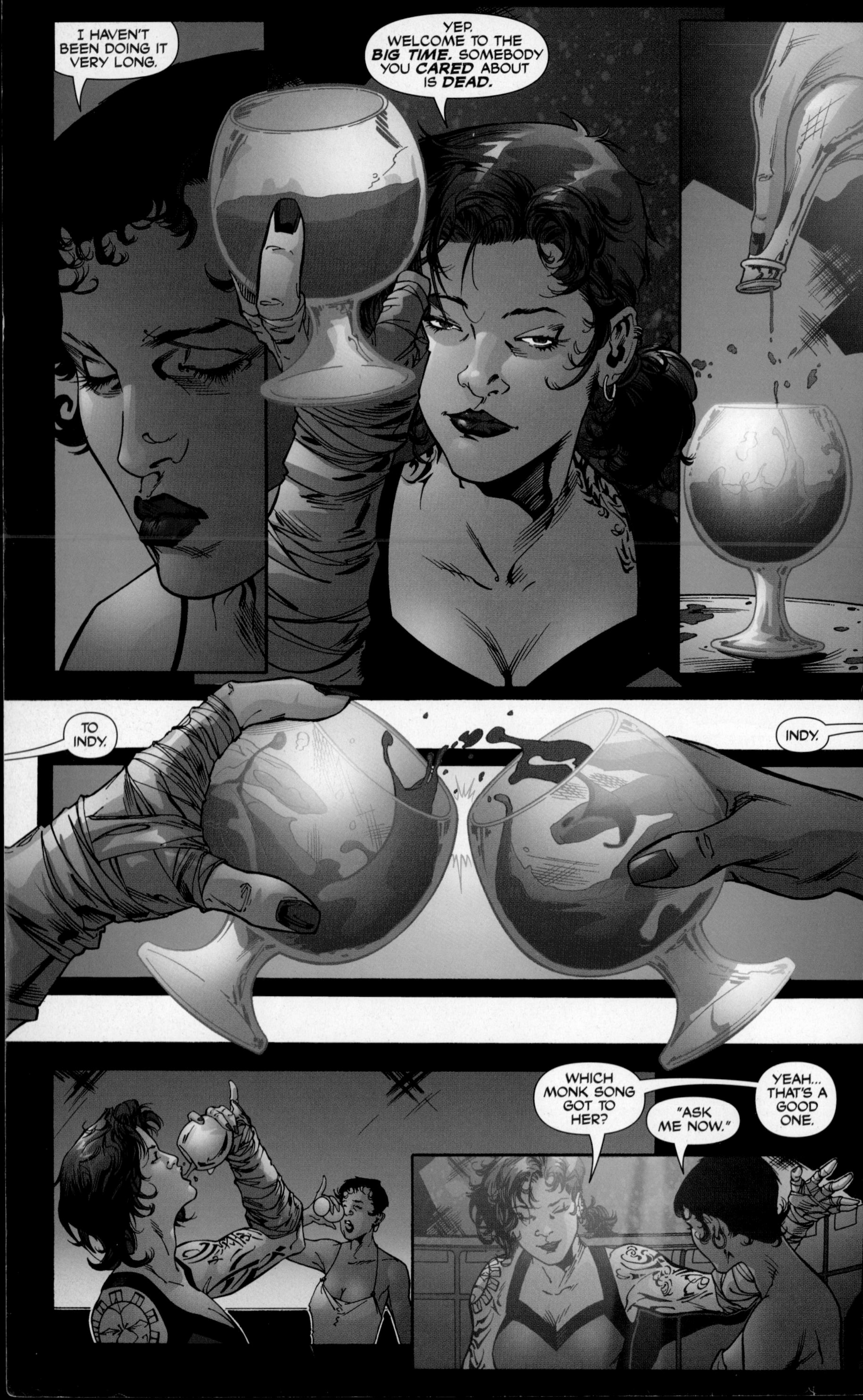
I HAVEN'T BEEN DOING IT VERY LONG.
YEP. WELCOME TO THE **BIG TIME.** SOMEBODY YOU **CARED** ABOUT IS **DEAD.**
TO INDY.
INDY.
WHICH MONK SONG GOT TO HER?
"ASK ME NOW."
YEAH... THAT'S A GOOD ONE.

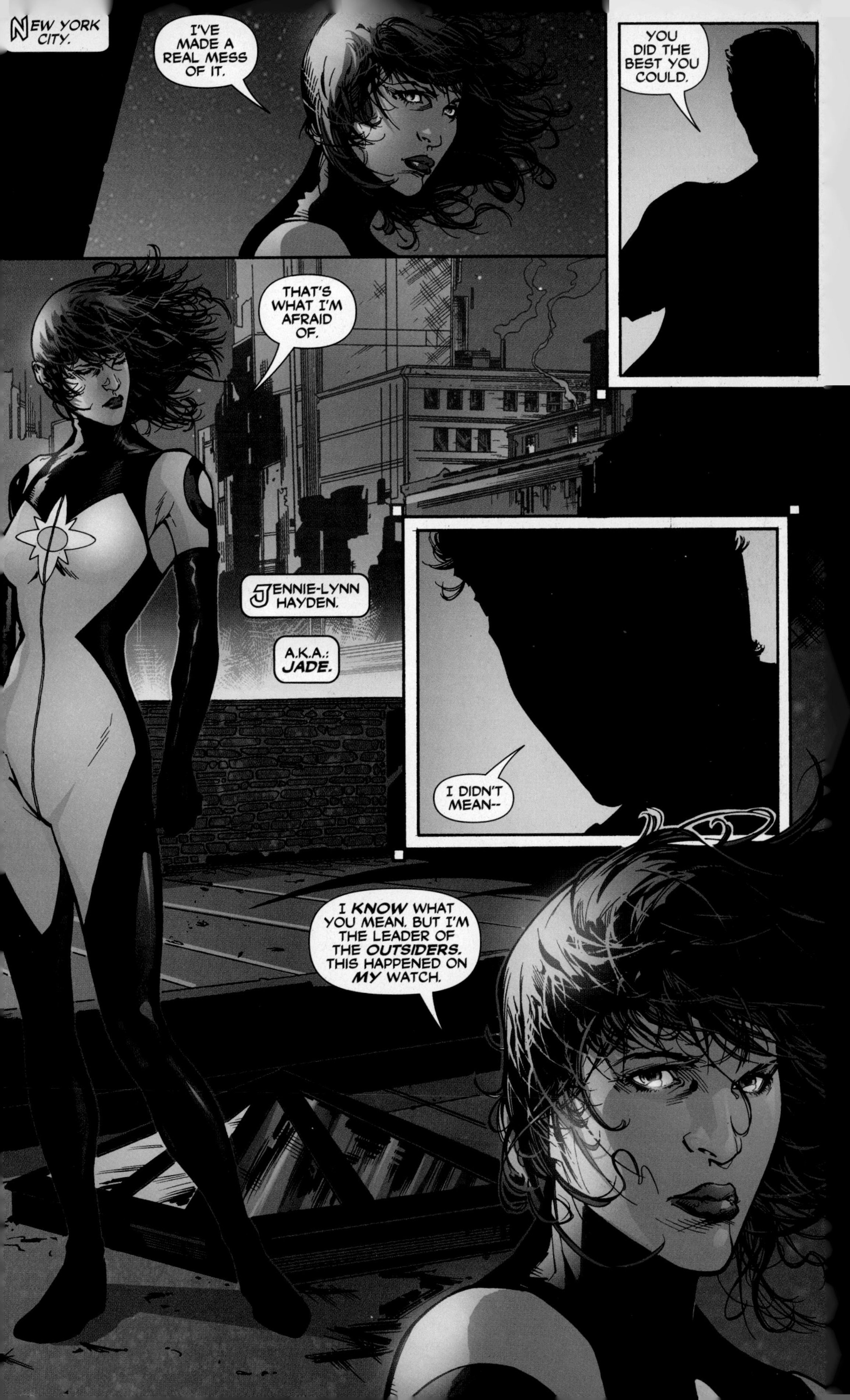
NEW YORK CITY.
I'VE MADE A REAL MESS OF IT.
YOU DID THE BEST YOU COULD.
THAT'S WHAT I'M AFRAID OF.
JENNIE-LYNN HAYDEN.
A.K.A.: JADE.
I DIDN'T MEAN--
I KNOW WHAT YOU MEAN. BUT I'M THE LEADER OF THE OUTSIDERS. THIS HAPPENED ON MY WATCH.

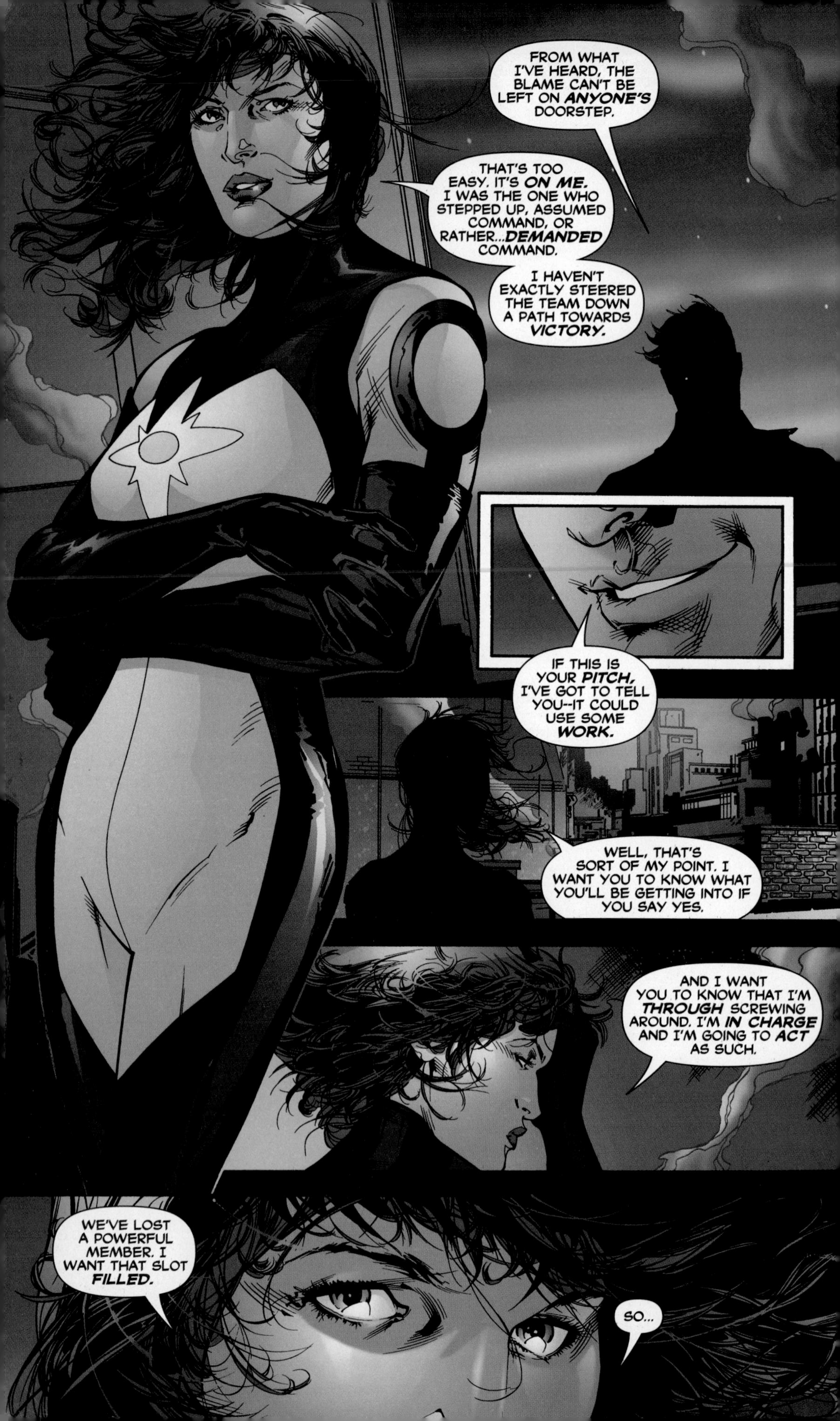
FROM WHAT I'VE HEARD, THE BLAME CAN'T BE LEFT ON ANYONE'S DOORSTEP.
THAT'S TOO EASY. IT'S ON ME. I WAS THE ONE WHO STEPPED UP, ASSUMED COMMAND, OR RATHER...DEMANDED COMMAND.
I HAVEN'T EXACTLY STEERED THE TEAM DOWN A PATH TOWARDS VICTORY.
IF THIS IS YOUR PITCH, I'VE GOT TO TELL YOU--IT COULD USE SOME WORK.
WELL, THAT'S SORT OF MY POINT. I WANT YOU TO KNOW WHAT YOU'LL BE GETTING INTO IF YOU SAY YES.
AND I WANT YOU TO KNOW THAT I'M THROUGH SCREWING AROUND. I'M IN CHARGE AND I'M GOING TO ACT AS SUCH.
WE'VE LOST A POWERFUL MEMBER. I WANT THAT SLOT FILLED.
SO...

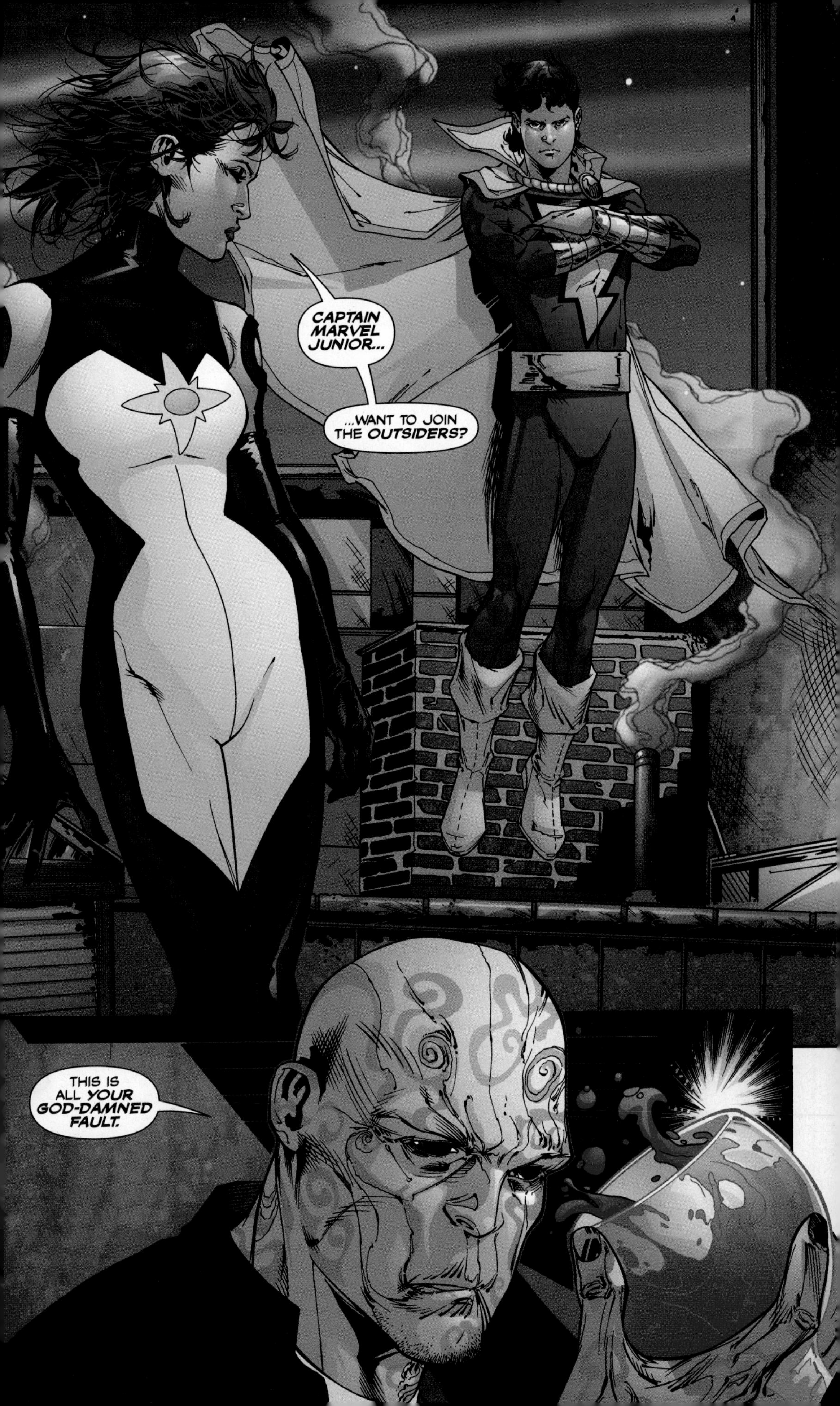
CAPTAIN MARVEL JUNIOR...
...WANT TO JOIN THE OUTSIDERS?
THIS IS ALL YOUR GOD-DAMNED FAULT.

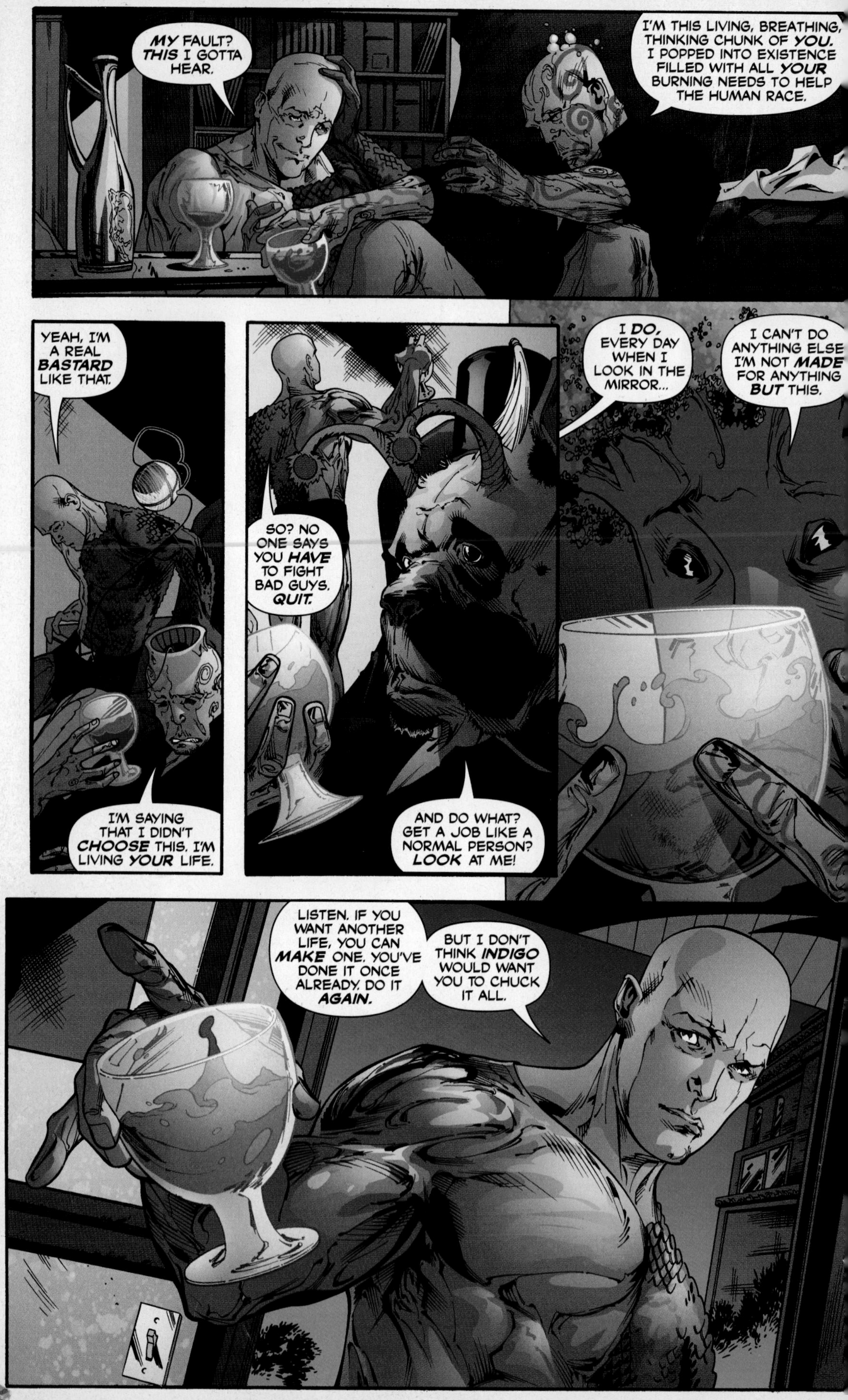
MY FAULT? THIS I GOTTA HEAR.
I'M THIS LIVING, BREATHING, THINKING CHUNK OF YOU. I POPPED INTO EXISTENCE FILLED WITH ALL YOUR BURNING NEEDS TO HELP THE HUMAN RACE.
YEAH, I'M A REAL BASTARD LIKE THAT.
I'M SAYING THAT I DIDN'T CHOOSE THIS. I'M LIVING YOUR LIFE.
SO? NO ONE SAYS YOU HAVE TO FIGHT BAD GUYS. QUIT.
AND DO WHAT? GET A JOB LIKE A NORMAL PERSON? LOOK AT ME!
I DO, EVERY DAY WHEN I LOOK IN THE MIRROR...
I CAN'T DO ANYTHING ELSE. I'M NOT MADE FOR ANYTHING BUT THIS.
LISTEN. IF YOU WANT ANOTHER LIFE, YOU CAN MAKE ONE. YOU'VE DONE IT ONCE ALREADY. DO IT AGAIN.
BUT I DON'T THINK INDIGO WOULD WANT YOU TO CHUCK IT ALL.

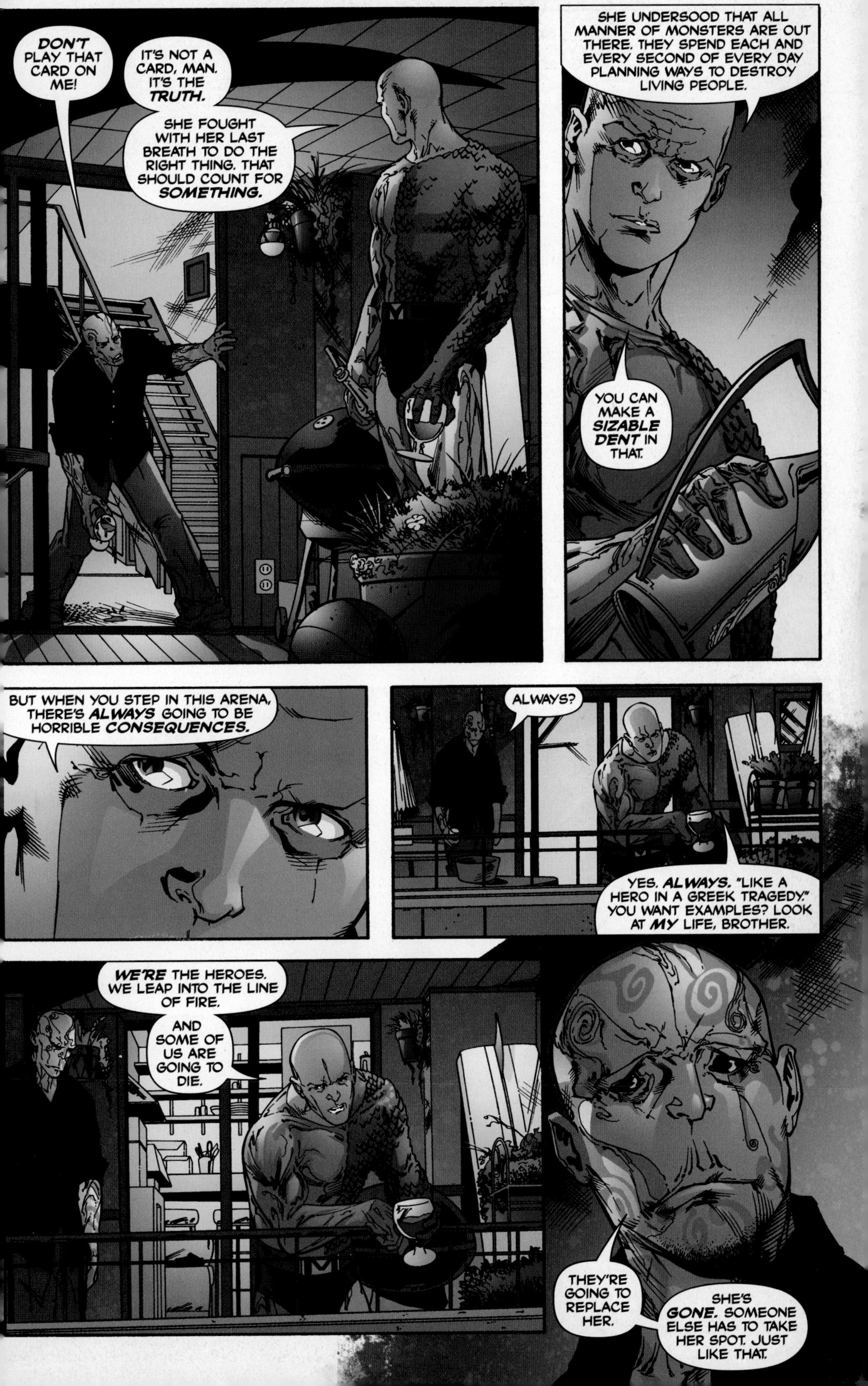
DON'T PLAY THAT CARD ON ME!
IT'S NOT A CARD, MAN. IT'S THE TRUTH.
SHE FOUGHT WITH HER LAST BREATH TO DO THE RIGHT THING. THAT SHOULD COUNT FOR SOMETHING.
SHE UNDERSOOD THAT ALL MANNER OF MONSTERS ARE OUT THERE. THEY SPEND EACH AND EVERY SECOND OF EVERY DAY PLANNING WAYS TO DESTROY LIVING PEOPLE.
YOU CAN MAKE A SIZABLE DENT IN THAT.
BUT WHEN YOU STEP IN THIS ARENA, THERE'S ALWAYS GOING TO BE HORRIBLE CONSEQUENCES.
ALWAYS?
YES. ALWAYS. "LIKE A HERO IN A GREEK TRAGEDY." YOU WANT EXAMPLES? LOOK AT MY LIFE, BROTHER.
WE'RE THE HEROES. WE LEAP INTO THE LINE OF FIRE.
AND SOME OF US ARE GOING TO DIE.
THEY'RE GOING TO REPLACE HER.
SHE'S GONE. SOMEONE ELSE HAS TO TAKE HER SPOT. JUST LIKE THAT.

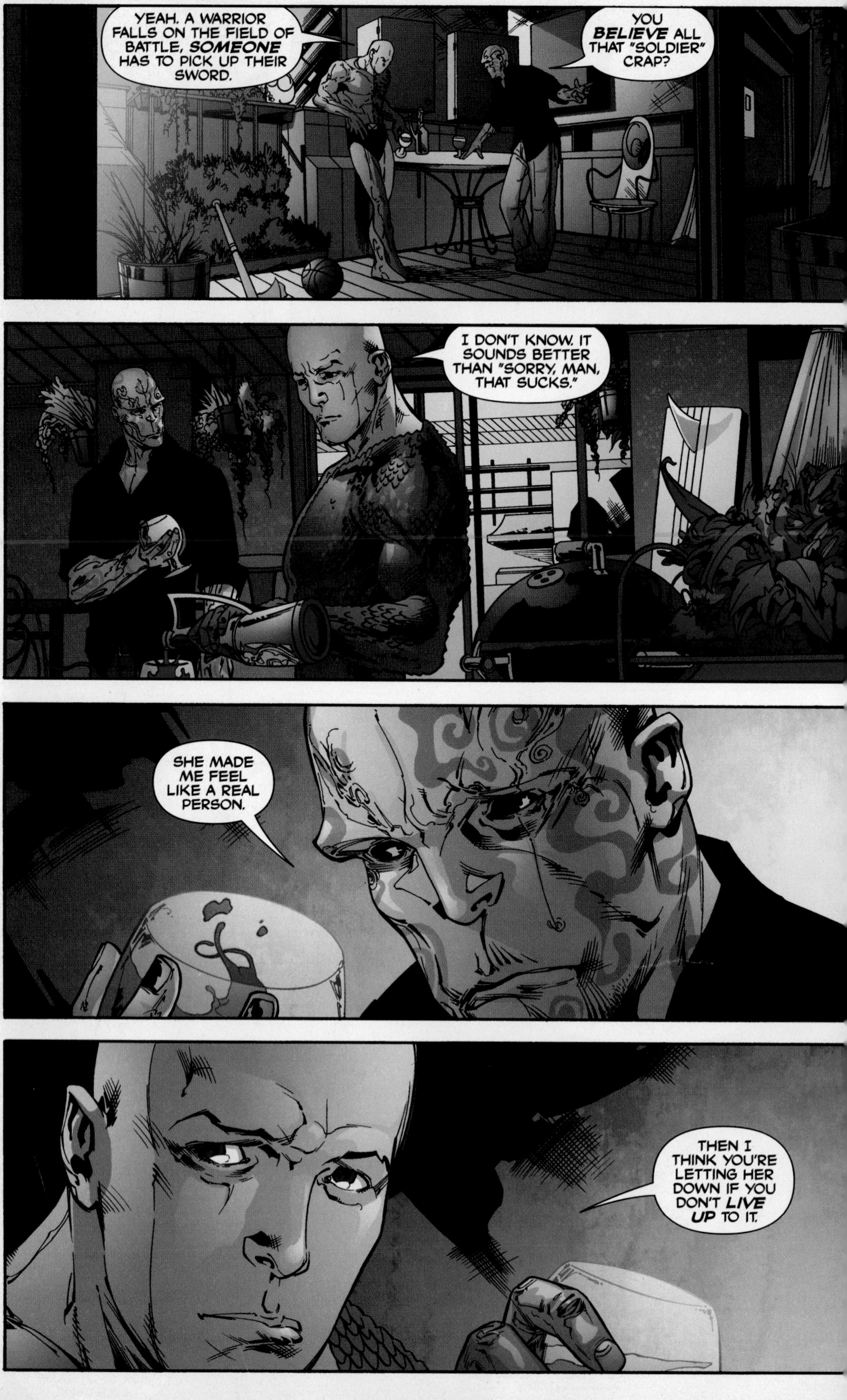
YEAH. A WARRIOR FALLS ON THE FIELD OF BATTLE, SOMEONE HAS TO PICK UP THEIR SWORD.
YOU BELIEVE ALL THAT "SOLDIER" CRAP?
I DON'T KNOW. IT SOUNDS BETTER THAN "SORRY, MAN, THAT SUCKS."
SHE MADE ME FEEL LIKE A REAL PERSON.
THEN I THINK YOU'RE LETTING HER DOWN IF YOU DON'T LIVE UP TO IT.

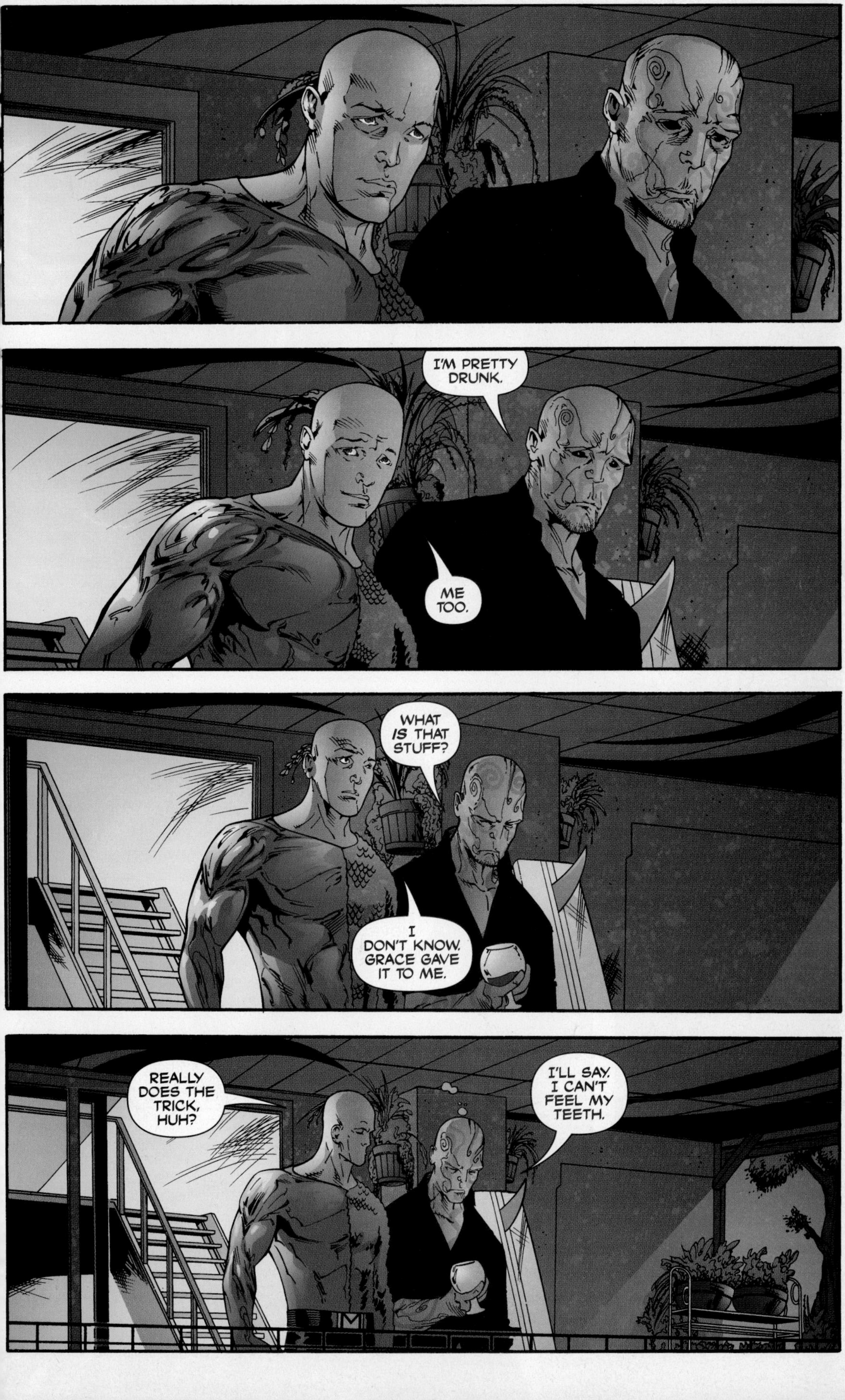
I'M PRETTY DRUNK.
ME TOO.
WHAT *IS* THAT STUFF?
I DON'T KNOW. GRACE GAVE IT TO ME.
REALLY DOES THE TRICK, HUH?
I'LL SAY. I CAN'T FEEL MY TEETH.

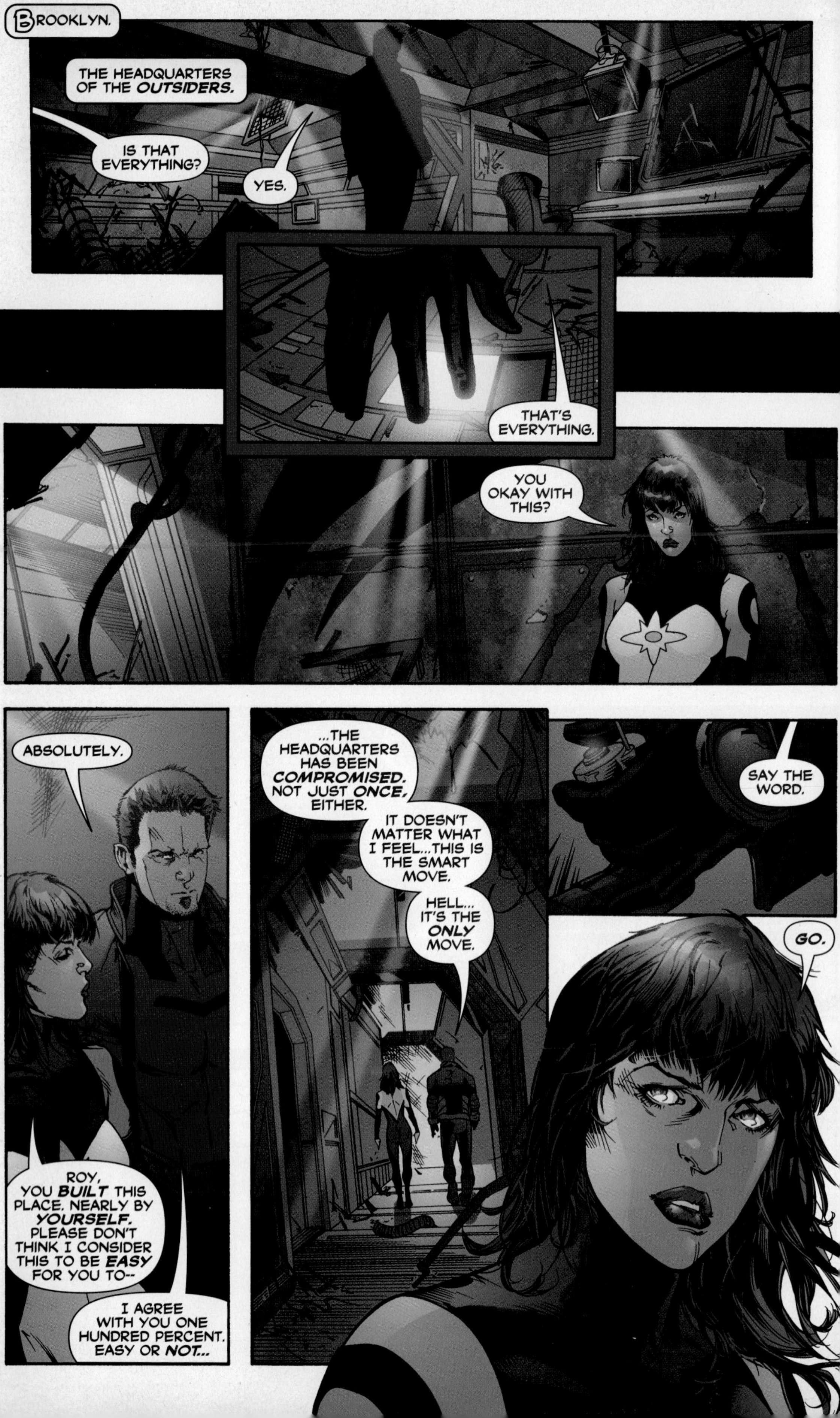
BROOKLYN.
THE HEADQUARTERS OF THE OUTSIDERS.
IS THAT EVERYTHING?
YES.
THAT'S EVERYTHING.
YOU OKAY WITH THIS?
ABSOLUTELY.
ROY, YOU BUILT THIS PLACE, NEARLY BY YOURSELF. PLEASE DON'T THINK I CONSIDER THIS TO BE EASY FOR YOU TO--
I AGREE WITH YOU ONE HUNDRED PERCENT. EASY OR NOT...
...THE HEADQUARTERS HAS BEEN COMPROMISED. NOT JUST ONCE, EITHER.
IT DOESN'T MATTER WHAT I FEEL...THIS IS THE SMART MOVE.
HELL... IT'S THE ONLY MOVE.
SAY THE WORD.
GO.

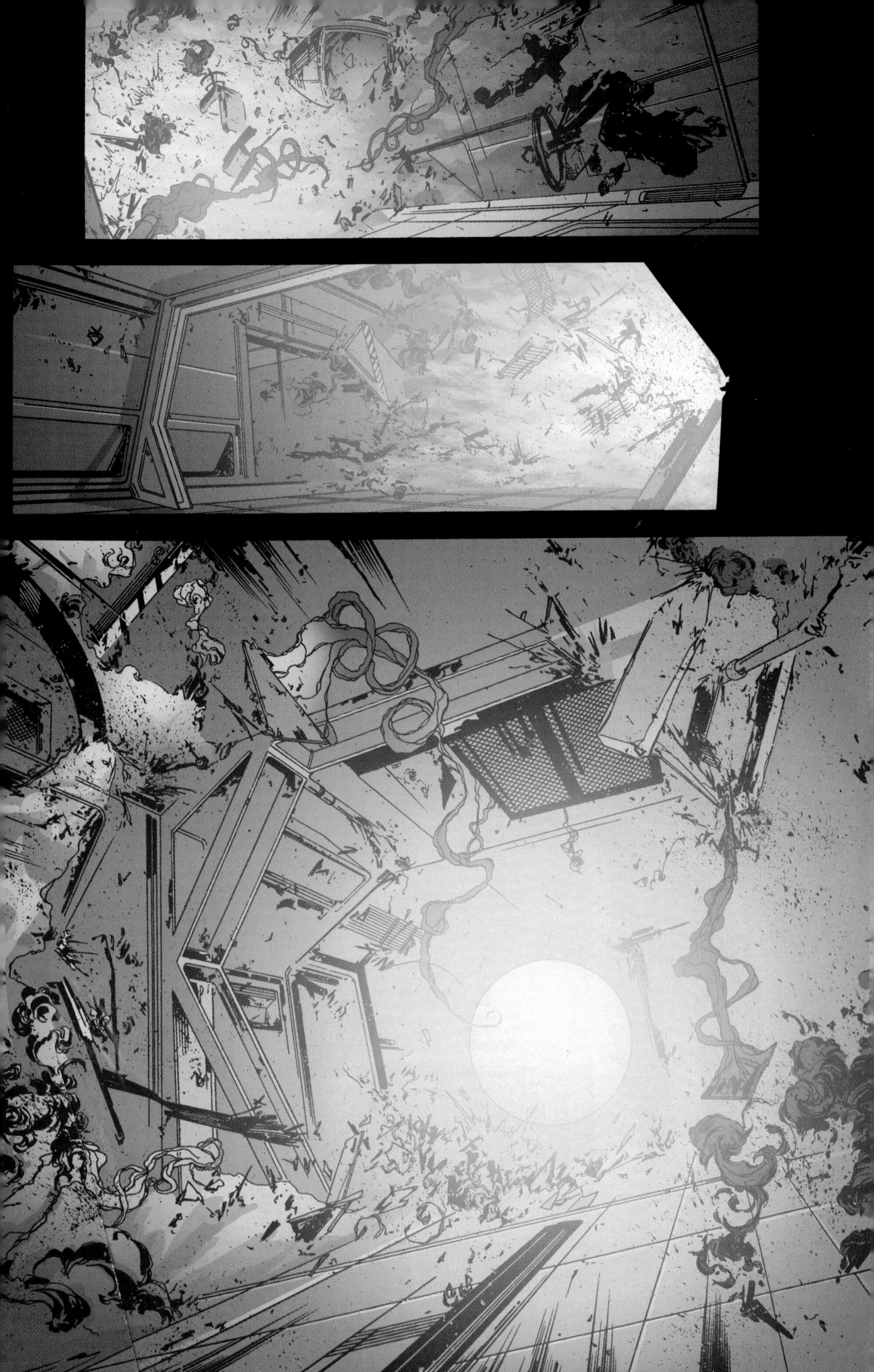

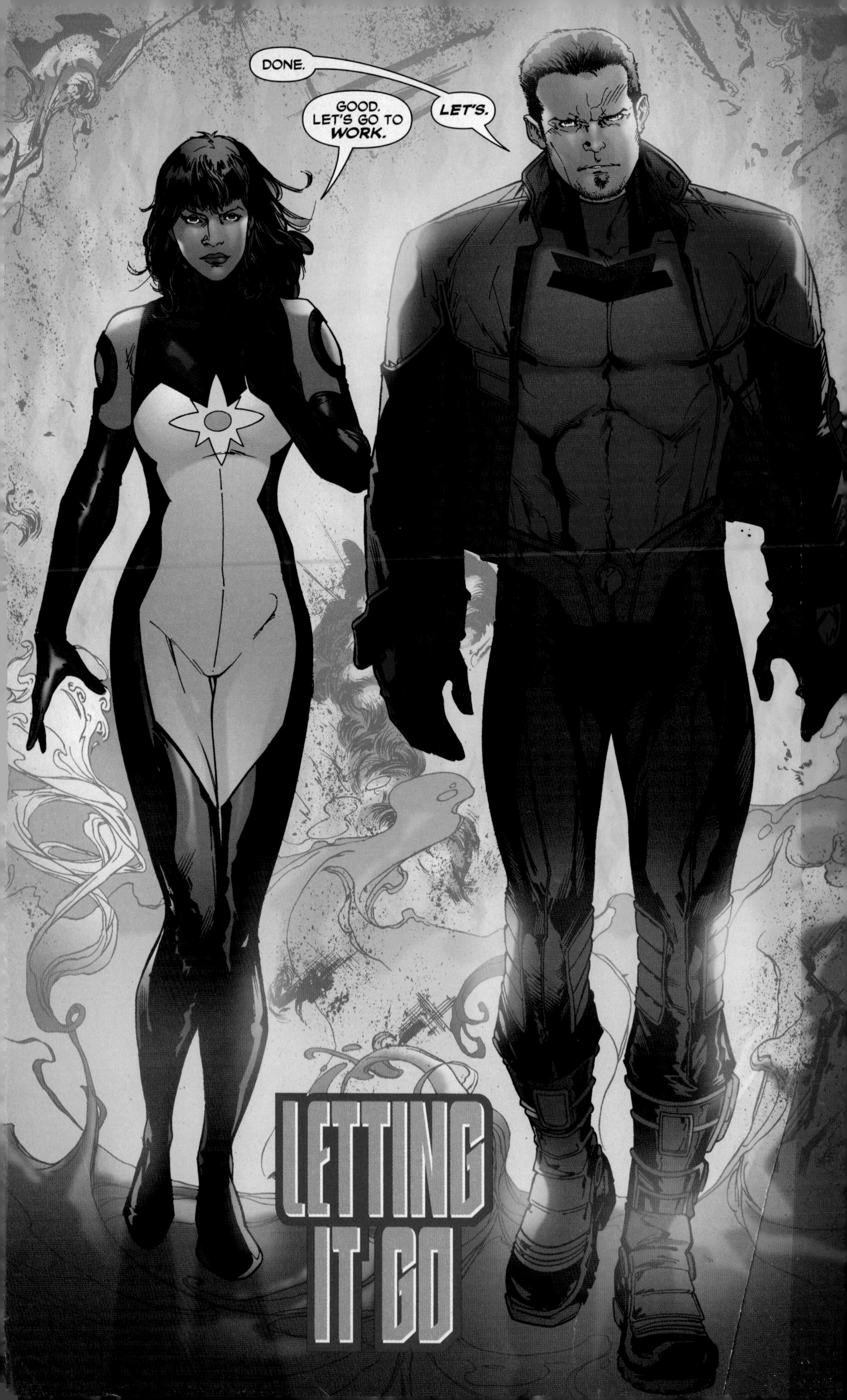
DONE.
LET'S.
GOOD. LET'S GO TO WORK.
LETTING IT GO

TEEN TITANS #24
ART BY MIKE McKONE & MARLO ALQUIZA

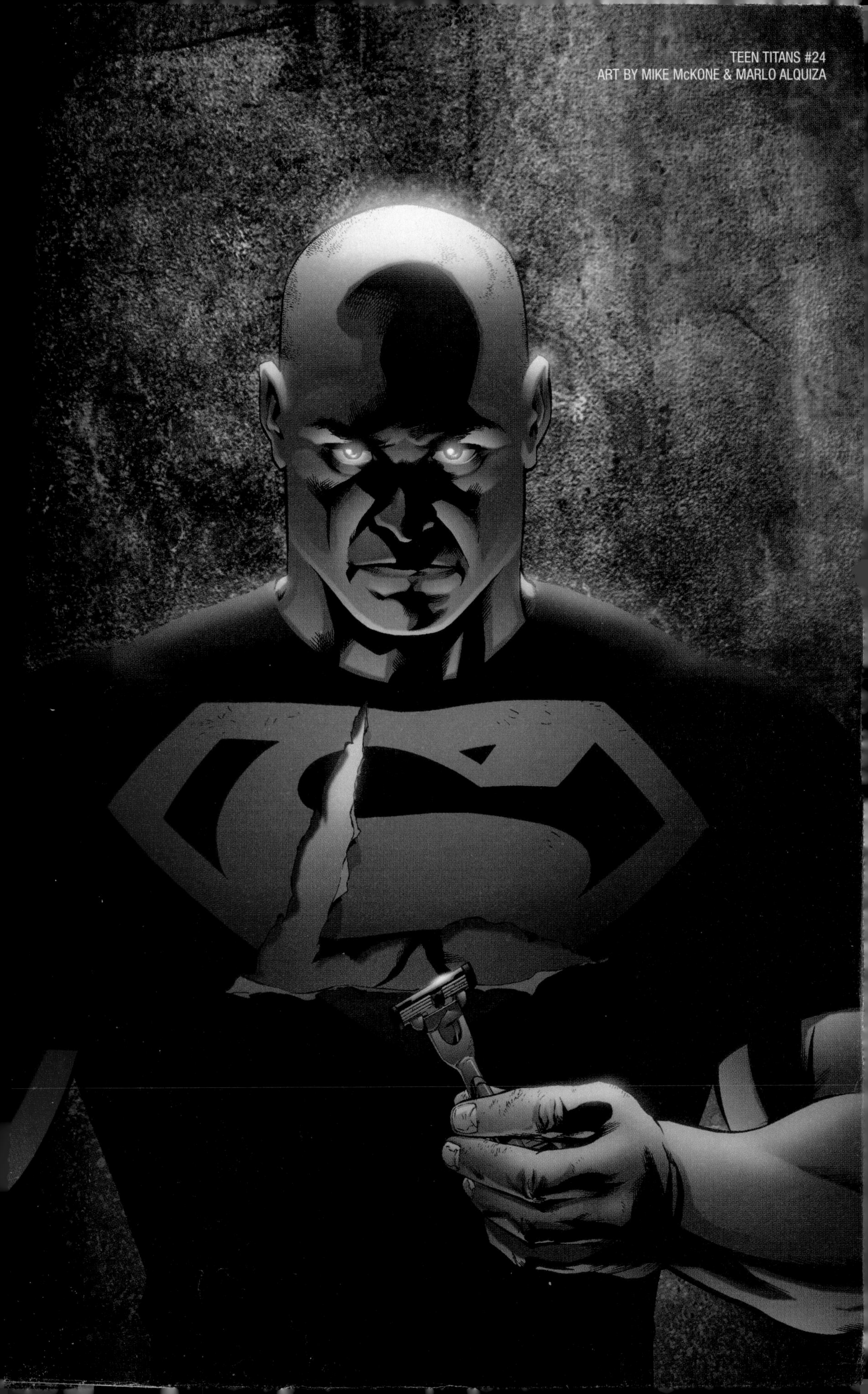

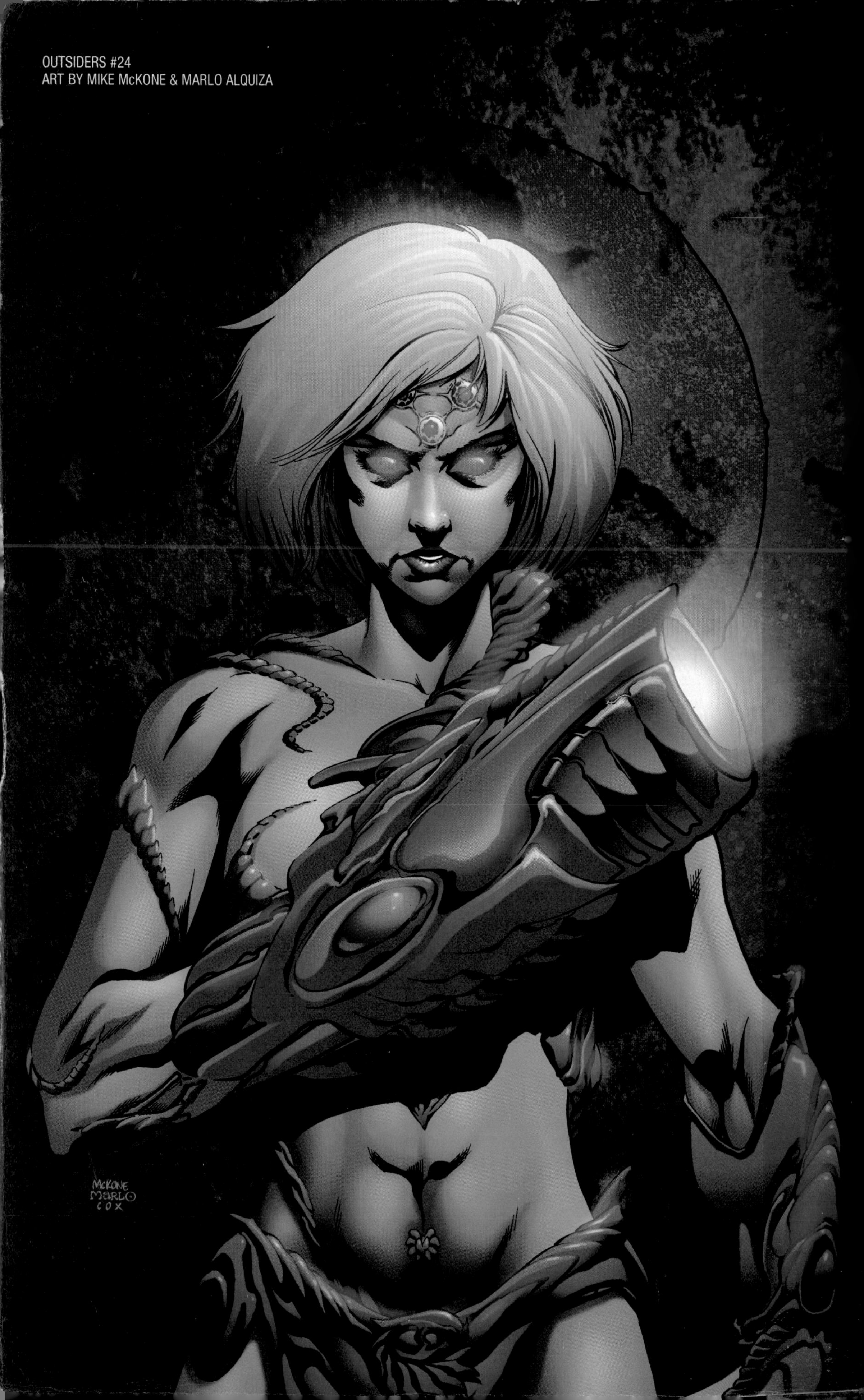
McKONE
MARLO
COX
OUTSIDERS #24
ART BY MIKE McKONE & MARLO ALQUIZA

TEEN TITANS #25
ART BY MIKE McKONE & MARLO ALQUIZA

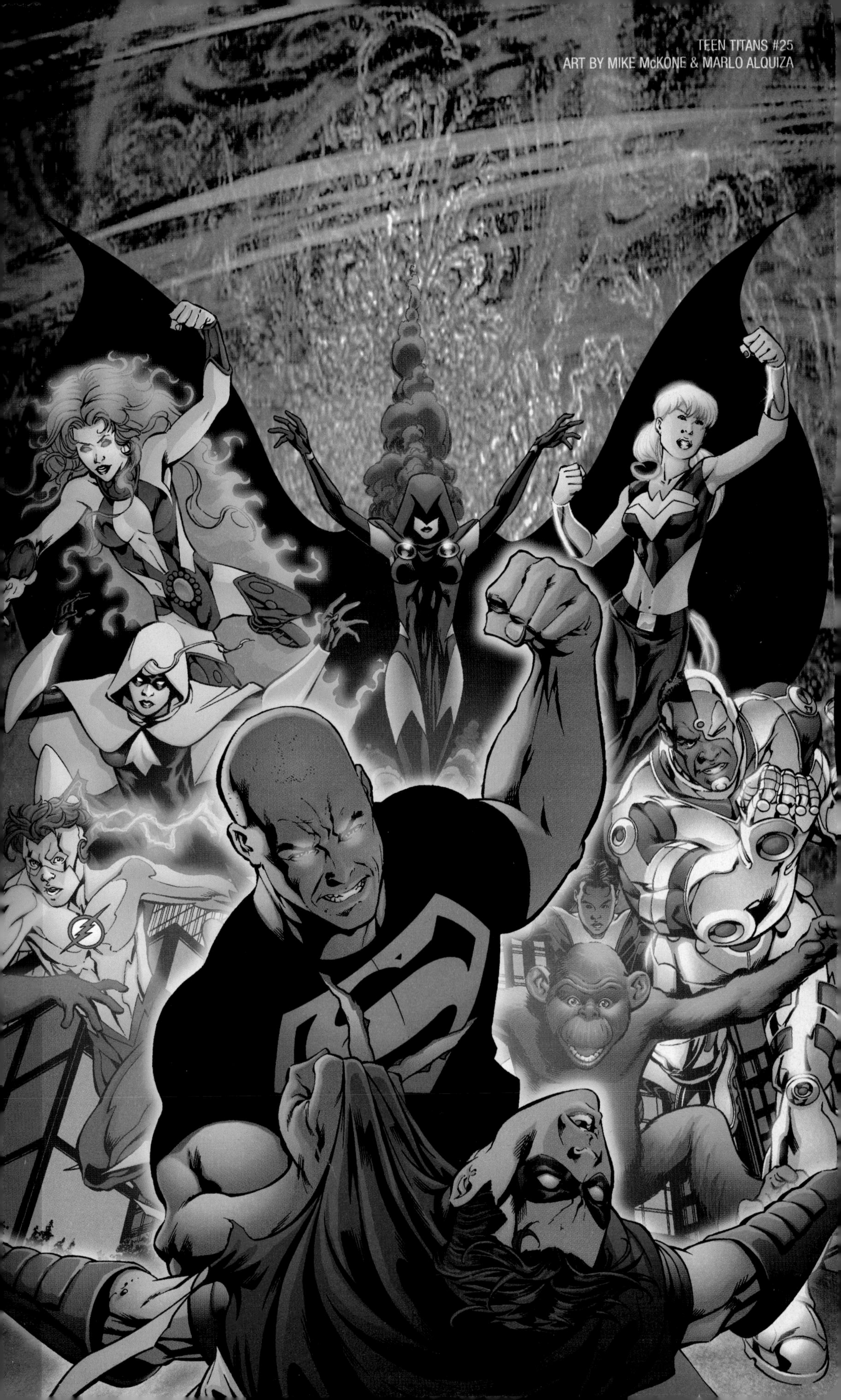

OUTSIDERS #25
ART BY MIKE McKONE & MARLO ALQUIZA

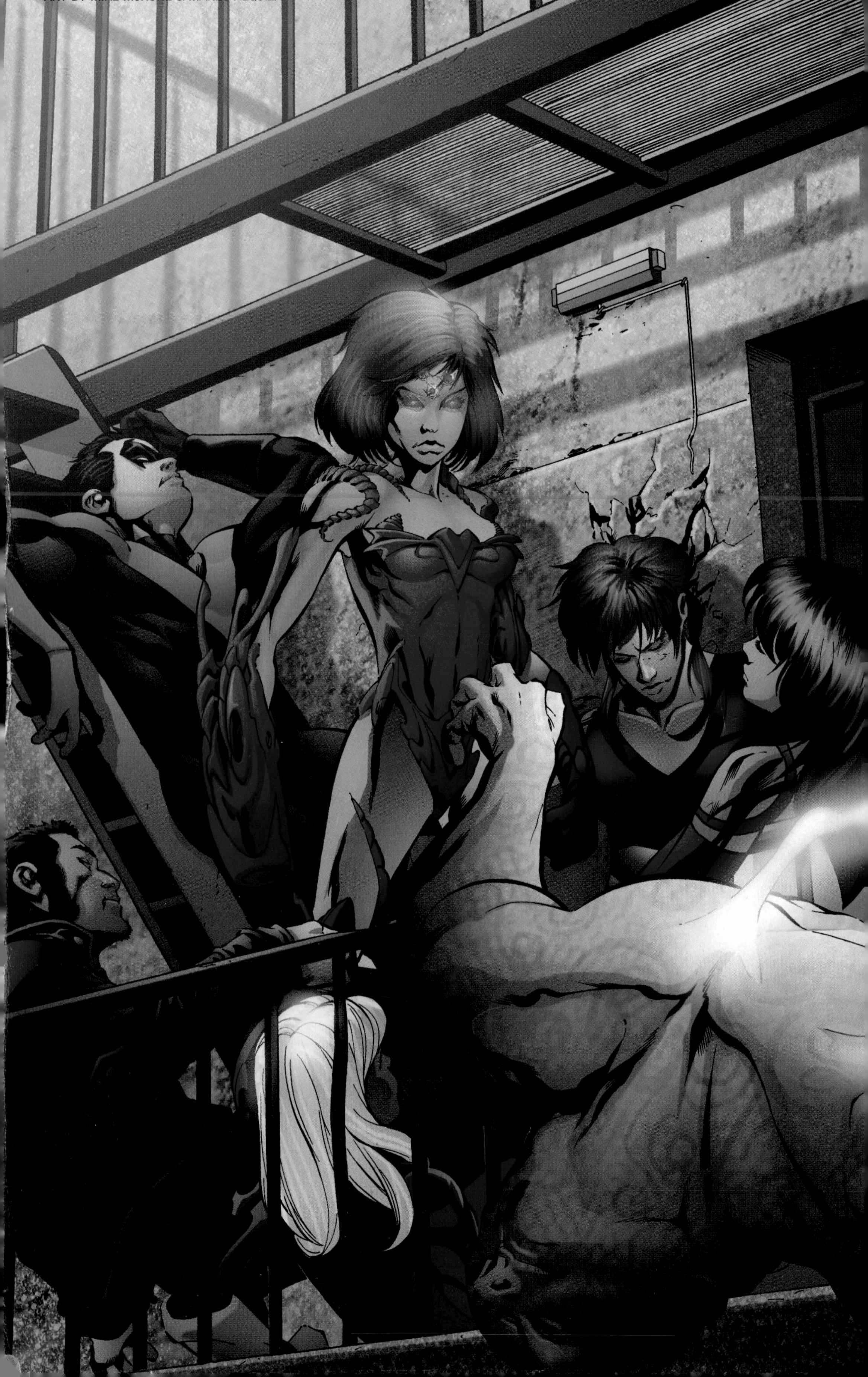

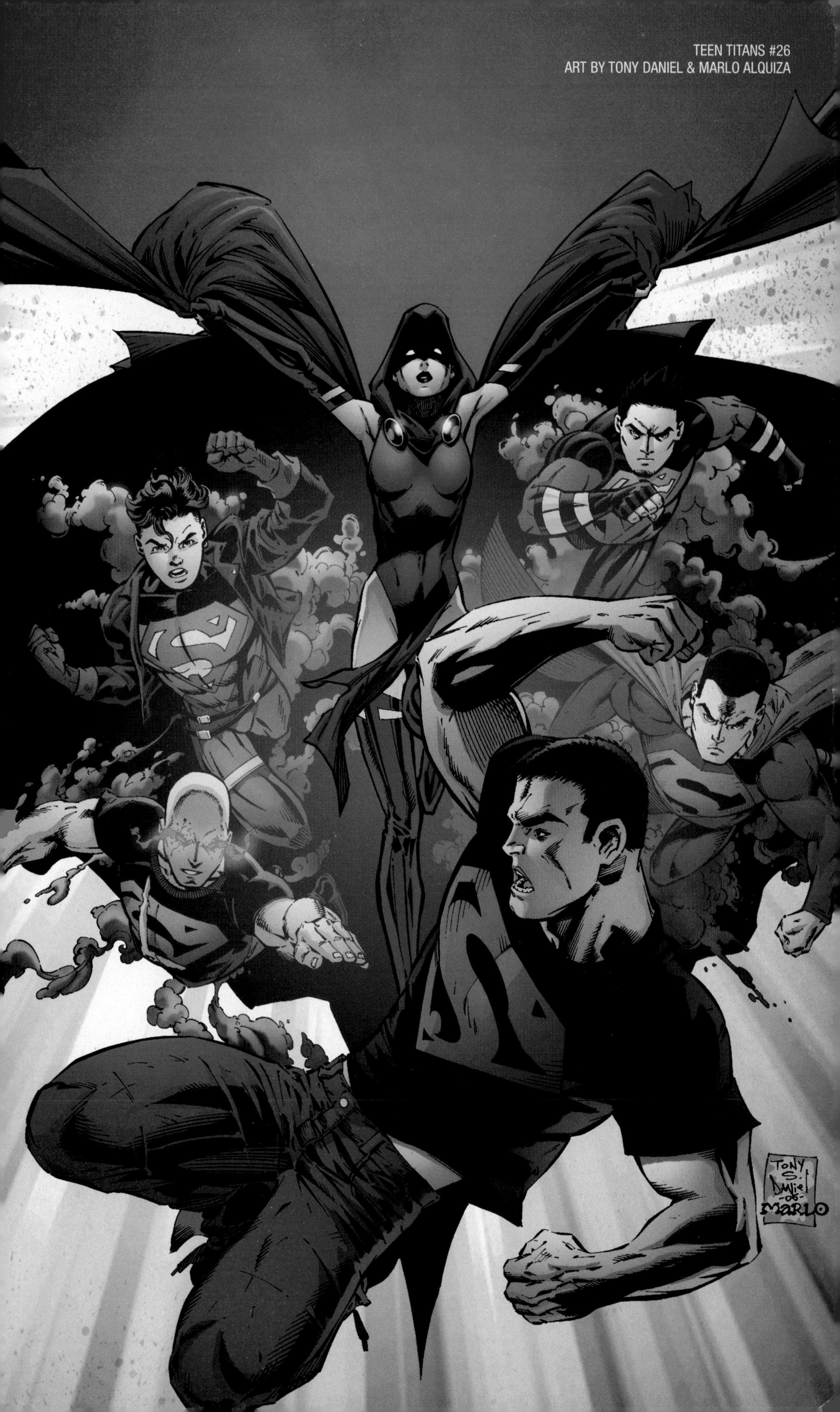

TEEN TITANS #26
ART BY TONY DANIEL & MARLO ALQUIZA

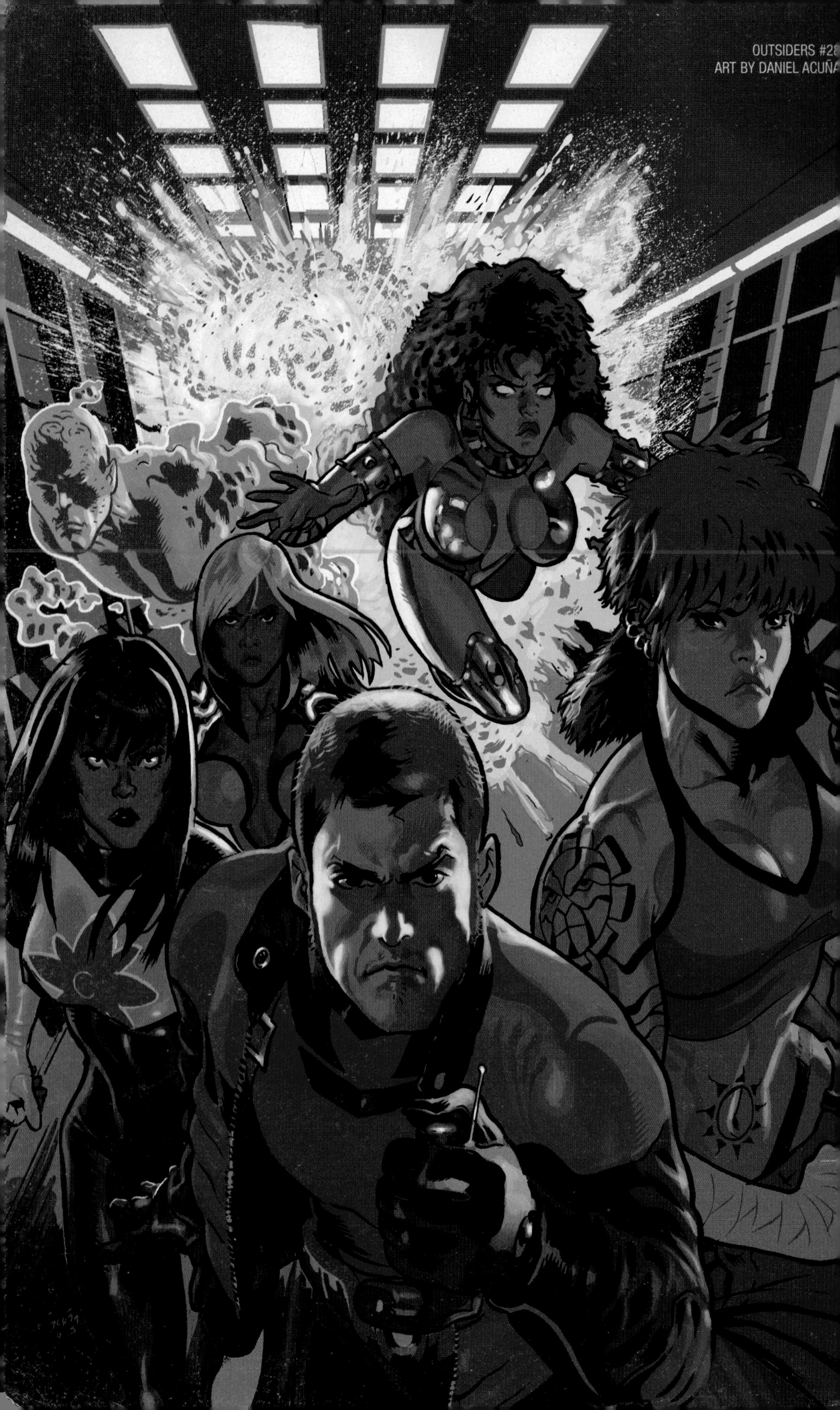

OUTSIDERS #28
ART BY DANIEL ACUÑA